The Civilization of the American Indian Series

THE WESTERN APACHE

THE WESTERN APACHE

Living with the Land Before 1950

BY

WINFRED BUSKIRK

Foreword by Morris E. Opler

UNIVERSITY OF OKLAHOMA PRESS : NORMAN AND LONDON

Library of Congress Cataloging-in-Publication Data

Buskirk, Winfred, 1908–
  The Western Apache.

  (The Civilization of the American Indian series; [v. 177])
  Revision of thesis (Ph.D.)—University of New Mexico, 1949.
  Includes index.
  Bibliography: p. 249
    1. Apache Indians—Economic conditions. 2. Apache Indians—So-
  cial life and customs. 3. Indians of North America—Arizona—Eco-
  nomic conditions. 4. Indians of North America—Arizona—Social life
  and customs. I. Title. II. Series.
  E99.A6B875 1986   306'.08997   86-40069
  ISBN 0-8061-1999-3

The paper in this book meets the guidelines for permanence and durability of the Committee on Production Guidelines for Book Longevity of the Council on Library Resources, Inc.

CONTENTS

FIGURES

MAPS

FOREWORD

by Morris E. Opler

In 1939 and again in 1941, Winfred Buskirk participated in archaeological field work on the Fort Apache Reservation in Arizona, an enterprise that provided him with a good deal of background information about the area and its natural resources. On various occasions during 1946, 1947, and 1948, he returned to the reservation with another mission in mind: to learn whatever he could about the aboriginal economy of the long-time residents of the vicinity, the Cibecue and White Mountain groups of the Western Apache tribe. In this effort he was spurred on by his interests in ethnobotany and ethnobiology and by his conviction that in the American Southwest anthropological inquiry concerning the economic and material aspects of life had received less attention than the more colorful and dramatic studies of ceremonialism, warfare, and social customs.

Though Buskirk was eager to fill in the gaps concerning Western Apache economic practices, he also sought to put them into context by relating them to the climate, to the characteristics of Western Apache territory, to its animal and vegetable resources, to Western Apache social organization, and to the influence of neighboring peoples and historical events. The account covers Western Apache economy of the 150-year period between 1800 and 1950, but particular attention centers on cultural activities before they were affected by the life-style of white Americans.

The Western Apache gave almost equal attention to four principal economic pursuits—raiding, hunting, the gathering of wild plants, and the cultivation of such crops as corn, beans, pumpkins, and gourds. This description of an economy is one of the most de-

xi

tailed and searching we have. For instance, hunting methods are depicted in the context of the tribal range, its geographical features, the influence of the social organization on the hunt, the weapons used and their manufacture, the training of boys for the hunt, hunting beliefs and rituals, the manner in which skins are dressed, and the animals and birds that are sought for food and other purposes. In the concluding chapter the author considers the cultural position of the Western Apache in the Southwest and the way in which their habitat and the surrounding peoples have influenced their behavior.

The writings of Grenville Goodwin, Keith Basso, and Charles Kaut are indispensable to a full appreciation of Western Apache culture, but the publication of this careful study of the economy is a happy addition to this distinguished company.

PREFACE

THIS book originated in 1949 as a Ph.D. dissertation at the University of New Mexico. Since then a few redundancies have been eliminated, and slight revisions have been made for clarity and brevity. No post-1949 data or bibliographical items have been added.

My purpose was and is to depict the way of life of the Western Apache as it was in pre-reservation times. Aside from explicit statements and obvious textual modifications, references to later times should be apparent from the context. The observations of people who came into contact with the Apache during the nineteenth century are dated, but most safely may be assumed to apply equally to earlier days. Several of my informants grew up in the 1870s and 1880s, when Western Apache culture was still much the same as it was before hostilities with the Americans began. Their memories and what they learned from that era's old people and their traditions carry the story back to about 1800.

I believe that most of the basic material and social culture described here is at least 150 years old and has changed little. I have tried to record changes that came about during the military occupation and have sought to show how the situation had changed by the time I completed this study in 1949. However, one of my priorities was to obtain information about Western Apache culture before it was affected by white American culture.

When something in this work has been recorded previously I have cited the literature, sometimes including additions or contradictions from my own informants. Mere confirmation has been noted on occasion, but more often it is not. The word *informant* refers to my own informants unless otherwise indicated.

Nearly all of the information I collected came from the Cibecue and White Mountain Apache groups, and unless specifically ascribed to one or the other or a subdivision of either, it applies to both. Informants often contributed data on other Western Apache, but most of the material is from the literature. It should be noted, however, that most of the material on the Cibecue and White Mountain groups applies to all the Western Apache. Older informants who had mingled with the San Carlos and Tonto groups and who had San Carlos relatives stated that the culture of all the groups was essentially the same.

My field work was carried out on the Fort Apache Reservation in Arizona in June, 1946; June–September, 1947; and March–April, 1948, a total time of about five months. Some material was obtained between April and June and in September 1939, and between June and August, 1941, but my primary investigations then were archaeological. My wife, Alice, who was with me in the field in 1946 and 1947, helped me a great deal with her inquiries and observations.

Many of the Apache provided information or confirmed data, but the most intensive work was with Bland Tessay and John Lupe of Cibecue, R 25 and Frank Tennajaeth of Cedar Creek, and Deklay and Mary (Mrs. Pete) Riley of Fort Apache. As nearly as I could determine, Tessay was born about 1881, Lupe in the early 1870s, and Deklay about 1860 or earlier. R 25 and Tennajaeth were born in the 1870s. Mrs. Riley was a forty-year-old woman who had always taken a keen interest in her people's past. My interpreters were Bland Tessay, a son of Frank Tennajaeth, Mary Riley, Vincent Altaha, and Lester Oliver, the last two being Tribal Council members who volunteered their services and would accept no compensation. The strong support of Lester and Cherry Oliver was of great value.

THE WESTERN APACHE

Chapter 1

INTRODUCTION

ALTHOUGH there are several substantial bodies of published material on the Apache, the preponderance of the literature concerns social organization, religion, and folklore. There are lacunae in our data on material culture and economic life, so an economic study can be a useful addition to the body of Apache ethnographic data.

The Western Apache tribe is of particular interest for such a study because of its mixed subsistence pattern based on agriculture, hunting, and the gathering of wild food plants. Some groups of the Western Apache rely heavily on agriculture, while others depend largely on hunting and gathering for their subsistence. This suggests a situation in which the functional mechanisms of change are still active and observable.

The basic descriptive section of this study presents in detail the fundamental aspects of Western Apache subsistence economy and associated material culture, namely, the procurement, processing, storage, and preparation of foods, along with rituals, beliefs, social implications, and attitudes concerning these phases of culture.

An obvious factor affecting the food-getting activities of the Western Apache was the subsistence economy of neighboring peoples. This comparative aspect of the problem, however, could not be effectively attacked by dissociating subsistence from other areas of the total culture. It will become clear that among the Western Apache, agriculture, hunting, and food gathering were intimately associated with their social and religious life and their value standards. Consequently, a study of the relationships in subsistence economy between the Western Apache and neighboring

3

groups had to be set within the larger context of placing the Western Apache, in terms of their total culture, among the Apachean tribes and the peoples of the Southwest.

Once the total culture of the Western Apache had been examined, their cultural position and cultural antecedents in the American Southwest could be appraised. There were immediate complications, however, because this group occupied an intermediate position, culturally and geographically, between agricultural peoples of the north and west (Pueblo, Navajo, and Pima) and hunting-gathering peoples on the south and east (Chiricahua and others). Furthermore, seventeenth- and eighteenth-century sources indicate that the Western Apache were probably a highly mobile group even in historic times and that they encountered many other diverse cultures.

Since subsistence depends largely on natural resources, environmental problems are inevitable. Therefore, throughout this study the development of the Western Apache subsistence economy is evaluated in terms of potential environmental determinants, the percentage of total natural-resource use, and the roles of interfering nonecological and historical factors.

Ethnographic Summary

The Southern Athapascans comprise a group of people who once ranged from southern Colorado south into Mexico and from central Arizona east to the Great Plains. In historic times, seven divisions have been recognized on the basis of territorial limits and cultural and linguistic differences: Navajo, Jicarilla, Kiowa-Apache, Lipan, Mescalero, Chiracahua, and Western Apache.[1]

The Navajo occupied a territory in the four-corners area of Arizona, New Mexico, Colorado, and Utah extending south at one time as far as the Mogollon Rim. They were the most atypical of the Southern Athapascan tribes. Politically, they were divided into many comparatively sedentary groups that functioned independently under the direction of a headman chosen on the basis of natural ability and ceremonial knowledge. Agriculture was the most important economic pursuit, with hunting secondary, but sheep raising later assumed major importance. Warfare was less developed than it was among the other Southern Athapascans. Socially, the Navajo were organized into nonlocalized, matrilineal, exogamous clans. There was a weak phratric system, a characteristic shared only with the Western Apache. The extended matrilineal and matrilocal family was the basic social and economic unit. Navajo religion focused primarily on curing and preventive medicine, secondarily on agriculture and hunting. Lengthy rituals, called chantways, were conducted by a class of singers. Many Pueblo items, rephrased and recast, are to be found in Navajo culture.

The Jicarilla occupied central and eastern New Mexico and the adjacent part of Colorado. They were divided into two culturally similar bands, the Ollero and the Llanero, which were further divided into local groups with recognized leaders. The extended matrilineal and matrilocal family was the basic social and economic unit. Although agriculture was practiced by some of the Jicarilla for some 250 years, hunting was the principal economic pursuit until stock raising replaced hunting and agriculture assumed more importance. The Plains culture's influence on the Jicarilla was marked, as can be seen in their hunting and warfare and their use of such items as the travois, parfleche, tipi, and buckskin clothing. Their religion was strongly reminiscent of the Navajo, with long curing ceremonies, but the Jicarilla also had shamanlike religious practitioners. Jicarilla culture as a whole more closely resembled that of the Navajo and the Pueblo than did other Apache cultures.

The Kiowa-Apache and Lipan were the most easterly of the Apache tribes. The former inhabited an area of the southern and western Plains and were satellites of the Kiowa. The Lipan, in historic times, occupied the Texas Panhandle and moved progressively south on the plains as far as the Mexican border. Little is known of Lipan culture, but the available information indicates that their material culture, like that of the Kiowa-Apache, was Plains in type. In nonmaterial culture, both the Lipan and Kiowa-Apache were closely related to the Jicarilla.

The Chiricahua ranged from the Mogollon Rim through southwestern New Mexico, west through southeastern Arizona, and south into Chihuahua and Sonora. They were divided into three bands, the Warm Springs (hereafter referred to as the Eastern

Fig. 1. *This conical-base black jar, found near Fort Apache in the 1940s, was made by an Apache potter of an earlier day.*

Chiricahua), the Chiricahua, and the Southern Chiricahua, which in turn were broken up into local groups. Both the bands and the local groups had leaders who were chosen because of outstanding personal qualities. The basic economic and social unit was the matrilineal, matrilocal extended family. Hunting and the gathering of wild plants were the chief subsistence activities. Agriculture among the Eastern Chiricahua was nominal, particularly between 1850 and 1950. Ritualism was highly developed in connection with the girls' puberty ceremony and the training of boys for war. Many individuals possessed personal supernatural powers, which were exercised for the public welfare and in individual cures.

The Mescalero of southeastern New Mexico appear to have been very similar, culturally, to the Chiricahua, who are much better known. Hunting was the principal economic activity, supplemented by gathering and by a sporadic agriculture. In material culture, they acquired many Plains traits.

Common to most Athapascan groups, including the Western Apache, were the brush- or grass-covered wickiup; the burden basket; the pitched water basket; conical-bottom pottery, with raised or incised decoration and flaring rim; the extended domestic family, with matrilocal residence the basic economic unit; matrilineal descent; permissible polygyny; variations of the sororate and the levirate; mother-in-law avoidance; the girls' puberty rite (except Kiowa-Apache); supernatural powers and religious rites acquired by individuals through dreams or direct contact with the source of power; curing rites; and the horror of death. The Apachean tribes resemble one another closely in their social culture but are less homogeneous in their material culture and economy than are the Pueblo. Apachean cultures show a varying amount of influence from both Plains and Pueblo but differ radically from the Pueblo in their greater emphasis on hunting, warfare, and a less sedentary life.

Relationships among the various Athapascan groups have been indicated in several areas of culture. On the basis of kinship, Opler[2] divided the Southern Athapascans into two groups: Jicarilla-Navajo-Kiowa Apache and Chiricahua-Mescalero-Western Apache. The Western Apache affiliate most closely with the Mescalero in kinship classification.[3]

Hoijer[4] placed the Southern Athapascans in the following linguistic divisions and subdivisions:

I. The Western Group
  A. The Navajo
  B. San Carlos (Western)-Chiricahua-Mescalero
    1. The San Carlos (Western) Group: San Carlos proper, White Mountain, Cibecue, Southern Tonto, and Northern Tonto
    2. Chiricahua-Mescalero
      a. Chiricahua
      b. Mescalero
II. The Eastern Group
  A. Jicarilla-Lipan
    1. Jicarilla
    2. Lipan
  B. Kiowa-Apache

Western Apache territory included roughly the area bounded by a line running from Flagstaff, Arizona, to and including the Santa Catalina Mountains northeast of Tucson, thence south of the Pinaleño Mountains to the confluence of the San Francisco and Gila rivers, thence north along the Blue Range to Springerville, and thence northwest to Flagstaff.[5] Neighbors to the north and northeast were the Navajo and the Hopi, Zuñi, and Keresan Pueblo villages. On the east were the Eastern Chiricahua[6] and, in the Rio Grande Valley, other Pueblo peoples. To the south were the Chiricahua, to the southwest the Papago, and to the west, progressively from south to north, the Pima, Yavapai, Walapai, and Havasupai. Beyond the immediate neighbors were other peoples: the Tarahumara and Opata to the south and the Maricopa to the west. The Western Apache ranged over highly varied topography. On the north they inhabited the southern edge of the Colorado Plateau, an upland country averaging 5,000 to 7,000 feet in elevation, much of it comparatively level. Mountains were high but less rugged than those of the Basin and Range area to the south. The San Francisco Peaks in the northwest (over 12,000 feet) and the White Mountains in the northeast (over 11,000 feet) were the highest points in Apache territory. Climate was severe throughout the winter and early spring, with frequent heavy snowfalls, but was invigoratingly pleasant in summer.

South of the Mogollon Rim and west of the White Mountains, the terrain broke sharply. Steep, rough slopes gradually gave way to mesalike remnants of former plateaus, which were severely eroded and cut by deep canyons. From the Salt River south lay a succession of abruptly rising mountain ranges that separated deep desert valleys. Although the elevation was much lower, varying from 2,000 feet to 7,000, the country was much more rugged than that of the Mogollon plateau country. The climate was mild in winter and hot in summer.

The Western Apache territories were arid except at the highest elevations. Average annual precipitation varied from ten inches in the south to twenty-two in the north, but average figures are meaningless because one year might bring rains of cloudburst proportion and the next practically none. The peak rainy season usually occurred in July and August, with another that lasted from November through March. Precipitation was usually light in April and nearly negligible in May and June. The frost-free season was four to six months long but sometimes longer, depending on the elevation.[7]

Life zones in this region ranged from Canadian to Lower Sonoran. A close approach to Hudsonian occurred on Mount Graham in the Pinaleño Mountains and Mount Thomas (Baldy) in the White Mountains, but these areas were of negligible importance. The San Francisco Peaks, at the edge of Northern Tonto territory, extended into the Hudsonian.

The Canadian zone embraced high plateaus and mountains from 8,500 to 12,000 feet in elevation. In the Apache country, most of this was in the White Mountains, where stands of Engelmann spruce (*Picea engelmanni*), blue spruce (*Picea pungens*), corkbark fir (*Abies arizonica*), and white fir (*Abies concolor*) frequently were broken by mountain meadows and stands of quaking aspen (*Populus tremuloides*) in burned-over areas. Below these was found Douglas fir (*Pseudotsuga taxifolia*).

The Transition zone, from about 7,000 to 9,500 feet, contained Douglas fir; yellow pine (*Pinus ponderosa*), the dominant type in this zone north of the Gila River; and, in the lower part of the zone, Gambel's oak (*Quercus gambelii*) and alligator-bark juniper (*Juniperus pachyphloea*). South of the Gila River, the dominant pine in this zone was Arizona pine (*Pinus arizonica*). In summer the pine forests were carpeted with grasses, legumes, and composites.

The Upper Sonoran zone ranged roughly from 4,500 to 8,000 feet. Through the upper levels of this zone, yellow pine mingled with the dominant vegetation, which consisted of piñon pine, junipers, and oaks. In the north the pine was piñon (*Pinus edulis*); in the south it was nut pine (*Pinus cembroides*). The Utah juniper (*Juniperus utahensis*) and the alligator-bark juniper were dominant in the north; in the south the Utah juniper was replaced by the oneseed juniper (*Juniperus monosperma*). The oaks consisted of Emory's oak (*Quercus emoryi*), the Arizona oak (*Quercus arizonica*), the blue oak (*Quercus oblongifolia*), and, at the lower elevations, the scrub oak (*Quercus turbinella*). Deciduous trees found along streams and drainageways were the ash (*Fraxinus velutina*), sycamore (*Platanus wrightii*), cottonwood (*Populus fremontii*), and species of maple (*Acer*). Common shrubs and plants included manzanita (*Arctostaphylos pungens*), squawbush (*Rhus trilobata*), mountain mahogany (*Cercocarpus* spp.), mimosa (*Mimosa biuncifera*), barberry (*Berberis fremontii*), snakeweed (*Gutierrezia tenuis*), rabbit brush (*Chrysothamnus* spp.), *Lycium pallidum*, bear grass (*Nolina microcarpa*), sunflower (*Helianthus* spp.), yucca (*Yucca* spp.), agave (*Agave* spp.), and cacti (*Opuntia* spp.). In parts of this zone, particularly along the Mogollon Rim, were open areas of scattered piñons and junipers and perennial grasses. The dominant grasses were species of Bouteloua, Sporobolus, Aristida, Muhlenbergia, Hilaria, and Stipa. With these occurred cacti, yucca, bear grass, and sagebrush (*Artemisia* spp.). In the Lower Sonoran zone, at elevations below 5,000 feet, were mesquite (*Prosopis juliflora*), creosote bush (*Larrea tridentata*), various cacti (*Opuntia* spp., *Cereus giganteus*, and others), saltbush (*Atriplex* spp.), and other xerophytic types. Along the streams were ash, cottonwood, and willow (*Salix gooddingii*). Growing with these were many ephemeral herbaceous plants.[8]

Fauna of the Canadian zone included the Merriam elk (*Cervus merriami*), mule deer (*Odocoileus homionus*), spruce squirrel (*Sciurus fremontii* var.), porcupine (*Brethizon epixanthum*), Arizona weasel (*Mustela arizonensis*), black bear (*Ursus americanus*), beaver (*Castor canadensis*), mountain sheep (*Ovis canadensis*), and numerous species of small rodents and birds.

Mammals of the Transition zone were the elk, mule deer, Abert squirrel (*Sciurus aberti*), chipmunk (*Butamias* sp.), ground squirrel (*Callospermophilus lateralis*), wood rat (*Neotoma* sp.), beaver, porcupine, jackrabbit (*Lepus* sp.), cottontail (*Sylvilagus* sp.), bobcat (*Lynx rufus*), cougar (*Felis concolor*), wolf (*Canis occidentalis*), coyote (*C. latrans*), badger (*Taxidea taxus*), skunk (*Mephitis* sp.), raccoon (*Procyon lotor*), bear, and small rodents. Birds included the Merriam turkey (*Meleagris gallopavo merriami*), band-tailed pigeon (*Columba fasciata*), and jay (*Cyanocephalus* sp.).

In the Upper Sonoran zone were whitetail deer (*Odocoileus virginianus* var.), the peccary (*Tayassu* sp.), mule deer, antelope (*Antilocapra americana*), mountain sheep (*Ovis canadensis* and *O. mexicanus?*), Arizona gray squirrel (*Sciurus arizonicus*), ground squirrels (*Citellus* spp.), prairie dog (*Cynomys* sp.), wood rat, beaver, rabbit, cottontail, cougar, bobcat, gray fox (*Urocyon cinereoargenteus scotti*), coyote, wolf, skunk (*Mephitis* sp. and *Spilogale* sp.), badger, raccoon, and small rodents. Among many birds were quail (*Genus?*), mourning doves (*Zenaidura acroura*), owls (*Otus asio?*), jays, ravens (*Corvus* sp.), and crows (*Corvus* sp.).

Lower Sonoran mammals were peccary, jackrabbit, cottontail,

jaguar (*Felis onca*), coyote, raccoon, badger, skunk, and small rodents. Birds included Gambel's quail (*Lophortyx gambeli*), the roadrunner (*Geococcyx californianus*), and the turkey vulture (*Cathartes aura*).

The Western Apache comprised five large groups (or superbands), all closely related in language and culture but each feeling itself distinct from the other groups.[9] These in turn were broken up into bands (Goodwin classified some as semibands), each of which was composed of several local groups. Listed below are the groups (superbands) and bands:

1. White Mountain group
   a. Eastern White Mountain band
   b. Western White Mountain band
2. Cibecue group
   a. Carrizo band
   b. Cibecue band
   c. Canyon Creek band
3. San Carlos group
   a. Pinal band
   b. Arivaipa band
   c. San Carlos band
   d. Apache Peaks band
4. Southern Tonto group
   a. Mazatzal band
   b. First semiband
   c. Second semiband
   d. Third semiband
   e. Fourth semiband
   f. Fifth semiband
   g. Sixth semiband
5. Northern Tonto group[10]
   a. Mormon Lake band
   b. Fossil Creek band
   c. Bald Mountain band
   d. Oak Creek band

Bands and semibands were further divided into local groups of a seminomadic character. In the local group were several family groups, which in turn consisted of a variable number of households. In a local group the majority were generally of the same clan, although some might be blood relatives of other clans, relatives by marriage, or unrelated. Usually the members of an extended family group were related within the limit of second maternal cousin or were relatives by marriage.

Local groups were directed by one or more chiefs, extended families by headmen, chosen on the basis of personality and proven experience and performance but usually from clans or lineages in which the office long had been held. The authority of these men rested in their prestige and the force of good example.

Blood relationship, particularly on the maternal side, entailed strong obligations. Maternal relationship was reinforced by the clan system and the customary matrilocal residence. Obligations and responsibilities of a man toward his wife's family also were strong.

Clans united the several Western Apache groups, bands, and local groups. These clans were matrilineal and exogamous. All members of one clan were considered blood relatives and were expected to aid one another in time of need. Clans usually were named after the legendary place of origin or first settlement and sometimes were also rather loosely called by the name of a related bird or animal. One clan might be related or linked to another or to several clans.

Although matrilocal residence was usual, it was not compulsory. Individuals and families were free to change their residence from one local group to another. Polygyny was permissible, but a man was expected to seek additional spouses only among his first wife's maternal family or clan sisters if eligible women among these were available. The affinal relatives retained a strong measure of control over a widower.

Hunting and gathering were the primary economic activities and were of equal importance, although in some families and groups agriculture assumed significance equal to that of hunting or gathering. Raiding and, to a lesser extent, trading were also important economic pursuits, but eventually the subsistence economy shifted to cattle raising, agriculture, and off-reservation employment.

The Western Apache lived in dome-shaped thatched wickiups that were grouped together in extended-family settlements. Cloth-

Fig. 2. *Cibecue informant Bland Tessay and an Apache wickiup of 1940s vintage.*

ing was made from hides and consisted of hard-soled moccasins with leggings to midthigh, a breechclout for men, a long skirt for women, and optionally worn upper garments. Serviceable weapons and undecorated pottery were made. The only field of material culture in which the Western Apache excelled was basketry. Coiled trays, ollas, twined burden baskets, and pitched water baskets were of unusually fine workmanship.

Women did the cooking and camp work, dressed hides, gathered foods, and built the wickiups. Men hunted and performed all dangerous tasks or those requiring more than average physical strength.

The principal deities were Sun; the culture hero, Slayer of Monsters; Changing Woman, mother of the culture hero; and a rather vague deity named In-Charge-of-Life. There was in addition to these a class of spirits (*gan*) who were believed to dwell in mountain caves; masked dancers or clowns represented these spirits.

Supernatural power was thought to be possessed by many plants and animals.

The theme of the four directions permeated all Western Apache ritual. Color-direction symbolism linked east, the most powerful and holy of the directions, with black; south with blue-green; west with yellow; and north with white. East and west were considered male, north and south female. Except where witchcraft and death were involved, sequences always ran clockwise and began with the east. Ritual numbers were four, eight (or twelve or both eight and twelve), and thirty-two. Although color-direction symbolism is also characteristic of the Pueblo, their associated colors and directions and their sequences differ from those of the Western Apache.

Ceremonies of a traditional type were performed in connection with the girls' puberty rite, warfare, illness, and hunting. Most curing ceremonies and many of those connected with agriculture and hunting were personal ceremonies gained through dreams or other contacts with the supernatural.

Western Apache folktales and myths contain many parallels with those of the Pueblo and other Southern Athapascan groups. There are tales in which Coyote figures as a trickster and culture hero and stories of Turkey as a culture hero, of heroes conceived through the agency of Sun and Water, of an underground world, of a disastrous flood, and of the destruction of monsters by a culture hero.

Chapter 2

AGRICULTURE

Farming Sites

White Mountain: Eastern Band. The principal Eastern White Mountain farming sites were located on the East Fork of the White River from Fort Apache to the foothills of Mount Baldy; at the head of Bonito Creek, a tributary of the Black River; at the head of Turkey Creek; near the head of the Black River; on Eagle Creek at what was later the Double Circle Ranch; at Point of Pine west of Eagle Creek; and from the head of Cienega Creek running into Eagle Creek.[1] Other sites were at Seven Mile Canyon, Corn Creek, and Canyon Day Village below Fort Apache. The last-named site was shared with the Western White Mountain band and was generally considered their territory. A possible site was five miles up a small, unidentified tributary of the upper Gila, but this may have been a site planted by the Eastern Chiricahua.[2] Latter-day sites were on the East and North forks of the White River and at Canyon Day, Seven Mile Canyon, and Turkey Creek. There were many farms at Bylas on the San Carlos Reservation.

White Mountain: Western Band. The Western White Mountain farming sites were at Canyon Day, the mouth of Cedar Creek, upper Cedar Creek, and Bear Springs.[3] Some sites along the Salt River below Cedar Creek were also occupied. Latter-day farming sites were at Canyon Day, on upper Cedar Creek, and at Bear Canyon.

15

Cibecue: Carrizo Band. The Carrizo band farmed along Carrizo Creek above the U.S. Route 60 crossing; on the North Fork of the White River from Post Office Canyon to eight miles above Whiteriver; and on the head of Forestdale Creek.[4] These people used to spend much time around Show Low and north of the Mogollon Rim as far west as the Cibecue meridian, and they farmed near Taylor, Shumway, Snowflake, and in other areas. They ceased to use this area, except for occasional hunting or gathering forays, about the middle of the nineteenth century because of Navajo pressure but were still on the Carrizo and North Fork in the mid-twentieth. One family cluster remained at Forestdale.

Cibecue: Cibecue Band. The Cibecue band farmed on Cibecue Creek and its tributaries from Salt Creek to four miles below the Day School. Patches were farmed along Salt Creek for nearly five miles and along upper Cibecue Creek to White Springs. There was a smaller settlement at Spring Creek west of Cibecue.[5] According to informants, people at one time lived on Spring Creek to its junction with the Cibecue and the Cibecue itself was populated down to this point. The last people died on upper and lower Spring Creek about 1918. People lived on middle Spring Creek until 1947. There were none there in 1947, but an informant stated in April, 1948, that he was going to plant some corn on a dry farm there.

Cibecue: Canyon Creek Band. Farming sites were on Oak Creek; in Gentry Canyon running into Canyon Creek; on Canyon Creek; just below the mouth of Lost Fork Canyon; and on Cherry Creek at the east foot of the Sierra Ancha.[6] People used to live on upper Canyon Creek from three miles below the Oak Creek junction clear beyond Chediski to the OW Ranch; they also occupied Oak Creek. Other occupied sites were Pleasant Valley down Cherry Creek to Roosevelt, Crouch Creek, and the top of Walnut Creek, but it is not certain that any of these were farming sites.

Cherry Creek east of the Sierra Ancha was reputed to be the best site in this band area. People left Cherry Creek in the 1870s because of military operations and white encroachment; the area was detached from the reservation. Some Apache had irrigated farms on Gledson Flats north of the Salt River, but this site was evacuated about 1905. People had left Canyon Creek by 1907. Goodwin,[7] who investigated the area about 1937, and Opler[8] reported the Canyon Creek area (specifically some of the Oak Creek–Grasshopper settlements) still occupied. By 1947 just two families were left in this region, and these occupied dry farms at Chediski but did not remain throughout the year.

Some of the Canyon Creek band held land at Spring Creek (which Goodwin included in the Cibecue band territory). In the 1860s or earlier there were some good dry farms near Blue House Mountain about midway between Cibecue and Canyon creeks.

San Carlos: Pinal Band. Some Pinal band farming sites were located along six miles of Pinal Creek; these later were called Wheatfields. Others were at the confluence of Pinal Creek and the upper Salt River and on Salt River from the mouth of Pinal Creek to the mouth of Tonto Creek. Farms in Coon Creek Canyon were shared with the Apache Peaks band and Canyon Creek band (Cibecue). A site at Dick Springs Canyon and the Gila River was shared with the Arivaipa band.[9]

San Carlos: Arivaipa Band. Farm sites were at the head and mouth of Arivaipa Canyon. Farms at the mouth of Dick Springs Canyon were shared with the Pinal band.[10]

San Carlos: San Carlos Band. The San Carlos band had few farms, and all on the San Carlos River from Victor's Bluff to Seven Mile Wash.[11]

San Carlos: Apache Peaks Band. There were no farms in the Apache Peaks band territory. Some of these people had small units on the San Carlos River at the mouth of Seven Mile Wash and about a mile below. Others had farms with the Pinal band at Wheatfields. A few shared farms at Coon Creek Canyon with the Pinal band.[12]

San Carlos Group. San Carlos communities were located at Bylas, Calva, Peridot, and Rice or New San Carlos. The San Carlos practiced agriculture less than the Cibecue, probably less than the White Mountain, but more than either of the Tonto groups.[13]

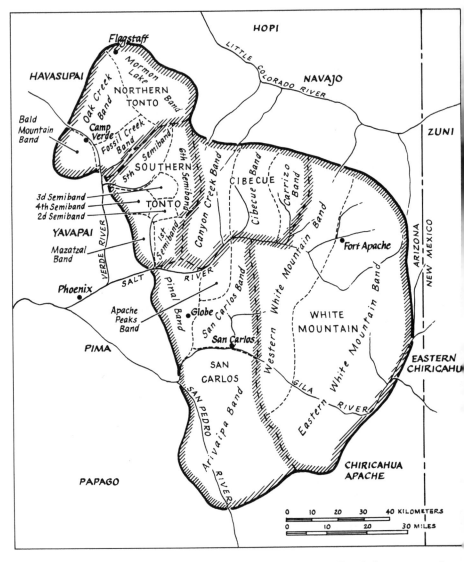

Map 1. *The Western Apache groups, bands, and semibands in east-central Arizona.*

Southern Tonto. The Mazatzal band had farms on Tonto Creek from its mouth to a point above Gem Creek.

Sites of the Second semiband were along Spring Creek, at Gisela, and at the juncture of Rye and Tonto creeks.

Third semiband farms were at Payson, Round Valley, Green Valley, and Star Valley.

Farms of the Fourth semiband were at Bluefarms at the north end of the Mazatzal Mountains.

The Fifth semiband had farming sites in the vicinity of White Rock Mesa north of the East Verde River, at Weber Canyon north of the East Verde, on the East Verde just below the Payson-Pine road, at Pine, on Pine Creek near Natural Bridge, at Strawberry, and on the South Fork of Strawberry Creek.[14]

Northern Tonto. The Northern Tonto farmed least among the Western Apache groups. The Mormon Lake band did not have farms, claiming they lacked water or suitable ground and were too exposed to the Navajo, Havasupai, and Walapai. The Bald Mountain and Oak Creek bands also lacked farms.

The Fossil Creek band had a few tiny units on Fossil Creek, on Clear Creek, and on the Verde River below the mouth of Deer Creek, but most of this band had no farms.[15]

Some of the Tonto were at Gisela, Camp Verde, and Payson.[16]

Topography, Soils, Site Selection

The rugged terrain of the Western Apache country and the scarcity of water severely limited the area suitable for cultivation. Lack of tools, except the digging stick and the stone ax, further limited the choice of locations. In field selection, the prime requisite was water. Sites had to be close enough to stream level so that a dam could be built and a ditch led in without too much labor. The site also had to be reasonably free of large vegetation and fairly level.

Agricultural possibilities varied in the different group territories. White Mountain informants said there was plenty of undeveloped land, which could be cleared and planted, and anybody who wanted one could have a farm. There are records of new land being cleared

on East Fork,[17] and sometime between 1845 and 1855 the Eastern
White Mountain allowed some of the Carrizo band to settle in their
North Fork territory and develop farms.[18]

Informants claimed the Cibecue band had more developed arable
land than any other band. Others called them the Corn-Feeds-the-
People Folk, and friends and relatives came up from the San Carlos
group at harvest time to get corn.

To the west, the Canyon Creek band had distinctly limited farming opportunities. It was difficult to find places where water could
be put on a field easily. In the upper Canyon Creek–Oak Creek
district, there were only thirteen landowners or landowning families in the 1880s, before the advent of white farm agents, and they
held some twenty-seven to thirty farms. About fifty families bor-
rowed these farms or helped on them for a share of the produce.
There were far "too many helpers" for the amount of land. The fact
that one woman in this area used four farms from eleven to fifteen
miles apart indicates the difficulty of finding suitable sites.

Fig. 3. *Apache fields at Cibecue.*

Most farms were along the stream courses. Here, in the pre-American times, large trees, such as the cottonwoods that became so prevalent, were said to be scarce. Willow grew along the banks; bottomlands were covered with high "feather" grass (probably gramma). Farm sites were located where there was little vegetation and where a shallow ditch could be dug from the water level of the stream to the field. Farms tended to be long and narrow. In the Canyon Creek area they were sometimes 220 yards long and only 10 to 15 yards wide.

Some farms were not along streambeds. Some were watered by small springs. Some were placed along wet seeps such as were found along the hillsides at Cedar Creek and in the Bear Springs area. Others were planted where rainfall runoff could be diverted onto them from hillsides, as up Salt Creek above Cibecue and at Bear Canyon, or from damned arroyos, as at Bear Canyon. In the latter case, planting was not directly in the mouth of the arroyos but to one side, where the danger of flood damage was not so great. A few farms, such as those in the upland pine country around Forestdale, were dry farms.

Floodplains were never used as field sites. Probably such a selection would not have been feasible, as the heavy rainy season came during July and August, too late to flood a field before planting but at a time when crops might be washed out.

Soil does not appear to have had too much importance in the selection of field sites, but it was considered, at least by those who had an abundance of sites topographically suitable. Black dirt, not too sandy, was much preferred to red clay and excessively sandy soils. A Canyon Creek informant's grandmother liked to plant in the "black dirt with straw," which had washed in from the mountains, but would plant in all kinds of soil. The Cibecue denied ever selecting a site because of the luxuriance of the vegetation, but the White Mountain, perhaps because in the fortunate position of having more irrigable sites to choose from than they could use, often picked a spot for this reason. Heavy red soil was much disliked. Alkaline soils were planted and continued to produce if they were well drained.

In earlier days the Apache avoided living too near their farms because of danger from enemies. They preferred hilltops to valleys as camping spots, and the women carried water and corn to the top. According to old informants, in the Cibecue Creek area the people moved down from the mountains to the small hills along Cibecue Valley between 1880 and 1885. About 1895 they began moving into the flats, where most now live. Areas covered with a heavy growth of brush were selected for camp sites because they afforded concealment from enemies.

During the American military campaigns, the Apache tried to plant in hidden locations where their corn would not be discovered and destroyed. Even after their forced exodus from north of the Salt River to San Carlos, many old people hid and planted in inaccessible places.

Fertility

The soils of the Fort Apache Reservation have not been analyzed, though one such project was undertaken on the school farm at Fort Apache and the soil and moisture staff at the Phoenix regional office and the Whiteriver Agency hoped to conduct others. Neverthe-

Fig. 4. *This large petroglyph of a gan, or mountain spirit, was photographed at Whiteriver in 1947.*

less, the soils are known to be sufficiently fertile. Moisture is the limiting factor to good crop production.

The very extensive archaeological ruins on the Fort Apache Reservation and in other areas occupied by the Western Apache indicate that the territory once supported a very considerable prehistoric sedentary agricultural population. Hough,[19] writing of the Forestdale district, stated: "It is not surprising, therefore, that in this favorable environment pueblos of large size developed; the cause for wonder is that in this region the pueblo dwellers have not persisted to this day."

Bourke[20] devoted half a page to the bountiful crops of corn, pumpkins, wheat, beans, vegetables, and fruits raised on Cooley's Ranch up the North Fork of the White River. An unofficial report of the Whiteriver Agency in 1944 stated that corn yields of thirty bushels per acre were harvested on dry lands in a good year, although they might be totally lacking in a dry one.

I saw fine stands of corn and beans on both irrigated and unirrigated Indian fields and good alfalfa fields under irrigation. Missionaries at Whiteriver raised an abundance of garden vegetables for more than thirty years. At Kinishba Pueblo, some four miles west of Fort Apache, in an area with a juniper-yucca-cactus cover, a vegetable garden was planted for some ten years, without fertilizer, and regularly yielded an excellent return of tomatoes, onions, carrots, cabbage, potatoes, and the usual garden produce.

The Apache claim that they have always fallowed (*rested* is their term) their fields. A family owning four to six small farms might plant two or three a year, possibly four. They believed it necessary to rest a field for a year every two or three years. One man said the people formerly rotated crops, insisting that fields must be fallowed; now, he said, the modern people do not rotate crops but "plant corn, corn, corn, all the time." Another man remarked that a field was always left idle for a year after a planting because the yield was not good if corn was grown on the same land year after year.

Although some of the modern Apache might have abused their fields, many certainly followed the ancient custom of resting them. Opler[21] stated that most of the land lay fallow much of the time, perhaps a third of a field being planted in any one year, then an-

Fig. 5. *About half of Kinishba Pueblo had been excavated and restored when this photograph was made. Kinishba, Arizona's largest prehistoric pueblo, is four miles west of Fort Apache.*

other third the next year. It was my observation in the seasons of 1939, 1941, 1947, and 1948 that more than half of the enclosed lands lay unused in any one year. Many fields in outlying areas, such as the old Canyon Creek–Oak Creek area, Spring Creek, and others, were used only sporadically if at all.

An unofficial report of the Whiteriver Agency stated in 1944 that 4,000 acres were under irrigation and 3,000 acres were being dry-farmed. It is doubtful that these fields were farmed actively; the figures probably represent acreage cleared and available for farming or a total of all acreage previously used. The official annual report of the agency for the calendar yaer 1947 showed a total planting of 1,018 acres (107 acres in forage crops, 865 acres of corn, 29 acres of beans, 17 acres of garden crops). If anything, this is slight, as it would be easy to overlook planted acreages in a report covering such a large area of scattered fields. In fact, I noted some wheat acreage that was not reported. The amount of cultivable land reported might have been large because probably not all of the reported irrigable lands were being served by usable irrigation systems. However, the figures do indicate that perhaps six of seven improved acres were unfarmed in 1947 and that of the irrigable land perhaps two of three acres were unused.

Animal manures were never used in former times. Indeed, the idea of using them would have been repugnant, probably, as it was believed that contact with some animal excrements might cause sickness and it was not customary for one to commit a nuisance in a field. Some manures were used in later times, although not to the extent that the government farmers would have liked. Probably most of the Apache would have had no ideological objection to the use of horse manure. Their failure to use manures more than they did was due to the difficulty of collecting and spreading them and to a lack of understanding of their value to a field.

A White Mountain man stated that his people used to burn the grama grass on a field because the ashes were good for corn but that weeds and cornstalks were taken to the edge of the field to burn and their ashes were not scattered. Others confirmed that weeds were thrown clear of a field, and even though they might later be burned the ashes were not put on the field. Although corn-stalks might be raked into piles in a field and burned, their ashes were not spread. In the 1940s, weeds were pulled or hoed and left in the field. Beans were almost invariably pulled, vine and all, and removed from the field for harvesting. The agency farmers en-couraged the practice of growing and plowing under cover crops to improve a field, but they encountered little success.

The Cibecue groups did not plant many seeds, and they thinned the corn if the plants appeared too numerous. The White Mountain followed the same practice unless they were unsure of the quality, in which case they planted many kernels to a hill so those that sprouted could "feed upon the extra grains." Pumpkins and beans often were crowded between the rows of corn, however; many also planted these crops separately. This type of planting was still fol-lowed by many. I saw an unirrigated field at Cedar Creek in which corn, pumpkins, and beans were much too closely planted for any but an irrigated field. The agency farmer said many Apache had the impression that the closer the plants were placed, the better.

At San Carlos, fields were sometimes double-cropped. An infor-mant who had lived there as a boy stated that this was done in pre-American days. The Mexicans taught the Apache to raise winter wheat and then to plant corn after the wheat harvest. The informant had seen this done in the 1880s but was told the practice was much older. He said it was still followed but was never adopted by the White Mountain and Cibecue groups. The harvesting of a crop of barley at San Carlos in 1875, followed by immediate replanting to corn, was mentioned by Clum.[22]

Climate and Calendar

With the arrival of Standing Moon and the gentle "time to plant wind" in March, it was time to think of planting. Sometimes planting time could be determined by moons or by solar observation, but in practice other phenomena were relied on. At Canyon Creek some watched the progress of the sun against certain landmarks as indicating planting times; according to Canyon Creek and White Mountain informants, some of the San Carlos and White Mountain also did this. There was no official sunwatcher.

Planting times were determined by plant and animal behavior rather than celestial observations. When the grass turned green and the mesquite yellowed with flowers and the spring birds came along below the Salt River, the upper Canyon Creek people knew it was time to return to their planting grounds. When the large cottonwood trees budded and began turning green, it was time to begin planting. Another indicator was the flowering of wild plants.

At Cibecue was a large cottonwood tree that was watched by all the people for their planting cue. When this tree was killed by lightning, the calendar was substituted.

The people of Cedar Creek began planting when the cottonwoods began to leaf and the mescal plants flowered. On the East Fork the cottonwoods, chokeberries, and other wild plants were watched for signs of budding and leafing. When the cottonwood was in full leaf, it was time for the second planting of early white or sixty-five-day corn. Here the sun was not watched.

Informants agreed that the return to the farm sites was made in March or April. One said the planting of corn (and later wheat and potatoes) in the upper Canyon Creek area began as early as March, although it might be as late as April or May. April and early

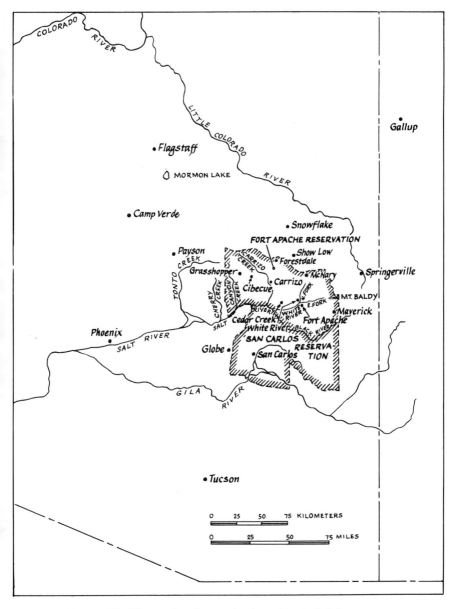

Map 2. *The Western Apache country in east-central Arizona.*

May were the usual planting times given, this varying somewhat with elevation and climate.

At Chediski, where killing frosts sometimes occurred in September, corn was planted earlier than at Oak Creek and would be ready to harvest about the end of August or in early September. On Turkey Creek and at other areas of high elevation, such as Forestdale, planting was begun in April, whereas on the lower North and East forks planting was in May and June and could even be delayed until July. Planting was early in White Springs, above Cibecue, since the area was shaded and the crops protected from the summer heat.

Harvest was determined by maturity of the crops, frost, or convenience, and among the White Mountain also by solar observation and the morning rising of the Pleiades.

An attempt was made to harvest the crops before the first frost. One informant stated that in former times in the Oak Creek district corn was harvested and stored by August 19. Pumpkins were not gathered until October, however. White Mountain harvests ranged from September to November, depending on planting time and type of corn.

Latter-day Apache planted by the calendar. Corn was planted late April or May (whites at Whiteriver considered the Indian planting somewhat late). At Cibecue some dry farms were planted April 1 and some April 15 in 1948. Wheat was planted in March, as were potatoes. Beans, once planted at the same time as corn or a few weeks later, were planted in July, and in 1947 some were planted August 1.

In the more heavily populated areas, such as the Cibecue and the North Fork–East Fork districts, the frost-free season extended, on the average, from mid-May to mid-October. Higher, in the yellow-pine belts of Chediski and Forestdale, frosts occurred as late as June and as early as September.

Normally, rainfall was heaviest in August, with September almost as heavy and July a close third. Although these are the months of most precipitation according to available weather data, Apache informants always said July was the rainiest month; June rain was usually negligible. An old medicine man said June was the only month when his rain-bringing powers were ineffective. Winter rains were often heavy, and March had an average precipitation of nearly two inches. The Apache believed that rains could be expected after the coming of a new moon and that there might be frequent storms until the moon became full. The crescent of the moon was thought to hold water that was released as the moon approached its full state.

Ownership and Inheritance

The five Western Apache groups had well-recognized territorial limits. Farming sites belonged wholly to the group within whose territory they lay and almost never were shared by people from different groups. Groups were divided into bands, each with its own territory. Farming sites were shared only by people belonging to bands of the same group if they were located on or very near the border between two bands.[23] Such a situation existed between the Eastern and Western White Mountain at Canyon Day, the Cibecue and Canyon Creek bands at Spring Creek, and the San Carlos bands.

The exclusive holding of territory by a group broke down under the reservation system. White Mountain, Cibecue, and San Carlos Apache moved into one another's old territories as the result of inter-marriage, employment opportunities, desire to be near agency facilities, or because of relocation by military authorities. White Mountain, San Carlos, and Tonto were to be found on the San Carlos Reservation; White Mountain and San Carlos people held part of the Cibecue; San Carlos, and even a few Chiricahua, lived in the old White Mountain and Cibecue territory.

Farming sites were associated with clans. Usually they were thought of as belonging to a dominant clan, although the lands were actually owned and planted by members of several clans, some of which might be related or linked. Ordinarily, none but members of the owning or related clans or blood relatives could develop or hold land at a site, although temporary use might be permitted.[24]

Farms often were held by individual men or women. A man who took me on an inspection tour of his farm was very proud that it was "all mine" and that he had made the irrigation improvements. Farms owned by more than one individual usually were spoken of

Fig. 6. *White Mountain informants Deklay, an old Apache scout, and Mary Riley at an East Fork farm.*

as the property of one person.[25] A farm operated by a family generally was spoken of as belonging to the husband, regardless of actual ownership, because he was the head of the family.[26]

Farms might be owned jointly by siblings, by a family, or by a family cluster of two or more households. Frequently they were held in trust by a widow, widower, uncle, or other relative for minor children.

Usually, farms owned by an extended family were at the same farming site. Outsiders marrying into a family ordinarily gave up farms at another site, but some kept them and returned to them for the farming season.[27] There might be ownership at scattered sites, however, as was frequently the case in the late 1940s, when a man might have farms at both Cedar Creek and Canyon Day or at North and East Forks or at Cibecue and Carrizo, Spring Creek, or upper Canyon Creek.

The number of farms owned by an individual or a family varied, but owners were more likely to have several than just one. There might be as many as four, five, or six small plots to a family among the White Mountain. On upper Canyon Creek, where land was scarce, of thirteen owners or owning families, one had four farms, another had one, two had two, and nine had three.

It was extremely difficult to estimate the number or percentage of Apache owning farms. In the 1880s, according to old informants, some thirteen families held land in the Canyon Creek–Oak Creek district, while more than fifty had no land of their own. Informants stated that "everybody" or "almost everybody" had land in the old days on the Cibecue, at Carrizo, at North Fork, and at Cedar Creek. Gifford[28] recorded that his Cibecue informant, who was from Carrizo but long had been a resident at Cibecue, said that the majority of the Cibecue group did not have land. This was undoubtedly true of the Canyon Creek band and might have been true of the Carrizo band, but it is doubtful that it would have applied to the Cibecue band. Cibecue informants indicated that practically everybody once farmed, although it is quite likely that many were not outright landowners.

Goodwin[29] stated that probably not more than 60 percent of all the White Mountain Apache owned or shared farms and that at any given site associated with a local group probably not more than 45 percent would own or share farms there, an additional 15 percent having farms elsewhere.

Trees and wild plants on a farm belonged to the owner. Goodwin[30] said stones, clay, and firewood on a farm belonged to the owner, and one of his informants stated that an owner could refuse to let others get water from a spring on his land, although in practice water would never be refused. Later, planted trees were privately owned, but trees planted on another's land belonged to the landowner.

Clearing a plot gave no title to contiguous land. A neighbor could clear a patch next to it without permission. This did not result in quarrels, since only small areas were planted and excess land was available. Normally, if a man desired to plant a different kind of corn from that of his neighbor, he would go downstream a quarter of a mile to prevent cross-pollination.

Land was never sold in early times. Transfer, other than for temporary use, was by gift or through inheritance. Later, ownership was vested in the tribe by the constitution adopted under the Reorganization Act, and the Apache Council transferred land from one user to another. Improvements on a place were owned individually and could be sold, in which case the council was asked to approve the buyer's use of the land. In practice the de facto ownership and transfer of land went on very much as it always had under Apache custom. If a man did not use a farm for two years, the government farmer might threaten to ask the council to take it away from him and redistribute it.

Farms might be given to blood relatives or affinal relatives joining a group. An individual changing his place of residence or local group affiliation was likely to give his farms away if he received new ones or the use of new ones at his new home. Goodwin[31] mentioned specific cases, all involving a transfer to blood kin or fellow clansmen. When drought ruined many of the farms in the Bear Springs area about 1864, many of the relatives, inlaws, and clansmen of these people sent for them and gave them new, uncleared sites or divided their own farms with them.[32]

Both sons and daughters inherited farms from either the maternal or paternal side of the family. In the case of grown children, place of residence largely determined which of them inherited. Married daughters living at home were likely to receive the property, married sons living away from home relinquishing any claim in their favor. Married daughters living elsewhere also might give up their claims in favor of children still at home.[33]

Goodwin's[34] survey of family clusters and the lands used provided many illustrations. I also collected a number of specific examples and explanations of land ownership, use, and transfer, most of them involving inheritance by direct descendants.

An Oak Creek woman and her husband cleared four farms, which they jointly owned, "but the woman's family had the most interest in it." After the husband's death this woman and her daughter and son-in-law continued to operate the farms. After the son-in-law's death in 1890 the Oak Creek farms were abandoned to relatives, and the group, consisting of grandmother, daughter, and very young grandchildren, moved to their farm on Spring Creek, where they had relatives (already this and the other farms were spoken of no longer as the older woman's but as her daughter's). The Spring

Creek farm later was used by a grandson until his death, after which it was unused.

A farm at Chediski was operated in season by a man of undetermined clan or affinal relationship. After three years at Spring Creek, the little family removed to Cibecue, where they were lent a farm on lower Cibecue Creek by the chief Z 1, whose children were their relatives. After they had farmed this land for two years, the chief O 1 came down from upper Cibecue Creek and said to them, "I want all you people to come up to my place and stay with us. I have the biggest piece of land there and nobody to plant it." (They were clan relatives of the O group). There they stayed, and one of the grandsons inherited the home site and farms they were given by O 1.

The former Cibecue people were said to have practically died out, the latter-day owners in many cases being people who came from elsewhere after 1900, including some from San Carlos and the Carrizo, Canyon Creek, and the White Mountain bands. At first, as incoming men married at Cibecue, the wives were "the boss on the land." Later, if the man worked it well for a few years, he became boss. However, the wife might divorce her husband at any time and keep her land. If the woman should die, the widower remained boss. When widowers inherited, it was for their children or, in the absence of children, because the wife had no close blood relatives or because these did not wish to dispossess him.

A unit on East Fork was owned and occupied in turn by great-great-grandmother, great-grandmother, grandmother, mother, and, in the 1940s, an occupant who hoped her children would stay there when she died. Perhaps the most common type of inheritance is from mother to daughter, because of the prevalence of matrilocal residence.

When a man cleared a piece of land, his wife and his children became his heirs. Farms were divided among all children or among all who wished or needed them. The oldest child might inherit a wife's farm. If there were no children or if these did not want it, a farm would go to brothers, sisters, nieces, nephews, cousins, or other relatives or clan relatives. In one instance at Cibecue a boy (the son of a man unusually wealthy by reason of property and steady employment) lived for years with an old man not related to him and inherited from him, in the absence of other close claimants, his house, lands, and a good many cattle.

Selection of the person to inherit property was influenced by the expressed wishes of the deceased, by closeness of blood relationship and social bonds in life, by need, and by proximity of residence. The decision seems usually to have been settled by the family (close relatives and clan relatives) without quarrel, although there were occasional disputes requiring a chief's arbitration. A site might continue to be used and owned by a family or family cluster, title becoming vested in the group.

Occasionally, sites were abandoned and later occupied by other clans. This occurred when a feuding clan was forced to leave Carrizo. It also happened during the military campaigns of the 1870s and 1880s and during periods of drought. Although such land might still be referred to as that of the clans who formerly occupied it, title rested indisputably with the current owners, for it was abandoned land when they took it.[35] Land that was abandoned or not used by its owner might be taken by another, but the owner might reclaim it at any time.

Blood, clan, and affinal relatives, or friends, often were granted the use of unneeded farm lands. Farms so lent could be reclaimed at any time, but the arrangement was likely to continue indefinitely. In later times, farms occupied on loan became, at the death of the original owners and by reason of long occupation and use, the inherited property of descendants of the borrowers.

Occasionally, a temporarily abandoned field was preempted and planted by another without permission. If the owner asked for it, the preemptor had to return it. The owner could destroy the crop and plant his own, or the two might agree to share the already planted crop or to divide the field—"either way he want it." Occasionally, such a situation would result in a dispute that was settled by the chief.

When temporary use of a farm was granted to an outsider unrelated by blood, affinity, or clan, approval of the clan chief or local group chief was asked as a matter of courtesy and was almost invariably given.[36] Fields occasionally were lent to be worked on shares, but this was the only form of rental.

There was always occasional quarreling over the ownership, use, and inheritance of farms. Informants indicated that quarrels were most frequent in the Cibecue area of the Fort Apache Reservation. The cause might have been the influx of new people into Cibecue, or it could have been, as the White Mountain claim, that the Cibecue were more inclined to cantankerousness and quarrelsomeness than other Apache. Disputes at Cedar Creek were infrequent.

According to a Canyon Creek man, in the old days some "cranky" people would plant or harvest more than their share of a field and serious disputes and fights would ensue. Sometimes an aggressive person would trespass on part of another's field already planted.

According to Goodwin,[37] disputes over ownership almost always occurred at new sites where ownership had not been long established. The man who first marked off a plot of ground and began to clear it had prior rights, but occasionally someone might try to preempt part or all of it. These quarrels were usually settled on the spot, but a fight might ensue, in which case a chief might intercede.

One such dispute came to my attention in which two foster brothers fenced property. When one died, his wife inherited his share. After her death, her brother would not allow the surviving partner to occupy the property. Eventually, the dispute was taken to the Apache Council, but it was the general opinion that the land should revert to the tribe and be redistributed.

Information on crop ownership was somewhat contradictory. Either a man or a woman might own a crop, and the same person who owned the crop in the field owned it after the harvest. Yet where a family operated a farm, the woman appeared to have greater claim to ownership, regardless of who owned the land.

A crop was divided with all one's marital and blood relatives if they needed it. Either the man or the woman could give away part of the crop. If a man owned the crop, his wife could give part of it away sometimes without consent, but if a woman owned the crop, the husband could not give it away.

Standing crops were invariably burned or abandoned if the owner died, although, in a family field, some, perhaps half, might be spared as the share owned by the bereaved spouse and children. Destruction was accomplished by the kinsmen of the deceased, not by the widow or widower. This was still a common practice in the 1940s.

Boundaries

Groups and bands of the Western Apache had recognized territorial limits, although others might travel through them to raid or at times to hunt or gather wild foods. Large and prominent geographical features, such as mountains, hills dividing valleys where water ran, or rivers, marked the boundaries. Clan farming localities and individual farm sites were generally known and recognized.[38]

In former times there were no fences, and apparently none were needed, as there were not enough horses in the area to menace the fields.

Both White Mountain and Cibecue people claimed that there was no difficulty in distinguishing boundaries between fields and that there was usually a ditch boundary. Gifford[39] stated that stone boundary markers were used by the Cibecue and White Mountain, but this was not confirmed.

Relatives or family clusters often farmed five or six plots in a common field. The Cibecue designated individual areas within a common field by cutting the tips of adjoining rows. This was denied by the White Mountain.

When the number of horses increased to the point where they became a menace to crops, brush fences were erected. Green oak brush was piled in irregular fashion to enclose a field or, more commonly, several fields. If a fence enclosed more than one field, the owners helped one another erect it. Oak-brush fences lasted two or three years; as soon as they rotted, another layer of fresh boughs was piled on top.

Juniper brush was used for fences at Cedar Creek and very probably elsewhere when readily available. Cactus or thorny brush was never used, although in later times cactus sometimes was used to protect watermelon patches from small boys.

Wire fences were first used in the Fort Apache area in 1889, at the same time the people began to have "big" farms, according to informants. At Cibecue the first government farmer issued barbed

Fig. 7.
*Apache
farms at
Cibecue.*

wire in 1895, requiring in return one day's work per spool. In 1949 fields were universally enclosed by wire. Wire-and-post fences were not infrequently struck by lightning. When this occurred, a medicine man was called to make repairs and the damaged post was hidden so that no one would incur illness by stepping on it.

Boundaries of individual fields often were determined by terrain and vegetation. If size were not limited by these natural factors, a man estimated by eye the amount of ground to be cleared or planted. Sometimes boundaries were fixed by arrow shoot, but this was done only by people with big farms. In the arrow-shoot method, only the length of the field was determined, not the width.

To fix the length, the archer stood at a predetermined western boundary of his field, then shot the maximum distance to the east. Going to the point where his arrow fell, he shot again to the east. He might shoot two or three times, but never four. The reason for this method was not explained by informants, although one of them had used it.

Size of Farms

It is difficult to estimate with any great accuracy the amount of land cultivated by the Apache. Early observers used the adjective *small* and synonymous terms in commenting on Apache fields, but they left no more precise description. Goodwin used such terms as *small* and *tiny* throughout *The Social Organization of the Western Apache*. Elsewhere [40] he spoke of aboriginal White Mountain fields as being small, one-half acre or so.

The White Mountain Apache often had four to six little farms per family, of which they might plant two or three and sometimes four. They did not attempt to plant large fields, only enough for a family. Cedar Creek Crossing fields were about two acres each, but such were divided into several plots, perhaps five on the average. This would allow two-fifths of an acre per individual plot. On upper Cedar Creek the measurements provided by informants with regard to the usual family field amounted to not quite three-fourths of an acre.

One informant estimated that in the Canyon Creek–Oak Creek area the farms were only one-half or three-fourths of an acre. When he gave dimensions (some of the larger farms were said to be one-eighth of a mile long by ten or fifteen yards wide along the narrow valley bottoms), resulting plots varied from less than one-half to slightly under three-fourths of an acre. Others were smaller; by pacing off plots estimated to be of comparable size to those which the informant remembered, I arrived at a figure of one-tenth to about one-twentieth of an acre. Arable land was scarce in this area.

An attempt to estimate the amount of land cultivated by the yield proved even more difficult. A White Mountain man said corn was raised in enough quantity to store for four years ahead. However, this appeared to be unusual, and the usual goal was enough produce for one year. Great care was taken in caching, as "corn was scarce in those days." Each family tried to maintain several caches, at widely separated points, for emergencies. A Cherry Creek man stated that the people there raised enough corn for one winter, but not two, because they had "poor people and children to feed."

At Oak Creek an informant's grandmother, who had four fields, harvested less than two sacks of corn. But helpers in this area were said to receive fifty to seventy-five pounds of corn, or two or three bundles of large ears plus the nubs they set aside. This woman raised only five or six large pumpkins, sometimes none, although other families raised five to ten. After the military occupation, she planted about ten hills of potatoes.

According to a Cibecue informant, an abundant crop before 1900 consisted of four or five one-hundred-pound sacks of wheat. Some indication of crop size can be gained from a Cibecue account of 1891 or 1892; seven horses made four trips each to carry it. The corn was packed 12 bundles to a horse. Since there were 10 or 12 ears to a bundle, this would have been 3,360 to 4,032 ears, probably in the neighborhood of 3,700 ears in all. In addition to this amount, the four boys who brought horses were given half a sack each. It is likely that a prior distribution had been made to people who had helped with harvesting or planting. Allowing a spacing of one corn stalk to the square yard (spacing was sometimes thinner, often thicker) and allowing one ear to the stalk (two ears was normal), 3,700 ears of corn would have been grown on about three-fourths of an acre; 4,000 ears would have required four-fifths of an acre.

When estimating the size of farms, it must be remembered that fields were planted (often with neighborly help) in one day. No case of more than a day being taken in the planting of a field was reported.

Fields in pre-American times were definitely smaller than those of the twentieth century. This was emphasized time and again by the older Apache: "Garden of grandmother a nice size—Indian garden got too big." "Apache never used to grow a big patch of corn, just a little patch. They said, 'Somebody find it, pull it all up.'" In early days they raised "not too many pumpkins, just five or six is all." "Didn't raise many pumpkins because field not big enough in those days." "Didn't plant big fields of wheat, just enough for family." Let us look at the size of mid-twentieth-century farms, which were larger than those of pre-Caucasian days. Opler[41] said the farms were small, that one man on the Fort Apache Reservation had several plots totaling twenty-two acres but that the average farm did not run to more than five acres, and that of this amount only about one-third is cultivated at any one time.

The figures that follow are averaged from Whiteriver Agency plats that were made in 1943. On the Middle Fork Cedar Creek ditch there were twenty-eight farms with a total average of 40.19 acres, or an average of 1.44 acres per farm. The largest farm was 4.9 acres, three were between 2 and 3 acres, ten between 1 and 2 acres, and 14 were less than 1 acre. On this ditch, one man owned five plots, four had four, two owned two.

On the East Fork Cedar Creek ditch there were twelve plots with a total of 29.05 acres, an average of 2.42. None on this ditch owned more than one tract, although several owners and those on the other ditch also owned plots in the Canyon Day area. Two farms here were between 4 and 5 acres in size, two between 3 and 4, two between 2 and 3, five between 1 and 2, and one was less than an acre.

On both Cedar Creek ditches there were forty plots totaling 69.24 acres, an average of 1.73 acres. No figures were obtained on the dry farms of the area, but most of those inspected certainly would not exceed 5 acres.

At Canyon Day village there were four ditches with ninety-three plots totaling 130.41 acres, an average of 1.4 acres. Some owners held more than one tract. Of the plots on these ditches, six were under 0.25 acre, eight between 1 and 2 acres, nine between 2 and 3 acres, five between 3 and 4 acres, one between 4 and 5 acres. The smallest was 0.20 acre. One school farm had 13.7 acres.

On thirteen North Fork ditches there were ninety-seven plots totaling 425.72 acres, or an average of 4.39 acres per plot. Included in this North Fork area were an agency farm of 26.10 acres, a school farm of 26.68 acres, and an agency orchard of 8 acres. If these are taken into account, the average individually held plot was only 3.88 acres. Two individuals held farms between 13 and 14 acres, one had between 12 and 13, one had between 10 and 11, two had between 9 and 10, one had between 8 and 9, nine had between 6 and 7, several had over 5, but most held way under 5 acres. This information on North Fork regarding size of plots and the number of different sizes was taken from five sheets showing perhaps eight or nine of the thirteen ditches.

No data were obtained for the Cibecue area, and none were available on East Fork or Turkey Creek. However, by visual inspection the farms at Cibecue and on the East Fork were judged to be no larger on the average than those on North Fork.

There were in the plats I examined in 1948 a total of 230 irrigated tracts of ground in the Cedar Creek, Canyon Day, and North Fork areas with a total of 625.37 acres. This averages to 2.72 acres per plot. If one takes into account four agency and school farms totaling 73.95 acres, the average size of the individually held plots is reduced to 2.44 acres. This is an estimated average for the farms which were so much larger than those of pre-American times.

There seemed to be no great desire for large or numerous farms among the Apache. According to Opler,[42] nearly every Apache family on the Fort Apache Reservation did a little farming under normal conditions. Not all the cleared lands were cultivated. There were many abandoned plots west of the Cibecue, at Forestdale, and at other places on the reservation, as well as virgin lands, that could be occupied by the ambitious. The Apache do not appear to be driven by the land hunger so characteristic of many Anglo-Americans or by the desire to possess or use more than enough to meet the needs of a family. Said one councilman: "We have five acres [which included a large home site]. That's enough. We don't want any more."

Irrigation

There appear to have been yearly and cyclical fluctuations in water supply. It is known that a drought about 1864 forced the abandonment of many farm sites in the Bear Springs area. Nevertheless, informants stated that drought was never so prolonged or so severe as to cause hardship or crop losses. It is quite possible that memory of such losses or hardships has faded. One man could remember a season when the North Fork of the White River was high enough to float logs, while his mother-in-law remembered a season when she could step across the North Fork at any place.

Springs were at one time much more numerous than they were in the 1940s, many having dried up after three quarters of a century. Apparently, there was never any ownership of springs. Whoever camped in their vicinity used them and cleaned them, when necessary, with hands and gourds.

The Apache believed they had irrigated as long as they had farmed, and it is certain they had irrigated for more than two hundred years.[43] Furthermore, they said, their irrigating technique always included dams. Irrigation was so much a part of the Apache agricultural complex that, except for favorable areas where seepage provided moist subsoils or some of the higher areas where there was plentiful rainfall, it was unthinkable to farm without irrigation. Farm sites were picked primarily for their accessibility to water. In the upper Canyon Creek area, where irrigable farm land was scarce, no dry farming was attempted, although it was possible.

Water was led to the fields by ditch, with or without the aid of dams. Fields were irrigated on the flat without ditching them. When shallow ditches were made ahead of the water to lead it to desired spots, these were leveled when the watering was finished; this practice is still used in unfurrowed fields.

Fields were leveled and kept level by transporting soil from high places to low ones and by throwing soil from high spots into the water, which distributed it to the lower areas. Very low spots were filled with brush, grass, and earth. A digging stick was the only tool used.

Ditches were dug from springs or stream banks; usually they were shallow and short. As they were dug, the water was led along to establish a proper level. Large rocks were pried out with sticks, two or four of these often being used in unison as crowbars. If necessary, a large rock was split by the application of fire followed by dousing with water.

The longest ditch informants remembered before the military occupation was one at Cedar Creek that served some thirty families and was about two miles long. Goodwin[44] observed that five to fifteen farms might be served by a ditch.

When the irrigation season arrived, ditches were cleaned and the vegetation along their sides burned. They were kept free of weeds during the period of use. Bear grass and gramma grass weighted with rocks were used as head gates and lateral gates.

Dams were not always necessary. Where used they were usually not true dams but short diversion dikes projected part way across a stream. All five dams serving the upper Canyon Creek area in the 1880s were of this nature, according to informants. Dams were made when the water was low. First, brush was laid down, then bear grass (*Nolina microcarpa*) was placed against it on the upstream side, after which a layer of gravel was piled on top, then earth, then more gravel, and so forth. Women and girls filled burden baskets by hand with earth, carried them to the dam, and dumped them. Breaks in dams were repaired with brush and earth before each irrigation.

The White Mountain built dams with willow, bear grass, gramma grass, gravel, and earth. Juniper trees were used in the construction of large dams. These were dragged to the site by horses, then covered with stones, brush, and bear grass.

The narrator in Goodwin's "Experiences of an Indian Scout"[45] described a dam built at Cedar Creek, presumably in the 1860s if the text is interpreted correctly. However, some of the technique smacks of military engineering. First a series of tetrapods was set across the creek in line. These were made of four poles driven into the creekbed and had a base about three feet across and a height of three feet. Rocks were placed between the tetrapods, men doing this work, then bear grass and dry bark were tied into the tetrapods in bundles. Bear grass was laid lengthwise along the upper side of the tetrapods from one to another. Over the bear grass was packed dry inner bark of cedar and cottonwood, both men and women working. This inner bark was pounded soft and wadded in. In front of the bear grass a wall of flat stones was built as high as the tetrapods. Between this wall and the bear grass was a space that the women filled with gravel and dirt. The whole task took two weeks. The dam was watched, and if a leak appeared, it was repaired. Fields and gardens were never watered by carrying water to them. Irrigating was considered a woman's job, although anyone might do it and men often helped. If there were sickness in a family, they might ask a friend to irrigate for them or a chief might request someone to help them. Neighbors helped one another construct dams and ditches. These were considered community projects. In some localities farm owners were notified by a "ditch boss" when ditch or dam work was necessary. This was usually an elderly man who took a special interest in farming, supervised such work, and apportioned the water.[46]

When they were hoeing and irrigating, the Apache sometimes addressed crops. The Cibecue said, "Grow fast, don't bother it worms, make a good crop." The White Mountain always prayed when irrigating.

People struck by lightning could irrigate and do all farm work except planting, according to the White Mountain, but an incident was told of a Cibecue man's forbidding his wife to irrigate because lightning had struck her camp.

When water was turned into a ditch, the headman of a community received it first.[47] Chief Diablo was at the end of his ditch and got water last of all, thus obtaining more time to irrigate.[48]

Occasional quarrels that developed into killings arose over land and water at Oak Creek. Usually such quarrels were composed by chiefs or influential men. Goodwin[49] stated that water disputes were usually reguarded as women's quarrels. A chief or man of influence might break a dam and turn the water from the ditch if his intervention failed to stop the wrangling.

The military and civilian agents encouraged and assisted in the development of irrigation projects in the 1870s and subsequently, partly to keep the Apache occupied and provide a substitute for the meats and wild plant foods they were no longer free to forage for, partly to make possible a concentration of population near the post at Fort Apache, where they could be kept under closer supervision.

Parts of these projects appear to have been poorly planned, as they did not supply the expected water and some ditches quickly washed out because of improper construction and poor engineering. In the Oak Creek–Canyon Creek district before 1891 the agency constructed ditches along the hillsides to provide everyone irrigable land, but there was never enough water from the spring that was tapped.

During the Civilian Conservation Corps period of the New Deal, many improvements were made in the irrigation facilities, but these were damaged severely by the heavy rains of 1941. I saw some small dams and ditches, built or renovated by individuals, that showed evidence of considerable hard work. The Apache took pride in this accomplishment.

Erosion took a heavy toll of farm lands, particularly in the western part of the reservation. Much good land on the Cibecue washed away—some at Cedar Creek and Carrizo and all of the irrigable land at upper Canyon Creek. The channels of streams that supplied water at Canyon Creek and Cedar Creek deepened so much that diversion was impossible. Others eroded to depths below the water tables they tapped. By 1949, most lands at Carrizo had become unirrigable.

Part of the situation undoubtedly was the result of the more intensive use and clearing of land and the intensive grazing that followed the military occupation. White lessees overgrazed the reservation, and much of the natural grass and vegetation cover was destroyed. The reservation was still grazed heavily during the 1940s, but within its capacity.

Floodwater, Irrigation, and Dry Farming

The Apache did little farming where irrigation facilities or moist subsoil were not available. Informants said there were good dry farms where corn was raised around Blue House Mountain in the Cibecue territory in the early 1860s and before. In the Forestdale area, corn, beans, pumpkins, and melons were successfully raised without irrigation before the district (except for one or two families) was abandoned.

At Oak Creek, lands were dry-farmed after 1891, in which year the ditches and many of the farms were washed out. Although there had never been enough farms at this location, no attempt was made before this time to plant where water was not available. In the 1940s at Cedar Creek, once-irrigated lands were dry-farmed. The same was true of some farms on Carrizo Creek.

There were a number of spots where moist subsoil from a river, springs, or seeps ensured good crops. In the Bear Springs area between Cedar Creek and the White River there were several such areas, but a drought in the mid 1860s forced evacuation of most of these. At one time there were many moist areas along the hillsides at Cedar Creek; these were planted, but they later dried up. The San Carlos band in pre-American times raised little patches of corn, wheat, and pumpkins in the damp soil along the bottom of the San Carlos River, according to Goodwin.[50]

At one time small dikes were built of rocks and earth in the Bear Springs area to divert rain runoff onto the fields. Small dams were built across dry arroyos before the rains, and the water thus caught was let into the fields.

On Salt Creek above Cibecue, where the land was dry, ditches or dikes were used to divert runoff after rains, but this practice gave way to sporadic plantings.

In the East Fork area, where the farms were irrigated, one energetic woman attempted manual diversion of water after rains, but few people emulated her. Failure to do so was ascribed to laziness and to fear of being outside during a storm, as doing so was tempting or disagreeable to Lightning.

It was denied that any attempt was ever made to use runoff waters in any areas occupied by the Canyon Creek band. A Cherry Creek man stated that irrigation was always necessary in the lower country but that in the high country there were some dry farms.

The government farmer at Whiteriver encouraged people to plant corn and beans on dry lands.

Division of Labor, Helpers, Attitudes

The Apache, both men and women, liked to farm. Hard work and industry in farming, as in hunting, gathering, basket making or any other economic activity, was an ideal. Chiefs in their daily morning talks exhorted the people to work hard, and during the farming season, such talks always included admonitions to do the necessary farm work, to raise large amounts of corn, to help one another.

Although there was a feeling that farm work, especially after the planting, was women's work, there was nothing degrading or menial about it. There was nothing, in other words, that would prevent a man from doing it, and, when available, men did participate in all types of farm labor.

Women perhaps took a more serious view of farming than did men. One man said that "in the old days the woman was the head of it; the man he don't much care; the man, he's apt to make the mistake; women have always been the better farmers. Just as among whites some were too lazy to farm. Some who had farms would not work them. Some would rather go out and hunt, but some were too lazy to do anything and were always begging food."

Preferences in working hours varied. Some preferred to work before sunrise, then breakfast, then continue until it became hot. About four or five o'clock in the afternoon they returned to the fields and worked until dark. Some women, older children, and men rose before dawn to work. Others preferred to wait until after breakfast.

Old people believed that the Apache worked harder and more conscientiously in earlier days than they did in the mid–twentieth century. They were said to go farther to plant and to keep their fields better. In the 1940s, many fields were untended because both men and women "like to ride around" or "go some place and drink."

The Apache did not display a desire to raise more than necessary for his own needs, and they showed little interest in improved methods of cultivation. Opler[51] believed the reason for this to be the lack of a market for Apache products. Traders and the agency did not buy Apache produce, although some of the traders bought beans on occasion. Fresh vegetables were supplied to the traders by missionaries, school farms, and outside truckers. An Apache who was encouraged to raise a field of potatoes could not sell or give them away. Therefore the Apache were inclined to raise only what they needed, and for this the traditional methods were sufficient. It is also quite possible that the lack of interest in improved methods was a matter of cultural values or goals.

The agency vacillated in its attitude toward agriculture for many years, and this was discouraging. Farming lapsed during the Roosevelt administrations, when the work-relief program, road work and later war allotments provided cash income.

Goodwin [52] said the dignity of subchiefs and wealthy men placed them above certain types of menial labor and that they did not work on their farms but hired poorer people to help. To a certain extent and in some local groups this was undoubtedly true. On war parties and hunting parties, the older and more influential men were exempt from such tasks as wood gathering and water carrying, which were performed by young men or novitiates. But there

Fig. 8. *Lumber operations at McNary and Maverick, Arizona, provided employment for many Apache in 1947. Timber from this pine forest at Maverick was used to build housing there and to provide revenue for the tribe.*

was no feeling that physical work of any kind was in any way demeaning.

In regard to economic pursuits, informants indicated that chiefs and men of influence felt a compulsion to set an example of hard work and industry. The chiefs Lupe (F 1) of the Cherry Creek district and Dazy (N 1) of upper Canyon Creek were said to have "worked all the time" in their fields. "Chiefs always worked the hardest," it was said. Dazy was the only man in his district to attempt the raising of sheep and chickens and to grow cabbage after the military occupation.

Among the White Mountain a chief would ask people to plant his field. While they were planting he would help cook the deer he had killed to feed them; afterward he would work in his field. Most of the White Mountain chiefs worked hard and set a good example for the younger men. Diablo on East Fork, perhaps the most influential chief of the Eastern White Mountain at the time of the military occupation, did not do farm work; he had captives at his camp who helped his family and dependents. Alchise, on North Fork, had the reputation of making his people work for him.

Chiefs always set the example in economic activity. They were the first to return to plant or to harvest. Some took an active part in directing these activities, sending certain men out to hunt, some to gather, some to plant. At Cedar Creek Crossing the chief directed in this manner and appointed some to plant for those he had sent on hunting or gathering missions.

Among some local groups, elderly men who took special interest in farming and who usually possessed agricultural ritual were called ditch bosses. They notified those sharing irrigation facilities when communal work was necessary, arbitrated disputes, apportioned water, and sometimes stayed at a site through the summer to watch it. At times they were hired to make the first ceremonial planting of a new field.[53]

Goodwin said no ditch bosses were to be found in the San Carlos Reservation in the 1930's, the men in charge of the ditches being government employees.[54] On the Fort Apache Reservation, men were hired to keep the ditches in good repair and supervise their use. On the Cibecue the foreman was known as the ditch boss and the position appeared to carry considerable prestige. He suggested to an owner what work needed doing and exhorted people to water when it appeared their crops were being neglected. It was difficult to determine how much of the prestige derived from the sanction of Apache tradition and how much was due to the ditch boss's own superior qualities and from his being the direct agent of the local government farmer.

Some women had great prestige and influence and were known as female chiefs. They took the lead in organizing farming and gathering activities among the women of their economic units. They were usually wives of chiefs, but not necessarily.[55] In a household the first wife was recognized as the female head of the encampment, and she directed the work to be done, including farming and food gathering. At her death the second wife normally took over, but this succession could vary.[56]

In early times men did not always participate in agriculture. Raiding and hunting took them away from home much of the time, leaving all agricultural activities to the women. When not otherwise engaged, however, men often helped with all forms of farm work. As a rule they did the heavy work, or at least helped with it, in connection with building dams, digging ditches, and clearing and preparing a field. Some of the White Mountain informants said they did the planting or always helped with it. Among the Cibecue, women frequently did all the planting, and among the White Mountain, a "lucky" woman might be chosen to drop the seeds after men had dug the holes.

There were no restrictions by which men or women planted different crops. Older men who were no longer able to engage actively in the chase helped in all farm work. Young unmarried men very frequently helped girls with their field work, the couples working side by side.[57] Goodwin[58] stated that men helped only in the preparation of fields, planting, and, at times, irrigation. My informants indicated that at times men took part in every agricultural process.

Women engaged in all agricultural work and were, in former times at least, considered to be better farmers than the men. If earth were to be carried for building dams, it was the women who transported it in baskets. Women were more apt to possess the knowledge of agricultural ritual connected with planting (dropping of seeds) and irrigating. At the harvest and after, they usually selected the seed and put the corn in the caches. Winnowing in baskets was done by women. Old women usually taught the young people how to farm.

Men took over a much larger share of the agricultural labor after the reservation was established. For one thing, war and the chase no longer required their time. The use of plows and horses and on occasion somewhat complicated machinery was too heavy and too difficult for women alone, although they might work in conjunction with them. Irrigating, harvesting, and weeding were performed very largely by women, although men helped much more than they had before.[59]

Goodwin[60] said it was not until after marriage that youths and maidens entered upon their full share of farm work. Boys and girls of this age were not allowed to help in harvesting because they were likely to be careless and spoil good ears of corn in stripping them from the stalks.

In a local group at Cedar Creek Crossing, boys and young men apparently did not help with farm work. They gathered along the sidelines to watch the men plant. In all other groups of which I had direct information, the whole family might help in planting and harvesting. In this, however, children did light work, such as covering up holes. Probably, in most cases, they worked because they wanted to work and because they wanted to take part in the family activity, not because they felt a compulsion to do so.

Old people, who had difficulty traveling, frequently were left at a farm site. Captives sometimes did part of the farm work or were left behind to help the old people with it.

Often during the preparation of a field, planting, and harvesting, a whole family worked together. Relatives, affinal relatives, and neighbors often helped. Where farms were planted one after another or when a number of people worked at a task, it was not necessarily relatives who worked together (although there was more obligation for relatives to help one another), but all neighbors. An exception to communal effort was noted in White Mountain harvesting, where one man stated that only the owning family harvested. It seems certain, however, that friends and relatives and share helpers might at times assist in this.

Relatives who would be expected to assist a family in its farming operations were brothers, brothers-in-law, nephews, uncles, and clan siblings. One Cibecue informant said brothers did not help and were not called upon for help, the implication being that a brother's obligation would be greater to his wife's family and that they would be entitled to all his labor. Another Cibecue group man qualified the statement that brothers-in-law would help with the phrase "if they were friendly."

A man's own father and mother might assist him. His sisters-in-law usually helped, as did his father-in-law and mother-in-law. A man always helped his wife's parents in any work in which he was needed, and he was also expected to help her brothers and sisters. Where a son-in-law and mother-in-law worked in the same field, the taboo relationship between them required that they work some distance apart (perhaps fifty feet). If there were no corn or brush between them, they worked with their backs to each other.

Sometimes a woman worked alone; occasionally two people; at other times, a whole family; sometimes a group of relatives and neighbors. When youths courted maidens in the field, as many as four couples might work abreast.[61]

Often a request for assistance was made at planting or harvest. On other occasions, helpers appeared of their own volition and offered their services. It appears to have been the prerogative of those without farms or crops to help those who possessed them for a share of the produce, and it seems that those with big farms or crops felt an obligation to accept such assistance. Chiefs in their morning exhortations admonished those without farms to assist those who had them with planting and harvesting.

Families without corn, whether they lacked land or because they had remained south at the gathering grounds too late to plant or because they were too lazy to plant, worked for others. Whoever had the largest crop received the most help. This worked a hardship on the farmers in such areas as upper Canyon Creek, where they were outnumbered by nonfarmers nearly five to one. At harvest time there were "too many people to help."

"Poor" people sometimes worked for a "rich" man "just to eat." When a family worked for another or for a chief, they were given food for their immediate needs but none to take home; "when it got ripe they would let them have some—not much." In other areas, helpers kept green ears or nubs or poor ears or ears from which the husks were stripped and later were given one or more bundles of large ears when the harvested crop was transported to the owner's camp.

Goodwin[62] noted that some 40 percent of the White Mountain did not have farms but could obtain produce in return for planting, tilling, or harvesting for wealthy men with large farms who solicited labor. Elsewhere[63] he spoke of wealthy men and chiefs hiring helpers for produce or for cooked corn, which they took home in pots or baskets. Chiefs might support poor relatives who worked for them.

Whereas some helpers were hired, in many cases help seems to have been given in a spirit of neighborliness. A local group often operated as an economic unit. Families were notified when planting time came, and two women ground corn to feed all helpers. Help was given on a reciprocal basis; fields were planted in rotation in this cooperative manner. In later times helpers were told, "I got the tulapai [corn beer]," and this was all they were given. They might drink part or all of it on the spot or take it home, as they wished. It was not unusual for an Apache to hire another for cash to herd his cattle, get his horse, haul wood, trim fence posts, and do other jobs. One man was given half a sack of acorns, about fifty pounds, for watering another's beans while the latter went gathering.

There was some exchange of farm products for meat or hides. Sometimes this was a formal transaction, for example a basket of corn for a buckskin. More often the trade was informal or amounted to an irregular exchange of gifts. While nonfarmers frequently gave meat for agricultural products, they did not make hunting a profession or attempt to specialize in furnishing animal products.

I have seen families in the field with a mother-in-law (because of the tabooed relation with her son-in-law) by herself in a far corner; brothers-in-law plowing together; a father-in-law with several resident sons-in-law hoeing corn. An East Fork woman of great ability and energy with good farm property kept several men busy clearing a new field, building up a woodpile for winter, and doing other chores. Every now and then people came for food or asked for corn. The workers included, among others, the woman's son-in-law, her husband, and an orphan boy who said, "She is awful good to me. She helps me a lot. I like her better than anybody." There was a feeling that the so-called wealthy should provide employment for people who were not so well off. A trader, descendant of a chiefly family, was reproached for doing his own work (driving and loading and unloading a supply truck, for one thing) when he could so easily hire it done.

Implements

Digging sticks of various lengths and shapes were used in early times as agricultural implements. Oak was considered the best wood. Green sticks were run back and forth through the fire and heated to straighten or bend them into the desired shape. One end was sharpened and hardened in fire. There appeared to be no use of abrasive stones in sharpening a stick. There were no footrests or auxiliary handles.

An all-purpose digging stick used in the upper Canyon Creek district was described as about sixty inches long and slightly crooked in the middle. In this district, both short sticks and long ones were used. Digging or punching holes was done from a standing (with the longer stick) or kneeling position. On hard ground a rock was sometimes used to hammer the stick, which was then prized up; this was usually done with the short stick and from the kneeling or sitting position.

Digging sticks used in the Cherry Creek district were described as thirty to thirty-six inches long and round like a hoe handle except on one end, which was sharp and flat for a few inches. This tool was used as a weeding hoe, the farmer resting with right knee to the ground, right hand high on the stick, and gouging to the left. This type of stick was also used for digging ditches. In planting, the same stick, or one somewhat more rounded at the end, was used. When planting, a hole was dug while kneeling on one knee.

The East Fork digging stick was of oak, about forty inches long, and heavy. It was chisel shaped on one end. The operator forced the point of the implement into the ground next to his knee on the left side of the body. Weeding was done from the same position. Digging sticks were sharpened with a hatchet stone and hardened in fire.

On Cedar Creek a thirty-six-inch digging and planting stick was used. It had a chisel-shaped end. It, too, was used with a side motion to the left.

Goodwin[64] said clearing and tilling was done with a digging stick, seeding with a planting stick. Often all operations were performed with a single all-purpose stick, which, with its slightly chisel shaped or flattened end, could be used for clearing, digging, scooping, punching, and even weeding.

A flail was used for harvesting. Flails used to harvest beans were six feet long, not too thick, and were used either in a sitting position or standing, but usually sitting. Only the one size of flail was used. In shelling corn, a six- or eight-foot flail about one and one-half inches in diameter was used.

The Apache did not use the Hopi-type rake or fork for removing corn stalks from the field but employed the limb of an oak tree.

Metal hoes were first obtained, according to tradition, from the Pueblo Indians north of the Mogollon Rim and later from the Mexicans. Shovels were acquired in the same way. Tools were few and highly valued. Often one or two implements were used by a whole community. The scarcity and value placed on them is illustrated by the statement of a Cherry Creek man that the poor always came to rich men or chiefs for agricultural products, not necessarily because they had no farm but because they lacked metal tools to work it—"maybe they got land but no hoe, no axe, no tools."

The U.S. Army and agency officials introduced the wagon, the plow, and other farm implements among the Apache. They also distributed shovels, hoes, and axes in large number and probably introduced the sickle, rake, and pitchfork.

Wagons and harnesses were issued from time to time after the establishing of Fort Apache in 1869. Palmer[65] noted that about 1890 the government provided the Indians on the Fort Apache Reservation with 150 wagons and two sets of single harness for each wagon. In 1948, I watched the agency blacksmith and his helper, both Apache, make a wagon box to order, including the metal strapping and bolts. It was to cost approximately ten dollars.

Fig. 9. *Haying time at East Fork in 1947.*

Fig. 10. *Apache women hauling milk cans filled with water at Whiteriver, Arizona.*

The principal family transportation mode of the 1940s was the horse-drawn wagon, sometimes enclosed with a canvas top; not many of the Apache owned cars or trucks. Men and boys often rode a single mount. The ownership of horses carried some prestige. One young couple with good government employment proudly showed off their recent purchase: three very inferior animals that they neither rode nor worked.

Plows were introduced early in the American occupation. The first to be used at Canyon Creek, the westernmost and most isolated farming community on the Fort Apache Reservation, was issued by the Whiteriver Agency in 1885. Plows quickly replaced shovels and hoes for groundbreaking, just as these had replaced the digging stick. When helpers came to assist a man in 1948, they arrived with plow and horses.

Harrows were used to some extent, although a log drag or section of brush was used as a substitute. Cultivators, mowing machines, rakes, and other farm machinery were not widely owned.

The Apache use of farm machinery was somewhat different from that of the average white farmer. Plowing usually was done with a single horse, sometimes a pair. In all of the plowing I observed, a rider or driver accompanied the plowman. When hitching a team, the agency farmer said, the Apache was as likely to hitch a mixed team of horse and mule as a matched team, even though two or more well-matched horses or mules were available. Many wagons were damaged because the traces were hooked up before the yoke was attached to the wagon tongue. Said the agency farmer: "The Apache are still primitive farmers."

Pests

Old Apache agreed that weeds were less troublesome in the early days, saying many were introduced after 1900. These included tumbleweed, cocklebur, Johnson grass, two or three varieties of morning glory, and various unidentified plants. Weeds once were pulled and thrown clear of the field and burned when dry, but in later times they were left lying where pulled or hoed. This might help to account for their latter-day prevalence.

Corn smut or other plant diseases were never troublesome. Diseased plants were not removed from the field.

Insects were said to be much less troublesome before the 1940s. According to the White Mountain, the most effective means of ridding a field of insects was to perform a rain ceremony and "wash them off." Cibecue informants said there were once religious practitioners with power to make insects leave a field by singing and praying and "talking to them."

Ashes were sprinkled on plants attacked by insects. Wood, preferably oak, was burned beside a field to produce such ashes, which were then sprinkled on the plants by hand. Ashes (any kind of wood ashes) were mixed with shelled corn in storage to repel worms. This was done only occasionally and by only some of the people. A more effective means of keeping corn free of worms was to store it on the cob.

Smoke was an effective agent in repelling a long, flat, squash-shaped flying bug. Logs, dried weeds, and yucca were fired to the windward side of a field to produce smoke. Stubble was never burned to eradicate pests.

Certain ritual methods of eliminating worms and insects were still followed in the 1940s. One of them was to collect worms in a jar of water, allow them to rot, then sprinkle them over a field. To repel grasshoppers, a "boss" grasshopper (a varicolored variety) and four other varieties were caught, wrapped in wild gourd leaves and tied with yucca string. These were carried to some distant place (as from East Fork to Carrizo). It was believed that the remaining grasshoppers would leave.

Crickets were considered the "music of the crop" and were never intentionally injured. If one were accidentally stepped on, its forgiveness was asked. During cold weather, crickets seen in exposed positions were picked up and placed in brush, "where it was warm." Prayers were addressed to crickets, requesting them to "help" with the crops. Informants stated that when the crickets made a unique sound on a particular day, it was mandatory for the hearer to make green-corn pudding. In autumn the crickets were said to make a sound equivalent to the Apache statement "It's time to harvest."

Beans once were free of pests, but during the 1940s the Mexican beetle was extremely prevalent. The agency farmer provided dust for people who would use it. The early type of Apache beans and large white beans, when planted beside pink beans, were said not to have been bothered by insects. In earlier days there also were few squash bugs.

The Apache picked insects from beans with their hands and crushed them. The nests of a red insect with black spots, which were made under the leaves of the bean plant, were also crushed. A flat "stink bug" was removed from pumpkins. A very small flying insect attacked watermelons.

The earliest plague my informants recalled was of huge green grasshoppers, "a different grasshopper," which ate the corn, small yucca, and leaves from all the trees in 1916 or thereabouts.

Cutworms were not pulled from the corn roots. According to a White Mountain man, they had not been a problem until recent times and the only pests that destroyed the corn were those that ate the silk.

Ants were considered a nuisance because corn would not grow near their nests. To get rid of them, a hole of about one thousand, seven hundred cubic inches capacity was dug in the field and filled with hot water. "Ants would run in and drown." The Apache did not urinate on anthills, since they believed this angered the ants and the offender would later be stung in retaliation.

Miner's candle roots and leaves of other plants were mashed up and soaked with corn before the corn was planted. It was believed that a gopher that ate a grain of corn so treated would swell up and burst. This procedure was not often used in later times; according to one male religious practitioner, it was "no good." Earth from the center of a gopher hole was sometimes soaked with corn before planting to prevent gophers from eating it.

When the land was irrigated, gophers were sometimes drowned. Water was led to all holes that were seen. If recovered, dead gophers were eaten. Rats and squirrels were killed in the field with rock deadfall traps.

Most Apache once possessed songs and prayers that were efficacious in preventing damage to crops by wild animals. Nevertheless, bears, deer, coyotes, raccoons, and skunks were at times troublesome. Various practical steps were taken to keep animals away. During the day, the presence of women in or alongside the field as they made baskets or dressed skins was usually sufficient. Sometimes a ramada or a tree platform was erected from which to watch for bears, which were shot if necessary. At night a single fire was built on a hill above the field—or fires might be built all around the field about fifty yards apart—to frighten away animals. If this did not suffice, juniper torches were carried into the field to drive animals away. Children sometimes stayed in the middle of a field and made noises with sticks at intervals throughout the night. When corn reached the roasting stage, a family might move to the edge of the field and hurl stones in it until the middle of the night.

Corn chewed or in any way disturbed by bears, coyotes, or other animals was eaten only by elderly people. Young people feared to eat it, as it was believed that it caused sterility.

Dogs never molested the crops. They were not trained to guard fields.

Bluebirds, blackbirds, and large crows (ravens) attacked the corn. Farmers camped in the fields to frighten them. Birds were not caught with corn pierced by a horsehair, as was done among some tribes. Dead crows and bluejays were nailed to posts in the fields to frighten others.

Scarecrows were used by the White Mountain only at the time the corn was drying. These were gramma-grass scarecrows made in human shape and placed on top of ramadas. Yucca-string "clotheslines" with strips of yucca hanging from them also were used. Later, muslin was substituted for yucca.

If an eagle or hawk should eat its kill in a field, the nearby corn was not used or even approached closely, as it was believed to cause insanity, headache, or a twisted mouth. Many children were said to die from contact with corn of this type.

Fences were not erected until the horse was introduced. A recognized code of settling livestock damage to crops was developed. The owner of an animal caught in a field was sent for, and paid a blanket, a buckskin, or other property according to the amount of the damage. This was usually paid willingly. An animal caught repeatedly in a field might be killed and eaten by the owner, but it could not be retained alive for his use. If a fine were not paid, the animal might have its tail and/or ears cut off. An animal belonging to a poor woman might be released, with no damages asked. On the rare occasions when the owner of an animal refused to pay damages, the case was taken to a chief or another influential man for settlement.[66]

Clearing and Preparation of Fields

Clearing was done with fire and digging sticks. Brush and grass were burned. The White Mountain believed that grass ashes were good for their corn. Some brush was pried out with the aid of a digging stick, and willow roots were pried out of the ground in this manner. Trees were left standing, for people liked a shade tree or so in a field, but many were girdled or felled in later times.

Small stones were removed from the field. Large ones were left, with planting done around them as around large trees. Some of the White Mountain left stones in their fields, claiming these helped the corn.

In the early days soil was broken with a digging stick, later with a shovel. This was done in February or March when the ground thawed. Before planting, a field would be thoroughly soaked and the weeds removed by hand.

When an old field was prepared for reuse, corn stalks were broken with the feet or pulled by hand, then raked into piles with an oak branch and burned. The ashes were left in place, not scattered. If grass covered the field, it was burned.

Corn (*Zea mays*): Seed Selection

In general, seed was selected by women. One informant stated that only women selected seed, but others said that at times a man, or both man and woman together, might do this.

The "leader" seed was selected ceremonially at harvest time. At the beginning of the harvest the White Mountain went into the middle of the field and chose the tallest stalks with two or three ears. It was desirable to find stalks with four ears, but those with only two or three ears were acceptable. Eight were selected, and

Fig. 11. *Seed selection among the White*
Mountain Apache.

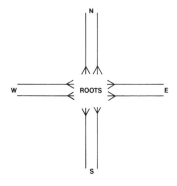

these were piled in the pattern shown in Figure 11 which "stood for a cross." Roots were inward, tops outward. The ears were then pulled from the stalks still standing in the field and piled in the center of the cross. Later, all eight stalks or only the ears were taken home. These were the leaders of next year's seed and were stored in a ground cache (now inside the wickiup). After the eight ceremonial stalks had been picked, it was necessary to find four ears of the "flat-headed, small, female corn," at least one ear of which was included in the seed selected. The remainder of the seed was taken from the largest ears and tallest stalks. This selection might be made in the field or at camp. Contrary to the Cibecue practice, the White Mountain did not sprinkle corn smut on the leader seed.

Among the Cibecue, only four ceremonial stalks were selected. These had two ears each, sometimes a third ("just a little fellow"). Two of these stalks were placed in an east-west alignment; the other two were oriented north-south to form a cross as shown in figure 12. Then the remainder of the crop was picked and piled on these four stalks. Dirt from a gopher hole was sprinkled on the pile east to west, then north to south, to produce a cross. The loose ears were tied together. The four stalks were tied in bundles of two and carried to camp. There the ears from the four ceremonial stalks were removed and saved to mix in with other seed. Corn smut was sometimes sprinkled over the ears from the four ceremonial stalks just before planting.

Goodwin[67] described, in a myth recorded from an Eastern White Mountain woman, the placing of four ears of corn, the largest and

Fig. 12. *Seed selection among the Cibecue Apache.*

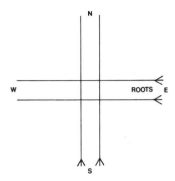

best, on the ground at harvest time. Each was pointing in a cardinal direction, butts to center. The rest of the crop was piled on these ears. Goodwin's footnote explains that the four ears were placed there to stand for all the corn, that it all might be as large and fine. After all the corn on the pile was tied in bundles, the four bottom ears were tied together by the husks. At the beginning of the husking, the first ear was thrown into the air, the thrower saying, "Let our pile of corn be so high." Turkey directed this harvest procedure. No mention is made of the use of the four ears for seed, but this seems probable.

In general, large or long ears were selected for seed. Sometimes these were picked from the tallest stalks or from stalks with the most ears. One informant stated that they were sometimes taken from the earliest maturing stalks. But as seed corn was selected more often than not after the harvest had been removed to camp, it seems doubtful that selection was often or consistently made on the basis of size of stalk or number of ears per stalk except in the case of the leader seed.

Taboos or preferences in the use of twinned and forked ears for seed varied. At Cherry Creek twinned ears were liked for seed, but not forked ears; however, both could be eaten. At Oak Creek both twinned and forked ears could be used for seed, but neither was eaten for fear such corn would make one ill or insane. The White Mountain used neither for seed but ate both.

Most informants stated that for seed corn kernels from all parts of the cob were used, provided they were sound. The shape of the kernel made no difference, although its size might. All but one of the informants said only kernels from straight-rowed ears were used; the dissenter said this did not matter.

The majority of the Apache preferred blue corn, although red and the soft variety of white were also popular. As a rule, black was not saved for planting. Flour corns were preferred over flint. Some Apache made a practice of saving only one favored color, some saved several colors or all. Most preferred to plant several colors. Among the White Mountain, where colors were planted in separate fields, the varieties remained true, but the Cibecue, who planted only one color to the row but often several colors in the same field or adjacent fields, said their corn always grew "all mixed up." Their tradition was that their original corn had been obtained in several colors from neighboring peoples but that after a few years it ceased to reproduce the colors they planted.

Seed corn was generally stored on the cob because cobs were less likely to be attacked by worms. It was carefully wrapped in bear grass and placed below the eating corn in the ground cache. Or it might be placed in a buckskin bag. If shelled, it would be cached in an old pitched canteen corked with straw, rock, and mud to keep out insects and rodents or stored in a sealed pottery jar. Seed and food corn were always stored in separate vessels.

Seed was usually saved for two years or more for fear of loss of a crop, but seed more than one year old was not used if newer seed were available, as it did not germinate well. If no planting was done for a year or so, seed might be stored until required or might be eaten.

Color varieties were nearly always stored separately, although they were on rare occasions stored mixed and even planted mixed. If pitched water baskets were not available, seed corn might be stored with other kinds of seeds and the different seeds and different colors of corn separated before planting. Different colored corn seems to have been stored together when the ears were of mixed colors or when there was only a small amount of corn.

Smut was not removed from seed corn. In shelling seed corn, care was taken not to damage the kernels. It was not beaten with a flail but shelled carefully with the fingers or a cob.

Seed corn was taken to the fields in a pitched water basket filled with water, then transferred to a basket tray when ready for use. If seed was stored in pottery jars, these were simply filled with water and taken to the field.

If seed was known to be good, only a few grains were planted to a hill, but if another's seed was used and its quality was uncertain, many kernels were planted; "then the corn would feed on the grains which did not germinate."

According to their traditions, the Apache secured seed from all surrounding peoples, both friends and enemies. At times they were known to have traded for corn,[68] both with outside tribes and among themselves. Some begged or bought corn from friends or relatives across the reservation. The army and government farmers introduced corn of unknown antecedents among the Apache. For these reasons it was to be expected that a considerable variation might be found in Apache corn. It was not known how old some of the Apache corn was. It was to be expected that several strains of pre-American corn survived, because when the government moved the Apache to the reservation at San Carlos, some remained at Fort Apache and they, with others in hiding, continued to plant in secluded places. Some of the Apache at San Carlos were known to have preferred their own seed to that issued by the government.

Corn: Planting

Corn was planted as early as March to as late as July. In the higher elevations, such as Turkey Creek, it was planted in April in order that it would mature before frost. On Cibecue Creek and the forks of the White River, where elevations average about five thousand feet, May was a normal time for planting. Sometimes the White Mountain planted a second crop a month after the first or when the first had reached a height of about six inches. Such late plantings were made with an early white or sixty-five-day corn not later than the time cottonwood leaves had attained full growth. There was no special planting of corn to be eaten green.

Corn fields were soaked a night to a week ahead of the planting date. Weeds were pulled after the ground had dried somewhat.

Corn often was planted after a heavy rain. On dry farms it was necessary to depend on such a rain.

The seed was soaked in a pottery vessel, pitched water basket, or skin bag before planting, a few hours to overnight among the Cibecue, all night before planting by the White Mountain. In early times many soaked the root of miner's candle and/or other plant material with the seed to kill gophers. An item soaked with the seed to produce abundant harvests was the "ears" (buds) of a weed that resembled those of corn; it was called "too many ears." The White Mountain also soaked kernels with earth from a gopher hole and oak leaves to bring good luck. In later times few people soaked their seed before planting and few, if any, added the above materials. At one time it was said that corn "come up right away," in about seven days, but later, probably because seed was no longer soaked, it broke ground after the tenth day.

Corn was planted irregularly, "just anywhere." Spacing varied from about twenty inches to eight feet, with an average interval of about three feet. The usual statement given by the Apache with regard to spacing was "two or three" or "one long step." One man said the White Mountain planted two or three paces apart, but the same man, who had been in the Navajo country, said Apache planting was closer and shallower than that of the Navajo. In the 1940s, when corn was planted by hand behind the plow, seed was usually dropped in every third furrow, although this might vary with individual taste and the size of the plow; some planted every fourth or fifth row.

By the 1880s some of the Apache, at least, planted with the digging stick in regular rows, with even spacing of hills two to three feet apart. It is quite possible that regular row patterns were planted earlier than this, but no account of it was obtained. Where trees or large stones were encountered, the row was continued beyond them; the obstacle was not circled. Rows were aligned by eye; there was no marking of guidelines with foot or stick.

Directional planting was affirmed only by those who had used the ritual planting. They (two White Mountain people) said it began in the east and continued up and down the field. Helical planting was described as an occasional practice at both Cedar Creek and East Fork. The first hole was planted at the center of the field, then holes were planted in order to the east, south, west, and north of this, after which planting was continued around and around in a clockwise direction. Helical planting was recorded by Gifford[69] for the Southern Tonto. There appeared to be no team planting by a staggered row of planters.

Holes were punched, either straight or slanting, or were scooped out with a digging stick. The depth of planting, as ascertained from oral statement and from measurement of illustrative holes, was from five to eight inches. The planter stood, kneeled, or squatted according to his preference. If the ground was hard, the digging stick might be driven in with a stone. The stomach or chest was never pressed on the stick to add weight. Holes were often dug at the side rather than in front of the planter. In this case, one knee was placed on the ground, the opposite hand at the lower end of the stick. The dry earth was first scraped away, then a hole was made in the moist earth. When men worked, they dug the holes. Usually the operator was followed by a planter. If a person worked alone, several holes were dug, then seeded and covered. The length of the planting stick varied from thirty to sixty inches, with an average length of perhaps thirty-six to forty-two inches. Soil was not loosened below the depth of planting.

Seeds were dropped in any fashion, with no set pattern of placement or number. Often a lucky person, a medicine man, or a woman with knowledge of prayers and songs would be sought to do the actual dropping of seed. Anyone so unlucky as to have been bitten by a snake or struck by lightning could not plant; neither could menstruating or pregnant women. Four, five, or six seeds to a hill was the average number, although statements were made that six or seven, seven to ten, and two or three might be dropped. All agreed that not more than ten would be placed in one hill.

Soil was replaced with the hands, moist first, then dry. Usually it was not tamped, although some pressed it with the hands or stepped on it lightly if the soil was dry. Holes were filled to ground level. Occasionally a mound an inch or two high was erected. No depressions were made around the hills, although latter-day San Carlos did this. Children sometimes filled the holes if this was not done by the planter.

It was standard practice to complete the planting of a corn field in a single day. This was accomplished by the cooperative work of several people who went from field to field until all fields were planted. Sometimes different parties worked in different fields simultaneously.

Planting was occasionally done at night, by moonlight, not because of any supposed benefit to the crop, but to prevent the soil from drying out.

If a crop was washed out, it was replanted, provided it was not too late in the season.

Most of the Apache agricultural ritual centered on corn. In early times everyone used song and prayer when they planted. In prayers the White Mountain asked "a girl that smile all the time" (a certain kind of "popped open" corn) to bring them a good crop. They also asked the mythical Corn People of each locality (each large agricultural site, such as Cedar Creek, Canyon Day, East Fork, and as far afield as Cibecue) to assist in ensuring a bountiful harvest.

At East Fork, planting was begun in the eastern section of the field and was accomplished by the following prayer: "I'm going to plant corn today. Dark [holy] gan's [spirit's] farm, all the crop he's got around his farm, I want a crop just like his. Our Blessed Mother [Changing Woman], God, Jesus" (the informant was a converted Catholic). The person went around the field four times repeating this prayer. There were also accompanying songs, but the informant refused to translate them, saying that anyone who sang these in summer or spring, except in the field, would be struck by lightning or bitten by a snake.

The Cibecue removed their moccasins while planting. If they failed to do so, it was believed that the corn would produce many leaves but no ears. In the 1940s, when plowing, some removed their shoes for the same reason. This practice was denied by the White Mountain.

It should be noted at this point that I recorded contradictory practices and denials wherever I found them. Often it is possible, if not probable, that these represented tribal or group or band differences. On the other hand, the differences might have been only local group or family or even personal variations within a common culture complex. Ritual and prayer were particularly subject to changes or variations over a period of time or from place to place.

My informants might never have encountered or heard of elements that were at one time part of the total Apache culture.

Corn: Care

The White Mountain occasionally broke the crusted earth to aid the growth of corn or pumpkin shoots. This practice was denied by the Cibecue.

Fences to break the wind or individual shields to protect plants from driven sand were never used by the Apache. Such protection was unnecessary.

White Mountain fields were damaged occasionally by flood. In these instances no one entered the field for four days. On the fifth day, if the corn had not been washed out or buried in debris, the roots were re-covered; bent stalks were straightened and tied to sticks, two to the stalk. After the corn became firmly rooted, the sticks were removed. Corn was not hilled.

At Canyon Creek, corn was weeded when it was about six inches high, at which time the earth was loosened around the stalks with a digging stick. If necessary it was weeded a second time, but not cultivated. At Cedar Creek, weeds were pulled when the corn was twelve to eighteen inches high. At East Fork the corn was weeded only once: when it was about eighteen inches high. At this time the earth around the plants was loosened. In early times, weeds were pulled or gouged out and thrown clear of the field. They might be burned after they had dried. Latter-day farmers left weeds where they were chopped or pulled.

The Cibecue thinned their corn and threw the excess stalks away; only the largest stalks were left. This was said to "make better corn." At Cherry Creek, every stalk exceeding ten to a clump was removed. In the 1940s, very few people did this. A Cibecue man said he preferred to use the surplus corn for fodder. The White Mountain also thinned their corn.

Irrigating was done early in the morning or late in the evening and occasionally by moonlight. Irrigation during the heat of the day was considered bad for the crop. Both men and women irrigated, although it was considered primarily a woman's task.

The Cibecue first watered corn when it had reached a height of six or eight inches. After this it was irrigated when necessary, "maybe two or three weeks apart."

The White Mountain irrigated two to four times: first in May, when the plants were about eighteen inches high; again a month later; and perhaps again in August. Rain ceremonies were often held in July when the corn reached a height of two and a half to three feet. These were directed by medicine men who led the prayers. The cost of the ceremonies was apportioned among the participants. When the crop had been watered two or three times or a good rain had fallen and the success of the crop was assured, farmers often left the farm for one to three months to gather wild foods.

Song and prayer accompanied irrigation and cultivation. The Cibecue addressed the corn, saying, "Grow fast; don't bother it, worms; make a good crop." No other ritual was practiced until the tassels formed. Then a woman possessing ceremonial knowledge walked around the field and sang, "Make a good ear; don't hail." If presented a gift, such a woman would sing for others.

Some farms in 1947 were suffering from lack of water, which was readily available, and some fields were choked with weeds taller than the corn. It was said that people would "rather ride around or go some place and drink" than care for their fields. When viewing such fields, I was usually told how much better they were tended in the past or how much harder people had worked. I saw other fields that showed every evidence of excellent care.

Corn: Harvesting

Late August and September were the normal harvest periods for all crops, although harvesting might be delayed or continued into October or even November. If not already at the farms, families and local groups returned for this purpose. At times only the mature ears of corn were harvested, the remainder being collected as they ripened. At other times all were harvested, and green ears were pit-baked and dried. Harvests might be hurried so that a group could leave to gather or hunt. Among most local groups the majority of the families spent the winter in lower country.

White Mountain harvest time varied with the type of corn and the time of planting. Early Hopi corn was said to mature in sixty-five days. A short, yellow corn growing about four feet tall was harvested in eighty-five days. White, soft Indian corn could be harvested ninety-five days after planting. Blue corn was slowest to mature, often being harvested in November. The fast-growing sixty-five-day corn was often planted late, perhaps in July.

There was no fast rule for the time of harvesting, nor was priority given one crop over another. Beans and pumpkins were harvested at the same time corn was picked.

The Apache determined when corn was mature by examining the silk. If dry, they opened a part of the ear and looked at the grains. If the kernels were still soft, they closed the ear; if not, it was removed from the stalk. Or they might wait until the husk and silk were dry. A chief would probably suggest at a morning talk that it was time to harvest or urge that the crops be gathered so that the group could go south to collect wild foodstuffs. Heads of families then instructed their groups to harvest.

There was usually no cooperative exchange of labor at harvest; only the immediate family worked. However, nonfarming helpers might be notified or volunteer. These helpers were either friends or relatives, women more often than men.

The first act in harvesting was to select the ceremonial stalks and choose the four female ears, as described in the section on seed selection. Then the ears were picked and thrown into a burden basket on the back. Ears were usually removed from the standing stalk, but in one harvest during the 1880s all the stalks were pulled and taken to the side of the field before the ears were removed. Sometimes the stalks were trampled as the ears were picked so that none would be overlooked. Bourke[70] saw stalks still standing in a harvested field.

The piled corn was usually husked in place, leaving enough husk to tie the ears together into bundles of eight to twelve. Bundles so tied or braided together were carried by hand. They also might be transported in burden baskets or saddlebags, in which case it was unnecessary to tie them or even husk them. If both men and women were involved, the men usually carried hand bundles, the women baskets, although White Mountain men basket-packed with chest and shoulder or head tumplines. Frequently, corn husks, stalks, and cobs were burned in a field after harvest.

Corn was dried two to four weeks. Bundles of ten or twelve ears were hung over a tree limb or an improvised drying rack. Drying on a ramada top (in which case the corn was turned) was also common and persisted into the late 1940s. One of my informants said ramadas had been in use only for the past seventy or eighty years.

When the corn had been dried thoroughly, part or all of it was shelled. Requisite dryness was determined by the shrinkage of the kernels and the ease with which they could be detached from the cob. If the crop was small, kernels were removed by hand; if large, flails were employed. The corn was placed on a hide or blanket, covered with a hide, then beaten with a flail six to eight feet long. Any grains left on the cob were removed by hand. After beating, the corn was winnowed, either by tossing it in a basket or placing a basketful on the head and letting the corn dribble out. Women did the winnowing.

When corn was shelled by hand, the butt of a cob was used to gouge out one or two rows on each side of the ear. The striking cob was held in the fist and jabbed against the kernels with a downward motion toward the operator. Then the ear was held in the left hand (for a right-handed person) and the right hand was twisted over the ear with an outward and downward movement; the heel of the hand detached the kernels. If a few rows had already been removed, the remainder might be removed by twisting the ear in the hands. Gifford[71] recorded the use of stone, bone, antler, and stick awls in shelling, but my informants said such tools were never used, only the blunt end of a cob.

It was a breach of good behavior for anyone not of the family to enter a field from the time the crops began to sprout until after harvest. This custom resulted from the fear that jealous individuals might ruin the crop by sorcery.

Ditch bosses or men with agricultural rites were frequently called on to perform a ceremony to hasten the ripening of the crops, according to Goodwin.[72] He[73] recorded and annotated a myth (described in the seed-selection section) in which Turkey directed the harvest procedure.

Corn: Storage

At least half the corn crop was stored. The remainder was consumed as needed or transported to the winter camp. An attempt was made to store enough to last until the next harvest.

Often there were many caches belonging to each family, distributed so that families would have food supplies available in several areas in case they were surprised by enemies. A family might have as many as five or ten caches, but not all for corn. These were located near the winter camps and farms. Crops of different years were stored in separate caches.

Corn was stored with the husks on or off. Often bundles of twelve ears or so were tied with yucca cord, or eight, ten, or twelve ears might be braided together by their husks. If two or three pitched water baskets or more were available for storage, the corn was shelled and placed in these.

Corn of different colors was almost always stored separately, although there were exceptions. Seed and food corn were stored in separate bundles or vessels. Partitions inside the storage pit were made from bear grass and cedar bark (*Juniperus* sp.). Different colors of corn might also be used to designate parts of the pit. Sometimes relatives (apparently members of an extended family or close group) used the same cache with such partitioning.

Rich people stored in pitched baskets, baskets, or pottery vessels. Poor people wrapped their corn in bear grass. Corn placed in grass spoiled if it became damp. The rich used as many as ten or twelve containers, sealing them with grass, stones, mud, or a stone cut to fit the opening, cemented with mud.

Seed corn was usually stored on the cob at the bottom of the cache. Other corn was stored either on the cob or shelled. If corn were stored on the cob, it was wrapped carefully in bear grass, although it might be put in a buckskin bag (this was a large bag shaped like a gunnysack, with the opening at the center across the short side). Shelled corn, both for seed and food, was stored in an

Fig. 13. *Geronimo's Cave at East Fork, which probably was never used by the well-known Apache, had not been fully explored in the 1940s. A large cache of spoiled corn was found in burden baskets in its depths.*

old pitched water basket (a new basket was never used for such purposes) or pottery jar. For cave or rock-shelter storage, olla-shaped baskets were often used.

Bourke and Barnes[74] in 1883 found in a cave up East Fork a cache of corn, devoured by weevils, stored in thirty finely executed and decorated baskets ranging from one to five feet high. They were told that this had been placed there years before at the death of a beloved member of the tribe. It was not possible to obtain confirmation that such storage for the dead had ever been an Apache custom. Informants denied the practice.

Cave storage or storage in holes in the rock below ledges or bluffs was also practiced. When the storage was of this type, stones were piled outside the openings, or the openings were walled up.

Ground caches were located in sunny spots by the White Mountain, on a slope by the Cibecue, to keep them dry. The Cibecue preferred sandy soil, often near or under a juniper tree. Cibecue caches were usually shallow, conical holes. Bear grass or grama grass (*Bouteloua* sp.) was laid on the bottom. Wrapped bundles or vessels were placed on this, then covered with a layer of bear grass. Over this, rocks eighteen to twenty-four inches in diameter were placed, then a layer of juniper brush and twigs was added. A covering of earth completed the cache. White Mountain caches were sometimes six feet deep, sloped conically down to a round base, and were just large enough at the top for a person to enter. A fire was built in the bottom to dry them. Bear grass and juniper bark were used for flooring and compartment divisions, and the whole was covered at the top with grass, rocks, and earth. No pole siding or roofing was used.

People prayed as they cached food or other objects. One prayer reported by a man who heard it in the 1880s was as follows: "I bury my corn here; don't nobody bother; don't coyote or bear or anybody dig it out; if you see him you change his mind." No further information on this prayer was obtained.

Men dug the storage pits, and women stored the food.[75] Adolescent girls watched while caches were constructed and helped carry food to them. After marriage, youths were taught the art of storage by their parents.[76]

Stored corn might be inspected to see if it were dry and undisturbed. The Apache took great care in storing corn because it was a scarce commodity. Pit-baked corn and parched corn were not ground-cached.

The White Mountain stated that they never stored corn or nuts in tree caches. A Cherry Creek man described the tree-caching of corn. Twenty to forty ears were assembled in a bundle some two feet in diameter and wrapped with bear grass. Hung from a tree, it would keep for about a year. Another method of preparing corn for storage was to impale an ear on each end of a sharpened stick. Approximately forty of these were then tied in a bundle. They weighed about seventy to eighty pounds and could be suspended from a tree or transported with ease.

Cellar dugout granaries were used after the military occupation and were still to be found in the 1940s. They were of varying size,

Fig. 14. *Bland Tessay and a semisubterranean storage structure. Food also was stored in caves or ground caches.*

averaging perhaps four or five feet in width by eight to ten feet in length. Their depth was about eighteen inches. Over the pit was placed a gable roof, which was covered with bundles of bear grass, then earth. In early times the entrance was walled with rocks; later wooden doors, which could be locked, were used.

I observed storage in baskets, pitched water baskets, cans, sacks, boxes, and bins. One house I examined had two ladderlike bundles of long-eared corn hung against the wall, plus a can and a box filled with the same product. In addition there was a large box or bin inside a shed and two large outside bins against another shed. Another house had a box of corn on the back porch, and in the wickiup owned by the same family were several baskets and cans of corn and a large pile of corn on the floor.

Corn: Names and Varieties

To their name for corn the White Mountain and Cibecue appended color and other descriptive adjectives. Variety names, which follow, were descriptive in terms of color: blue corn, soft gray-blue corn, striped red and white or yellow, almost red with white stripe, white, pink, yellow, red (almost black), black.

One particularly large-butted, long, curving type of corn was called gan corn or bear corn by the Cibecue and was used in curing. In one of the White Mountain myths, Turkey shook out "big corn," which Goodwin[77] identified as dark red corn.

Blue corn was said by the White Mountain to be the male and boss of all the corn. There was a "flat-headed, small, female" corn, not a variety, that was sought as a part of the necessary seed. A kind of "popped-open" corn was called "a girl that smiles all the time" and was used in prayers to the Corn People; this also was apparently not a variety.

The Cibecue "corn chiefs" or "corn captains" (these were medicine men, but nothing more was learned of them; possibly they were ditch bosses) had names and synonyms and associations for some of the varieties of corn. Black corn was also "sun-up" corn or "man's" corn and was associated with the east. White corn was also called "girl's" corn and was associated with the south. Yellow corn, associated with the west, was "sun-down" corn or "woman's" corn. Blue corn was "boy's" corn and was associated with the north.

Goodwin stated that each of the seven varieties of White Mountain corn was the property of a certain clan or clans but that corn definitely was not assigned to only one clan and that there was nothing comparable to Pueblo corn clans. Clans owning a certain colored corn were not restricted to the planting of that particular kind, but permission to save the seed of another kind was asked of the owning clan as a matter of form.[78]

Nine corn-owning clans were listed by Goodwin.[79] Two clans shared the ownership of white corn, and two shared black corn. The owning clan of round corn also shared the ownership of blue corn with another clan. Yellow and gray corns were each owned by a single clan.

The Cibecue group claimed to have had, before reservation days, corn varieties in blue, white, yellow, red, black, green, and speckled red with a light stripe. These were not preserved in a pure form, as they cross-pollinated after a few years.

The White Mountain stated that blue, red, soft white, hard white, yellow, and black were the most ancient types. Barnes,[80] who was stationed at Fort Apache in 1880, spoke of "Indian corn in the common red, green, blue, and yellow colors." I collected in the East Fork, Canyon Day, and Cedar Creek areas long ears of red, white, yellow, speckled blue and white, speckled red and white, and black corn.

Apache corn was shorter than modern American corn, varying from four to six feet and not usually over five. The number of ears varied from two to four to the stalk, with two being the expectable number. The pre-American corns were said to be faster growing than modern American. A soft white early corn was said to be harvested in sixty-five days, though it is doubtful that corn matures fully in this length of time.[81] A red corn with a light stripe that was called Hopi corn was reputed to mature in sixty-five days. A short yellow corn growing about four feet high was reported to mature in eighty-five days. Another soft white Indian corn required ninety-five days. Soft red corn was said to require a longer growing time than soft white, and blue corn required the most time of all.

Corn: Origins

Apache mythology associates corn with the gan or mountain-cave spirits. In one tale a gan married Raven Chief's daughter, took her to the underworld, then brought Raven presents of corn and seeds with instructions how to plant them.[82] In other tales,[83] Turkey shook corn from his wings and taught farming.

Old Apache, however, had realistic traditions concerning agricultural origins, and these derive corn from various surrounding peoples. The Canyon Creek and Cibecue stated that corn was first obtained from the "Hopi friend of Apache" and "Pima enemy of Apache." The Cherry Creek had traditions of obtaining corn from the Mexicans and from non-Apache Indians to the southwest.

An eighty-eight-year-old White Mountain Apache recounted the agricultural traditions he heard when he was a boy. He was told by his elders that they had in turn been told by their elders that the original seed and practice of agriculture had come to them from the Mexicans and Pueblo (which of the Pueblo is not known, as they are all called in Apache "People on the Rock"). Before this time, the tradition went, the Apache had lived only on wild products. This account, if reliable, would carry Apache agriculture back at least two centuries.

The man said white hard and yellow hard corn were first obtained from Mexico and that soft white, blue, and red were derived from the Pueblo.

Several Apache spoke of occasional nineteenth-century trading expeditions to the Zuñi and (in the case of the Cibecue) to the Hopi in which corn was brought back. Some of them believed that flint corn was introduced by white Americans, and none had heard of popcorn or sweet corn before the American occupation.

Although the Apache long had had contact with the Navajo, sometimes friendly, often not, none mentioned that corn or other plants were obtained from them.

Corn: Attitudes and Preferences

Corn was highly valued by the Apache. If possible, they had a small amount of corn food, in one form or another, each day. People liked to farm, and, apparently, those who farmed most were those with high social and economic prestige: the chiefs and rich people. Both men and women were interested in agriculture, but the women were the most concerned and were reputedly the better farmers.

People were enjoined by chiefs in the latter's daily morning harangues to plant corn, to take care of it, to work hard, to feed their wives and children. Young people were given similar advice by fathers, mothers, and grandparents.

The girls' puberty ceremony once included the grinding and cooking of corn as part of a girl's tasks to show her abilities. At Cedar Creek in 1948 a dying girl dozed or lapsed into periods of unconsciousness shortly before her death and told those around

Fig. 15. *Evelyn Ethelbah and her sponsor in the girls' puberty rite. Singers are in the rear.*

her, "We'll plant corn; it's a beautiful place" (the field she had seen), then died.

Although the latter-day Apache valued corn, they did not show as much concern over it as some of the Pueblo were reputed to display. One young woman took me across a field to show me her farm. A ditch had broken, and water was flooding some six to ten rows of corn and would obviously wash it all out. She showed no concern and made no attempt to divert the water into its channel. I saw horses tethered at the edge of growing corn, where they were allowed to feed on it. The Apache said they did not "feel bad," as did the Hopi, about accidentally injuring or cutting down any of their plants.

The Apache held colored corn in high regard. They preferred flour corn over flint. Some said they would rather have Indian corn than American or "tall Kansas" corn because it was softer.

In their preferences for seed corn they varied, some keeping and planting only one color, most preferring to plant more than one color. Most preferred blue, a few yellow, white, or red. Black was rarely planted because it was difficult to know when black corn was properly cooked, burned, or not yet done.

Blue corn meal was cohesive and made the best tortillas; other kinds "cracked easy." White corn meal was also desirable for tortillas, "but the rest, no." Yellow or white corn was most desired if consumed in the green stage; "red not taste good, blue hurt the heart." Yellow corn was favored for parching, white and red next. White corn meal was best for mush; blue and others were not used much. Yellow flint corn was best when pit-baked; used otherwise, it was too hard.

Corn: Uses (Other Than Foods)

The Apache used small corn stalks, which they removed while thinning, for beds, although twenty-four-inch hay grass was preferred for this purpose. Bedding material was piled on the ground to a height of four or five inches. In the 1940s, such stalks were used for fodder.

Corn husks were never used for dye. They were used occasionally to stuff matresses but were said to "make too much noise." Wide husks were used for wrapping corn bread or tamales, small ones for cigarettes.

At one time, cobs were used to make pipe bowls. They were also burned to produce coals for parching corn and were considered the best fuel for this purpose. In later times they were piled up for use in stoves. Husks, cobs, and stalks often were burned after harvest, there being no taboo against this practice.

Corn smut was rubbed on the face by girls to bleach the skin.

Big, large-butted, curved ears of corn, called gan corn or bear corn, were sometimes used by medicine men in curing. Only one ear was used. It was heated in the fire, applied to a patient's head, reheated, then reapplied several times. It was not learned what ailment this cure was supposed to relieve.

Pollen was shaken from the corn into a deerskin bag by the Cibecue for use in connection with ritual. If necessary, it was mixed with the preferred cattail pollen to increase the bulk. Goodwin[84] said yellow corn meal might be mixed with pollen or used in its place. Curtis[85] said pollen was mixed with meal and offered during prayers invoking an abundance of corn. My White Mountain informants said corn pollen was never used and cattail pollen might be mixed only with that of the piñon.

Corn: Recipes

Much corn was eaten before it matured, partly because green-corn recipes were liked, often because the previous harvest had been exhausted. Immature corn was sometimes boiled, cob and all, at the time the ears came into silk. Usually, only the smaller of the two ears on a stalk, the lower one, was plucked before maturing. The cooked cob was said to be good. Yellow or white corn was the preferred corn for such use.

Green corn on the cob was boiled or roasted. This was noted by Reagan.[86] Large green corn was ground and made into gruel.[87] Green corn was mashed, salted, and compressed into a cake that was baked in ashes.[88] Reagan[89] described a "wedding cake" and puberty ceremony "cake" that my informants denied was made. It was prepared, according to Reagan, from mashed green corn or from finely ground corn meal. A yeast preparation for "sweetening" the meal was made from the chewed root of *Euphorbia serphillifolia,* which was preserved in sacks in dried form. A piece of the root was chewed and kept in the mouth "for a couple of days," a virgin usually doing the chewing. The meal was then chewed with the masticated root or in the "freshened mouth" without it, and the cud was deposited in a vessel. At the time Reagan made his observations (probably about 1901), sprouted corn and partly sprouted wheat were used to produce the sweetening.

Reagan[90] saw walnut kernels mixed with mashed green corn and baked in cake form.

After the Apache learned to fry foods, green corn was sometimes cut off the cob and fried with deer fat and young pumpkin.

The process of pit-baking green corn was described by a Cibecue man. A pit four feet square and two feet deep was filled with crisscrossed wood, over which round rocks four to six inches in diameter were placed. Oak was used for firewood because pine killed the flavor. The pit was fired. After the smoke had abated, any wood still smoldering was removed. Green corn stalks were laid on the hot stones. Then the corn, either husked or unhusked and in single ears or tied in bundles, was thrown in. About one hundred pounds (four or five burden baskets full) was used. Corn stalks were placed over the corn and covered with earth about one foot deep. Meanwhile, a stick had been held vertically in the pit. This was removed, and through the opening that remained about five gallons (two large pitched water baskets full) of water were poured into the pit. The hole was then closed with earth. This operation was performed just before dark. Next morning, the corn was removed and cooled. It might be eaten immediately or shelled with a knife, dried three days in the sun, and stored. If stored, it would keep all winter, but not past spring. It was boiled for use as needed.

A White Mountain corn pit still in use when I saw it measured seven feet square and four feet deep. The stones used in the pit were rounded and were six to eight inches in diameter. Most were vesicular lava, although some were of limestone. Into this pit was dumped four wagonloads of green corn at a time, and about fifteen gallons of water was poured in for steaming.

No one who had been struck by lightning might participate in the steam baking of corn; it was believed that the grain would not cook under those conditions. There was a taboo on sexual relations among the participants during the time of cooking. A lucky person (one with power) was secured to light the fire. This was lighted first on the east, then the south, west, and north. It was believed that a family must continue to use the same pit to obtain satisfactory results. A family could not go from one pit to another, as with mescal.

Reagan[91] stated that green corn was steamed for twenty-four hours before being removed from the pit. Palmer,[92] who did not mention the use of water in pit-baking corn, said the process required eighteen to twenty-four hours.

Reagan[93] stated that at harvest time all green corn was separated and pit-baked.

Corn was often husked, spitted on the end of a sharp stick, and roasted by hunters. Burned kernels were removed with a stick before eating. An unhusked ear was sometimes placed directly in the fire or in hot ashes and roasted, then husked and eaten. Corn was eaten even when scorched by the fire.

A pile of corn might be roasted by covering it with brush and firing it. However, according to the White Mountain, it had to be carefully placed with the ears in an upright position, stems to ground. One husk had to be removed from each ear. Even children were said to know these requirements. Failure to observe them was believed to bring bad luck.

Corn was often parched before grinding. It was never stored in this state but was ground and used immediately. Ground corn, parched and unparched, was eaten by the pinch, mixed with other ground seeds and eaten by the pinch, and cooked, alone or in combination with other foods, into a "gravy" (mush or gruel).

Corn-meal dough was compressed, and small dumplings, as large in diameter as a finger, were dropped into a boiling pot of plain water or soup. Such dough was mixed only with salt and water. It was necessary to prepare two dumplings at a time, one in each hand; contrary practice was believed to bring bad luck. These dumplings were placed in a basket, speared with a sharp stick, and eaten. Small dumplings were also cooked with ground acorn meats.

Bread was made in a variety of ways. An "ash bread" was prepared from corn meal mixed with salt and water. This was placed on an ash bed, covered with ashes, and small coals raked over the top. After a time it was uncovered; if not completely cooked, it was turned over and re-covered with ashes and coals. When done, it was placed in a basket and water was poured over it to remove the ashes. It was then broken with the hands and eaten. Ash bread might also be wrapped in corn husks before cooking. In this shape it resembled a tamale.

At Oak Creek in the early 1890s a man who had been in the Hopi country made an earth oven in which he baked corn tamales and bread. This oven was said to make excellent bread but was not durable and had to be rebuilt after about four days. This was the only instance known by informants of the use of a Pueblo-type oven.

Tortillas were prepared by spreading a corn-meal batter on a hot stone. By the 1890s, at least, a small amount of government-issued white flour was mixed with the corn meal to make the tortillas less crumbly. Blue corn was favored for tortillas; white corn was also desirable. In later times, tortillas generally were made of white wheat flour and cooked on a wire grill.

Goodwin[94] quoted one of his informants on the process of making tortillas: "Take a metal hoe, set it on three stones in the fire and be sure you have hot coals in between the stones. Now mix up your corn-meal dough, roll it into a ball between your hands, then mash it down on the hot hoe blade. When you have mashed it so it reaches the edge, take it off." Bourke[95] said the scouts made tortillas in a metal pan, Santee[96] that hunters carried a flat piece of tin for this purpose. Reagan[97] stated that the Apache made a "corn pone," which was baked in or under the ashes or cooked in lard in a skillet, and a kind of saltless corn-meal "pancake" in a skillet. He described tortillas as being made of flour and baking powder, if available, on an inverted skillet.

Mush was prepared from corn meal alone, but meat or other plant foods usually were added. Mush was made from corn meal, to which might be added meal from ground parched beans, sunflower seeds, saguaro seeds, and other wild seeds. The corn meal might be ground from parched or unparched corn. The mush was normally eaten with the fingers and from a basket. Juniper ashes were used to flavor corn meal mush and to produce a green color. Gruels were prepared from corn meal boiled in soup and from parched corn meal boiled with mashed pumpkin.

Corn was used in many combinations with other foods. The whole grains of green corn that had been steam baked were boiled with meat or with plant foods. Corn was boiled with beans or with beans and venison together.

A flour that was eaten by the pinch, either dry or slightly moistened, was prepared from parched corn meal mixed with ground sunflower seeds, acorns, walnuts, piñon nuts, or lightly parched pumpkin seeds. Such flour—and flour prepared from corn and miscellaneous wild seeds—was also baked into bread cakes.

Corn meal was cooked as a sausage in the intestines of animals in the same manner as was blood.

Corn cobs were mashed and boiled in water with salt. For some this was a starvation recipe; others prepared it because they liked it.

Corn smut was often eaten raw in the field. At other times the smutty ear was taken home and boiled. On still other occasions the smut was removed from the ear, wrapped in corn husks, and boiled until solid, after which a stick was pushed into it. Finally, acorn meal was sprinkled over it, and it was eaten.

Corn and "hominy" were mentioned as being boiled with broken or dried bones. The use of true hominy was either a late practice or the term was misused by the informant, as the early-day Apache did not prepare hominy.

Beans

There is some doubt concerning the antiquity of beans (*Phaseolus* sp.) as an Apache crop plant, although they were known to be cultivated before the Anglo-American occupation. A Spanish document dated 1799 and translated in part by Whipple [98] stated that "the Coyotero Indians raise small quantities of maize, beans, and a few legumens."

The Cherry Creek people believed they had had beans long before the advent of the military. According to tradition, they had obtained beans (teparies, *Phaseolus acutifolius?*) from the Pima ("got lots of things from them") and from the Mexicans. However, beans were not, as were pumpkins and giant sunflower seeds, attributed to the Cave People (gan). The White Mountain did not plant many beans; some of the local groups or families did not plant them at all, and some denied that they had ever grown them before the soldiers arrived. They said they did not have prayers or lucky planters for the beans as they did for corn and pumpkins because beans "came from the whites."

At upper Canyon Creek, people began using beans introduced by the Americans after 1890. Before this they had a big white bean "like the lima bean" (*Phaseolus lunatis* or *Phaseolus coccineus?*) and small varieties of kidney beans (*Phaseolus valgaris*) in white, yellow, red, and black colors. There was also a small black-eyed bean (cowpea, *Vigna sinensis?*) that did not grow downward as other varieties, "just stick it out." Only pink kidney beans and pinto beans, both introduced in modern times, were grown in the Cibecue area in the 1940s.

The White Mountain had red, yellow, blue, and speckled beans, the antiquity and antecedents of which were undetermined. A yellow bean was grown at Cedar Creek, and a cream-colored bean speckled with brown (a pinto bean) was grown at Canyon Day. The pink and pinto were the favored types, and the pinto reputedly was obtained from the Mexicans.

The presence of black-eyed peas (*Vigna sinensis*) was denied by all.

The qualities of the various beans were believed, by the Cibecue, to vary. All were planted at the same time, harvested at the same time, and irrigated in the same manner. The newer varieties came up in about a week and a half, but the sprouting time of the old types was not known because they were planted and unattended until they were well grown. All stored equally well. Insects were said to bother the modern pink beans more than the old type and were said to have molested the large white bean (*Phaseolus lunatis* or *Phaseolus coccineus?*) hardly at all. (Possibly this is just an impression. Insects were said not to be numerous or very troublesome in the 1890s. In the 1940s the Mexican beetle made dusting necessary.) Pink "English" beans and the old Apache small white and large white beans were said to produce about fifty pounds to the patch, while the yellow and red beans yielded about one hundred pounds to the same patch (the size of this patch was not satisfactorily determined).

English beans were well liked. The Apache never cared much for the old Apache large white bean (*Phaseolus lunatis* or *Phaseolus coccineus?*).

Beans were planted in the early spring at the same time as corn. A variation of this occurred at upper Canyon Creek, where they were planted about two weeks after the corn "so they would get ripe the same time." In either case they matured at the same time as the corn and were harvested with it. After the turn of the century, probably under government tutelage, the Apache did not plant beans until July. In 1947, some were planted August 1 at Cibecue.

In both early days and later times, some Apache planted beans in separate plots, some between the corn clumps or with the corn and pumpkins. At Oak Creek a woman planted separate patches, rows one foot apart and hills one foot apart. Six or seven seeds were dropped in a four- to five-inch hole made with a planting stick. Others separated rows and hills by two feet or more.

Bean fields were always irrigated before planting. The usual practice was to water again when the plants were six or eight inches high, when they flowered, and when the pods formed. Subsequent irrigation was determined by need. Weeds were pulled and the earth around the plants stirred with a stick when the vines were small.

Beans were not soaked before planting except by the East Fork White Mountain; these people soaked them the same as corn. At Cibecue it was said they cracked too easily to withstand the soaking. However, they were moistened in a gunnysack of wet earth.

Large and small beans were always planted in separate rows. Different colors were usually stored and planted separately.

Some preferred a sandy soil in which to plant beans. The older generation of Apache said beans grew better in a high altitude and cold climate.

There was no ritual or prayer in the planting and care of beans as with corn and pumpkins. However, the prayers for corn served for beans and all other crops. Beyond some weeding and cultivation with a digging stick, little attention was given the bean crop. Beans were not trained on sticks or poles, although some supported them with wire or string trellises "learned at school."

Oak ashes were sometimes sprinkled on beans, as on other crops, to prevent attacks by insects. Insects might be removed with the hands and crushed. A red insect with black spots was so crushed, as were the nests it made beneath the leaves.

Green kidney beans were sometimes picked and boiled with salt, but they were usually not harvested until September or October, when they were ripe and hard. The whole bush was pulled, placed on a hide or blanket (occasionally, some Apache pulled only the pods instead of the whole vine), and beaten with a flail. The larger leaves and stems were then removed by hand and the beans winnowed by tossing in the air with the hands or pouring from a basket held on the head. At Cibecue, beans were sometimes trampled instead of beaten. This practice was denied by the White Mountain. The large white beans (*Phaseolus lunatis?* or *Phaseolus coccineus?*) were never beaten but shelled by hand.

A six-foot flail was used, usually operated from a sitting position. If necessary, beans might be beaten twice. The harvesting floor was about ten feet in diameter, the surface hardened by wetting and trampling. If the pods did not open, they were pulled off by hand and might be taken home to cook. A few beans were given to helpers.

In early times, beans were placed in pitched water baskets, buckskin sacks (twenty-five pounds or so), or pottery vessels and stored in ground caches or rock shelters. The crop then was small, "not over fifty pounds." Seed was selected on the basis of color rather than size but was inspected to make sure it was sound. In later times, some beans were stored in the pod.

Bean crops were said to be better about the turn of the century but were considered uncertain and poor in the 1940s. At that time, dust for the Mexican beetle was distributed without charge to those who wished it, but not all took advantage of the offer. The Whiteriver government farmer was trying to increase the planting of beans on unirrigated farms.

Mush was made from ground parched beans. Unparched whole beans were boiled with salt. During the summer, only enough beans for a single meal were cooked to prevent spoilage. Beans were also boiled with corn. Only in later times did the Apache fry precooked beans.

Pumpkins

Pumpkins (*Cucurbita moschata* or *Cucurbita pepo*) were one of the earliest Apache plants. As with corn, there were special songs, prayers, and lucky planters for them. Only one informant failed to include pumpkins as one of the original Apache crops.

Although an old crop, pumpkins do not appear to have been grown in great abundance in pre-American times. Families who planted corn every year did not always plant pumpkins. Upper Canyon Creek families used to raise five to ten large pumpkins. At Cibecue in earlier days, they raised "not too many, just five or six is all"; at Cibecue in the 1940s they might raise as many as a hundred, but many were not used: "Horse, burro eat it." At Cherry

Creek there were possibly somewhat more, for up to twenty were sometimes stored temporarily in layers of grass. At Cedar Creek only a few were grown, "just three or four or six," and the same was true of the other White Mountain. Bourke noted that in 1883, one hundred thousand pumpkins were raised on the Fort Apache Reservation.[99]

At Cedar Creek it was said that only one variety, a large yellow pumpkin, had been planted. At East Fork there was a round but not too large hard-shelled, greenish-colored pumpkin and a "crooked-necked squash" (*Cucurbita maxima?*). The latter was derived from Mexico.

One type raised at Canyon Creek was large—sometimes fifteen to twenty inches in diameter—long and soft necked, with a blue stripe. Other types were small—about ten inches in diameter—without a neck, hard shelled, and black, white, or brown striped. There was no orange-colored pumpkin. At San Carlos there were said to be yellow, gray, and other colors of pumpkins.

The Cibecue raised a large hook-necked pumpkin and a yellow pie pumpkin. A round black and green striped pumpkin "just like a cloud" matured earliest. It had a yellow interior. According to informants, it spoiled easily. The Hubbard squash (*Cucurbita maxima?*), with long neck and green or gray color, was the latest to mature; it stored better than most varieties and was used throughout the winter. A white, hard, short-necked pumpkin was midway between these in growing speed and storing qualities.

Pumpkins were planted five feet (two paces) or more apart, not in any pattern but randomly. Some Apache planted them in the corn rows, some around the edges of the corn field, some in separate plots. They were planted in moist ground with a digging stick, in a hole four to seven inches deep. Four or five seeds were dropped into each hole. The seed was sometimes soaked for about an hour before planting among the Cibecue, all night by the White Mountain. Seeds were not dampened or sprouted in wet earth. All varieties were planted at the same time and at the time the corn was planted. They were not planted with or close to watermelons. The plants appeared above the ground in about one week.

Pumpkins were weeded, irrigated, and the ground around them sometimes stirred with a digging stick at the same time corn was given such care. Those in separate patches were irrigated when about eight inches high, when the vine began to spread out, when they bloomed, and thereafter until ripe. Water was poured at the roots to make them grow large. Oak ashes were sometimes sprinkled on them to repulse insects. Flat stink bugs were removed by hand. The Apache learned from the whites to break off the ends of pumpkin vines to increase production, but only one man at Cibecue was said to do this. The Cibecue moved or rolled pumpkins to dry areas in the patch to keep them from getting wet and rotting; the White Mountain put grass under them.

Pumpkins were harvested the same time as the corn or later. They ripened from early fall until November. They were pulled from the vine, and no part of the vine was left attached as in the case of watermelons. Ripeness of the pumpkins was detected by the exterior's losing its shine and becoming rough and by the leaves' drying and falling. Some could tell when pumpkins were ripe by the color. They were not thumped to detect maturity. An attempt was made to harvest all pumpkins before the frost, as this would ruin them.

Green pumpkins were picked during the summer and boiled or baked in ashes. When the rind of pumpkin shone brightly, it was considered edible. At harvest time they were transported to camp in burden baskets, perhaps one large pumpkin to a basket. Helpers, if any, were given some for their assistance in carrying.

Pumpkins were never stored in prereservation days, although sometimes they were kept under a pile of grass for a limited period. Grass was spread and pumpkins placed on this, then more grass was added, then another layer of pumpkins, and so forth. Usually they were eaten as harvested or saved only a month or two. All were consumed by December at the latest. Those a family did not need were given to others. "They had to eat them up." Meat and hides might be given in exchange for pumpkins.

The largest seeds of the largest pumpkins were saved for seed. Color was no criterion for selection. Seeds were stored in a small pitched water basket and placed in a ground cache. Pumpkin seeds and those of the "crooked necked squash" were always stored separately. After seasonal migrations ceased, pumpkin seeds were stored in the wickiup. They were wrapped in grass with ashes and tied to the roof of the wickiup with three yucca strings to keep them warm and dry. Seeds to be eaten were kept in a vessel.

In the 1890s and thereafter at Cibecue, pumpkins were dried before storing. First they were sliced transversely, producing rings about three-eighths of an inch thick, them strung on sticks or a yucca string about one to one and a half inches apart. They were then hung between two trees for four or five days, after which they were stored in a sack. The pumpkin was seeded and cleaned through a hole in the end before being cut into spiral strips.

Another method of drying and storing pumpkins was practiced at Cherry Creek, where segments two inches wide and one to two feet long were cut from the pumpkins. These were dried on a tree or bush. When dry, they were suspended from the interior of the wickiup roof. They kept all winter, but not through the summer. They were never ground-cached.

Agricultural rituals were associated with the growing of pumpkins as with corn, these being the only crops of which this was true. However, prayers and songs for the corn were considered sufficient to cover pumpkins.

A prayer for pumpkins was described by an old White Mountain man with the injunction that it might be written but was not to be repeated to other Indians. It was a proprietary ritual that he wished to keep in his family. This rite was held at the time the runners were ready to spread. A young boy was sent out to pick a large supply of blue juniper berries. When he returned, he was blindfolded and sent into the pumpkin patch. He threw the berries in all directions, asking for that many pumpkins. He called out, "Gut, gut, gut" (this is the name of one variety of juniper berry; possibly there was another meaning), acting like a gan, and asked Changing Woman for as many pumpkins on the vines as he had thrown berries. After this prayer, it was said, the vines "really started blooming."

Newlyweds could not enter a field of growing pumpkin plants, lest the fruit shrivel and die on the vine. Other Apache stated that this applied only to nursing and pregnant women.[100] The basis of the taboo on newlyweds and pregnant or menstruating women is told by Goodwin in the tale "How the Squash Plant Was Obtained."[101]

The White Mountain denied that pumpkins were ever used for

vessels as were gourds, but a Cibecue had seen them so used in the 1880s. The meat of the pumpkin was scraped out with a stick and the hollowed rind boiled in a five-gallon tin, then hung by a yucca string about the neck to dry. The pumpkins used were yellow-white, brown, and spotted. They were colored red with a dye from a "soft red rock," which was boiled with them in the tin. Such a pumpkin vessel would last two or three years but was not considered as durable as a gourd.

The Cibecue used pumpkin seed to make a cosmetic grease for chapped skin, according to Gifford.[102]

A common way of preparing pumpkins was to boil them, mash them, and stir them in parched ground corn while boiling. Salt was added but was never applied to this or to any other Apache dish until it began boiling. Sunflower seed also was cooked with pumpkin in the same manner as corn.

Pumpkin halves or large slices were placed in an ash bed and covered with ashes. Before the pumpkins were eaten, the ashes were scraped away and the crust removed.

Whole pumpkins were opened and cleaned of their seeds and pithy matter. Either salt or some sweet material was then inserted and the pumpkin plugged, after which it was steam-baked with green corn in a pit oven.

Pumpkin seeds were eaten either uncooked or after parching. When lightly parched, they were sometimes ground with corn, moistened, and eaten by the pinch. Sometimes they were cut in thin slices and fried.

Gourds

Gourds (*Lagenaria siceraria*) were cultivated before the advent of the Americans. Only two informants had ideas about their origin, one stating that they were obtained from the Mexicans, the other saying Apache captives among the Mexicans had learned how to prepare them.

Two kinds of gourds were grown: a small one about the size of two finger joints, which was used as a rattle on cradleboards, and a larger one, which was used for canteens, cups, and dippers.

Seeds were sometimes soaked before planting, sometimes not. They were planted in four- to six-inch holes, three or more seeds to the hole (a Cherry Creek man said always four seeds). Some planted a few inside the brush fences, the vines being trained on the fence. If the gourds grew on the ground, they would be flat, which was not desirable. Others placed them at intervals around a field, perhaps four or five hills in all. Stakes were erected and the plant trained on these "to make a long tail." One man said that if gourds grew hanging on a stick they made a canteen, if on the ground they made a jug. They required more water than corn.

Seed was selected from gourds of a desirable shape, usually from a "long-handled" one, and such selection was said to produce well-shaped gourds. Seed might be stored in the roof of a wickiup in the same manner as pumpkin seed, or they might be stored with pumpkin seed in a pitched basket in a ground or rock cache. (Pumpkin seeds could be stored with gourd seeds but were never stored with seeds of the crooked-neck squash.)

Yucca string was often tied around the growing gourds to shape them, hourglass or double hourglass effects being obtained. Children often played with small gourds, so shaping them as they grew. Cultivated gourds with yucca string tied about the middle were seen at Cibecue in 1947.

In the 1940s, gourds used as cradleboard rattles had been replaced by beads and other gewgaws (in one case by the celluloid-framed picture of the father, who was absent in military service), although one gourd rattle was seen at Whiteriver in 1947. They were not used much by the 1940's for cups, dippers, canteens, or storage vessels. They were never used for face masks or for ornaments or for rattles except on cradleboards.

Size and shape determined use, small gourds being made into cups, long-handled gourds into spoons or dippers, large gourds into storage jars or canteens. They were not used to store water at home, only on long journeys, because it would taste bad, nor were they ever used as cooking vessels. They were used to store acorns, seeds, and salt.

To prepare it for use, a gourd was thoroughly soaked in warm water. A row of holes was punched close together with a bone awl if it were desired to split the gourd for a dipper. Then, by pressing, the gourd would separate, or it could be cut between the holes. It was dried in the field or hung up to dry but never covered with brush while drying. Seed and pithy matter were removed with a stick, and water was kept in the gourd for at least two nights (it was changed each day) to remove the taste. Sometimes gourds were boiled in a large can to remove the bitter taste. They were always bored or cut before they dried and hardened. They were pulled from the vine by hand, not cut. Gourds were never baked beside a fire to harden them. Utensils made of gourds would last for three or four years.

Gourds were decorated by grinding up red stone in hot water and rubbing this into the gourd to color it; yellow clay might also be used for this, but the colors were not lasting. Among the Cibecue, this was the only form of decoration.

Among the White Mountain, designs were burned onto the exterior of gourds—probably a case of Mexican or American diffusion. Common motifs were deer, butterflies, diamonds, crosses, moons, and half-moons. The White Mountain denied painting their gourds, painting being reserved for the pitched water basket.

Dorsey[103] wrote that huge gourds were used for water storage among the White Mountain, which use is contrary to informants' statements. Gifford[104] recorded large gourds grown by the Southern Tonto for water bottles too large for journeys.

One informant had been told by her great-grandmother that the Apache formerly ate small gourds. Goodwin[105] listed a clan, the Wild Gourd Growing People, that was named for its members' habit of eating wild gourds.

Melons

Watermelons (*Citrullus vulgaris*), as nearly as could be determined, were grown only after the reservation was established. At Canyon Creek seeds were obtained from the San Carlos whites. Bourke[106] noted that in 1883 the Indians on the White Mountain Reservation were reported to have raised twenty thousand watermelons, ten thousand muskmelons, and ten thousand cantaloupes.

Seeds were selected and stored in the same manner as pumpkin seeds. Melons might be grown in a corn patch or by themselves; in the 1940s the tendency was to plant in separate plots. Different varieties of melons were often grown together, but not in the same garden with pumpkins. Hills were planted two paces or so apart, about four to five seeds to the hill, at a depth of six or seven inches. Seeds were soaked the night before planting. Planting was done at the same time as corn.

In the 1880s a man at Oak Creek put horse manure in the water in which he soaked his seed and also planted the seeds with mashed horse manure. He always planted in the evening in order that the seed would remain moist. This man made beds four feet wide by ten feet long. He planted four or five hills of watermelons in the side of these by pressing the seeds into the earth with his thumb. Others did not follow this practice.

Melons were weeded and cared for in the same manner as corn. Vines were not broken off to increase production, but the Apache did thin all but five or six plants. Melons might be moved to dry ground or brush might be placed under them to prevent them from getting wet and rotting. When picked, about an inch of vine was left on the melon. This was believed to prevent spoilage.

Watermelons were eaten as soon as they matured. No attempt was made to dry them. Melons were never stored by burial in sand but might be covered with weeds and kept till November.

Tobacco

Most informants stated that tobacco (*Nicotiana* sp.) was never cultivated by the Apache but spoke of wild tobacco and substitutes that were used. One White Mountain man stated that tobacco was planted in the 1860s before the advent of the Americans. This was called mountain tobacco because they had to go far north to get it. It was very strong, "so strong one could smell the smoke across the valley, and tasted better and smelled better than the smoke white people use."

Goddard[107] in 1910 obtained an account from an aged San Carlos man to the effect that tobacco was planted.

Wild tobaccos (of unidentified species) were obtained on the north side of East Fork and in the Oak Creek area; very probably they existed in other areas, but inquiries on this subject were not exhaustive. At Oak Creek they were said to grow best if the plots were burned over before planting. In this connection, Gifford[108] noted: "Tobacco cultivated . . . [San Carlos, Cibecue, White Mountain] wild-tobacco seed after burning brush where it grew, not on farm. [San Carlos] tried growing Mexican tobacco in Wheatfield valley near Miami, failure." An informant stated that no care was taken of the crop after it was planted.

Tobacco was obtained from Mexico during raids. It was a scarce and valuable commodity. A man lacking tobacco would trade a large hide or blanket for a small supply. At times, those with tobacco shared it by passing a pipe from man to man.

Pipes were said to be elbow type, although tubular pipes were used before the 1870s. One informant said the last tubular pipe he had seen was one fashioned from white clay by a Tonto woman in the 1890s. Pipe bowls were made of clay and also from corncobs. A few were found in Pueblo ruins. Tobacco was smoked in corn-husk cigarettes as well as in pipes.

Young boys were not allowed to use tobacco, for it was believed harmful if used in excess by young men.

Tobacco was often used in prayer, and as an object of ceremonial importance; it was never handled carelessly. Throwing it from person to person rather than handing it gently was thought to bring bad luck.

Devil's Claw

There was no planting and cultivation, in the usual sense, of devil's claw (*Martynia louisiana*). However, the seeds of this plant were thrown into sandy places, washes, or beside a stream to have stands available close to camps. The seeds were never stored but always were gathered from wild sources.

When devil's claw was found growing in a field, it was allowed to remain unless the growth was too heavy. Only one informant, a Cibecue, recalled seeing devil's claw planted in a field. All others said the seeds were broadcast in places outside cultivated areas.

The black "hooks" of devil's claw were used, after splitting, for decorating baskets. The material was strong, resisted wear, and in a rain softened instead of swelling and cracking. *Martynia* seeds were often cracked and chewed for their juice, which was "just like milk."

Sunflowers

The large single-headed sunflower (*Helianthus* sp.) was grown by the Canyon Creek (westernmost) band of the Cibecue Apache. Sunflowers were also grown in the upper Canyon Creek–Oak Creek area in the 1800s (there is no information about whether they were present earlier than this) and in the Cherry Creek area in the 1870s and probably earlier. Bourke[109] wrote in 1895 that "a quarter of a century ago, or less, the Moquis, Apaches, Navajoes, and Pueblos used to plant them; under cultivation, the seed-disks attained enormous dimensions."

Gifford[110] recorded that sunflowers were grown by the Northern Tonto and the Southern Tonto and in a note[111] stated that the Northern Tonto got their seed from the Hopi and that the San Carlos got sunflower seeds from the Mexicans. Since the San Carlos are recorded on page 20 of Gifford's account as not cultivating sunflowers, one may wonder whether the "SC" (San Carlos) on page 665 is a misprint for "ST" (Southern Tonto).

The Canyon Creek Apache may have obtained their seed from one of the Tonto groups or from the Hopi or Mexicans (or possibly from the San Carlos or Mexicans if Gifford's "SC" on page 665 is not a misprint). Sunflowers were not grown by the Cibecue or Carrizo bands of the Cibecue or by either of the White Mountain bands. One man saw them cultivated on the San Carlos Reservation, but others who had lived there did not confirm this.

Very few of the Canyon Creek band grew sunflowers. At Cherry Creek people were afraid of them because they "came from caves" (from the gan, mountain-cave dwelling supernaturals), and only people with supernatural powers grew them. These restrictions did not affect the Canyon Creek group.

A purple-seeded Helianthus of unidentified species grew to a diameter of fifteen to sixteen inches, "as big as my hat." They frequently were so heavy that they bent the stalk and touched the ground. Seed was saved from the largest heads and stored in a vessel or hide sack.

Seeds were planted without prior treatment an inch or so deep and from one to two feet apart. At Oak Creek one family planted them around the edges of the watermelon patch, others in between corn rows or among beans and squash. At Cherry Creek they were planted only on irrigation ditches, as it was thought they would spoil other crops because of their cave origin. They were first watered when about eighteen inches high and subsequently if necessary but required less water than the other crops. They might be weeded.

Sunflowers were harvested during September and October as they ripened. The heads were removed, placed on a sunny slope, and allowed to dry for about a week. They were then put on a metate and the heads broken into pieces and the seeds loosened with a heavy stick. Finally the heads and seeds were placed in a basket tray and winnowed.

It is doubtful whether the cultivation of sunflowers was ancient. The marginal position of the cultivated plant among the two Tonto groups and the westernmost bands of the Cibecue (and possibly the San Carlos) would indicate a rather recent introduction, as would Gifford's information that seed was obtained from the Hopi and Mexicans. Also, some of the Canyon Creek band and people who had lived among the San Carlos denied that sunflowers were ever cultivated. This would indicate that they did not have a long-standing or firm place in the culture. The best evidence in favor of some antiquity is the belief among the Cherry Creek people that the seed of the large sunflower, together with the pumpkin and gan-dance headdresses, were given them by the Cave People.

During the 1940s, perhaps half a dozen families were raising sunflowers at Cibecue, all living around the home of a Cherry Creek man. The heads were not as large as they reputedly were at one time. In August, 1947, some immature sunflowers measured seven to eight inches across the seed disk; some stalks were seven feet high. In some patches there was an odd mixture of single-headed stalks with large heads and multiple-headed stalks with small heads; the latter were identical with the wild variety of the vicinity.

The plants at Cibecue might have come from seed brought in some years ago by a missionary rather than from the old Cherry Creek or Oak Creek seed.

Small Grains

Before 1900 but after the military occupation, the Apache planted oats but did not harvest this crop, which was used for forage. Rye was never raised.

Barley (*Hordeum* sp.) was raised before 1900 as the result of encouragement from agents and the military. It was sold to the government, traders, and freighters. Clum bought barley from the Apache at San Carlos in 1875, "the first time they had received money for their crops." After barley was harvested, the field was immediately replanted to corn.[112]

Reagan[113] stated that grain bins in Pueblo ruins on the Fort Apache Reservation contained corn cobs and barley heads from which the barley kernels had been removed by vermin. Possibly these heads were intrusive from the period when the Apache raised barley, or perhaps Reagan erred in his identification, for all the ruins known in this area appear to be pre-European. The Apache stated that they were first given barley by Americans.

Wheat was raised by some of the Western Apache before the American occupation. Lockwood[114] quoted from the letter of a traveling Indian agent, dated August 7, 1859, that the Pinal and White Mountain Coyoteros raised wheat, corn, beans, and pumpkins in abundance. Old informants from the Cherry Creek, Cedar Creek, and East Fork districts said they had raised a little wheat before Anglo-American times and placed this as definitely before the 1870s. Oddly enough, one at East Fork stated that the only old crops were corn and wheat. According to Cherry Creek tradition, their wheat was obtained from the Mexicans at an early time.

Apparently only a small amount of wheat was raised in premilitary days. At Cherry Creek it was "always" raised, but only at one place. Wheat raising was a distinctive enough pursuit that other Indians often called the Cherry Creek group the Wheat Field People. *Wheat Field Indian* was the regular term used by the Cibecue for the San Carlos Apache.

In early agency days, wheat was raised on the San Carlos, at upper Canyon Creek, at Cibecue, at Cedar Creek, at Forestdale, and on the White River. It was irrigated at all places except Forestdale. Sales to the government encouraged larger plantings. In 1883 the Fort Apache Reservation produced 12,600 pounds of wheat.[115]

After withdrawal of the military garrison, wheat raising practically ceased on the Fort Apache Reservation. One reason undoubtedly was the lack of a market. Another was that wheat was "too much work; nobody help." On the San Carlos Reservation, where there were binders and threshers, some soft spring wheat was still raised.

At San Carlos winter wheat was planted in November and harvested in the spring, after which the field was planted with corn. On the Fort Apache Reservation it was planted in March and harvested in July; no winter wheat was planted.

Wheat first was planted with a digging stick, the plants close together. Later it was planted with a hoe, the holes about four to six inches apart. No ashes were mixed with the seed. After the agency was established, wheat and other small grains were broadcast, often ahead of the plow. After plowing a harrow, a piece of brush or a log was dragged over the field. Wheat was irrigated about four times: once to make it sprout, once when ankle high, once at blooming time, and finally when the heads were filling out.[116]

In early times heads were picked or pulled; later, scythes and sickles were used. The wheat was carried to a threshing ground consisting of an earth floor that had been wet down and tamped hard. Four or five horses were ridden over it for about an hour while one man stirred the wheat with a fork. After this the straw was lifted and shaken with forks. Then the grain was thrown into the air with shovels to winnow. Finally women completed the winnowing process with baskets. Wheat grains trampled into the ground were scratched out with the fingers.

One man stated that at one time shortly after 1900 people might get four or five one-hundred-pound sacks of grain from their harvest. "People raised lots of wheat then," he said.

Women first ground wheat on metates, and some continued to do this. Others took their grain by pack horse to a mill established by the agency at East Fork.

Reagan[117] stated that winnowed wheat was usually washed and dried. My informants denied that this was ever a common practice.

Green heads of wheat were sometimes picked and held over a fire; the kernels were removed, placed in a pan, washed, and boiled with meat or bones. Ripe wheat was often parched in a frying pan, then ground and eaten without salt, either in its dry form or after being moistened.

Whole grains of wheat were boiled with salt and meat. Old people without teeth ground this cooked preparation on a stone before eating it. Mush was made of wheat, with salt added. Mush was sometimes made into a tamale with fat meat but without corn-husk wrappings.

Salted wheat dough was pounded into a thick tortilla (without soda or baking powder) and cooked in ashes. When cooked, the ashes were removed by washing. The washing did not cause the tortilla to become soggy, it was said, because the heat retained from the cooking dried it. Such tortillas also were cooked in Dutch ovens. Reagan[118] mentioned a wheat-flour bread baked in ashes in a wrapping of green corn husks and also baking-powder and soda bread in flat rolls that were baked in Dutch ovens. He said wheat flour was made into a biscuit bread fried in a skillet.

Miscellaneous Crops

Whipple[119] said cotton had been seen near the Western Apache rancherias. Gifford[120] recorded that it was formerly grown by the Southern Tonto. All of my information was negative. It appears doubtful that much cotton, if any, was raised by the Apache.

The small black seeds of Indian spinach, a small, red-rooted, large-leaf plant (probably lambsquarter—*Chenopodium leptophyllum* [Moq.] or Nutt or *Chenopodium incanum Watson*),[121] were broadcast in the vicinity of camps. Its leaves were eaten with soup or, uncooked, with mescal juice. The seeds once were ground and used as food and the sprouts were boiled with meat, according to Reagan.[122]

Potatoes were not cultivated until the Anglo-American period. Seed potatoes were obtained from the whites rather than selected from the previous crop. In the 1800s they were planted at the same time as corn and their care was very similar to that of corn. In one case at Oak Creek a family planted one row of about ten hills, some fifteen inches apart, in the middle of the corn field, cutting half a potato per hill for seed. Potatoes were dug in October or November before the frost and were used quickly, as no way of storing them was known.

In later times potatoes were planted in early April, usually in every second furrow of a plowed field. Not many were grown.

In 1883, according to Bourke, the Apache on the White Mountain Reservation raised 135,000 pounds of potatoes.[123]

Fig. 16. *Burden baskets filled with food for guests at the girls' puberty ceremony.*

Potatoes were boiled, with or without meat. An Oak Creek district informant stated that his group did not bake potatoes in ashes, fry them with grease, or fry cakes of mashed potatoes until the 1890s.

The sweet potato was not known to the Apache except as an occasional store commodity.

Chilis were not planted in aboriginal days, although at times some were brought from Mexico. At Oak Creek a small red chili (*Capsicum* sp.) was raised in the 1880s from seed obtained from white ranchers at Pleasant Valley. It was grown on the sides of earth mounds about six inches high and four by ten feet in dimension. During the 1940s the Apache raised a small amount of green chilis.

Alfalfa was raised in irrigated fields, cut with agency mowers, and stacked or baled.

The Apache were not excessively fond of fresh vegetables. In the 1880s at Canyon Creek cabbages (*Brassica oleraces capitata*) were the only vegetable raised, and they by only one man. In the 1940s some families raised carrots (*Daucus carota*), onions (*Allium cepa*), cabbage, tomatoes (*Lycopersicum esculentum vulgare*), cucumbers (*Cucumis sativus*), and lettuce (*Lactuca sativa*). They raised good tomatoes, and at one time even raised a small ground tomato. It was the Indians' experience that the traders would not buy their vegetables or even corn, fresh vegetables being obtained outside the reservation or from the school and missionary gardens. (The traders did, however, purchase beef and beans from the Apache.)

Apple (*Malus sylvestris*), peach (*Prunus persica*), and other fruit trees were introduced after the military occupation. Fruit trees were distributed by the government farmer, who made certain that the holes in which to plant them had been prepared before the trees were delivered.

Miscellaneous Ritual

Many items of belief, taboo, and ritual connected with agriculture have been discussed elsewhere and will not be repeated.

Agricultural rites, including prayers and songs, accompanied planting, irrigating, and cultivating. Sometimes old men walked around the inside of fields singing songs at the time the leaves of the corn turned dark but before it had tasseled. They also walked around the edge of the field sprinkling pollen. According to Goodwin,[124] the ditch bosses or other men with agricultural powers were called upon to perform a ceremony, just before the harvest, to hasten ripening.

Curtis[125] states that among the Apache ceremonies are "a rain dance, a puberty rite, a harvest or good-crop dance, and a spirit dance."

Prayer feathers were used in fields. The White Mountain placed turkey feathers at the four corners of a field to prevent flood. No effigies were employed. The Cibecue placed a turkey feather at each corner of the field and one in the center when rain was desired; this was believed to bring rain and to prevent hail. Bourke[126] wrote that when corn was planted the Apache medicine men buried eagle plumes in the field, scattered pollen, and sang.

When rain was needed, rainmaking ceremonies were conducted by medicine men with the requisite powers. A whole community might help pay for such a ceremony. The people probably participated with prayer and song on these occasions, but information on the extent of participation was lacking. A medicine man walked toward a rain cloud, made a buzzing noise, and talked and prayed for rain. Bourke[127] described a procession at San Carlos in 1884 in which a long-handled cross was used and a rhombus twirled to imitate the sound of a gust of rain-laden wind. Palmer[128] wrote that the White Mountain tried to produce rain by lighting many fires in dead trees. This was not confirmed.

A medicine man in his late seventies told me his powers of rainmaking had been effective in all months except June. He could no longer bring rain, he said, for he had already done it too many times and he was getting too old. When one of his sons reached twenty-one, he told me, he might teach him the rituals, but not before, since the power could be harmful to a young man. He would not teach me, he said, because a white man could not learn the procedure within the time limits in which it must be memorized and because it could not be written down. He himself had once learned a ceremony by writing down the names of gods and prayers and had been punished with pains in the hands and arms.

Solar eclipses were known to be caused by the position of the moon. These were thought not to hurt the crops, but everyone built fires throughout the camp and said special prayers to keep the darkness from becoming permanent.

Prayers could be said in a field to prevent hail. A medicine man might wave hail away by holding the palms of his hands together in front of and above him, then parting them, this motion causing the hail to go to the sides. In the 1940s, fees of five dollars were still paid for such services. If hail started to fall on one's farm, it was stopped by chewing four hailstones, spitting them toward the cardinal points, and praying. An owner might also stand with yellow pollen or a piece of turquoise and motion clouds away from his field with a hand.

The White Mountain did not plant a field struck by lightning, for it was believed that if a person ate the corn his family would "dry up" with tuberculosis. People did not speak of lightning during the summer, nor would they anger it by going outside during an electrical storm or a heavy rain. Obsidian was put at the four corners of a field to keep lightning away and also was tied to children to ward off lightning and "bad things." At Cibecue a large lightweight red pumice stone was kept at one camp to ward off lightning.

Among the Cibecue a medicine man was said to have slowed down the progress of the summer sun by walking fast and attempting to cover perhaps fifty miles while he talked and prayed to the sun to go slowly.

It was believed that raccoons could be prevented from entering the corn fields by covering their spoor with four "oyster shells" (fossils). These were found in the Black River region.

It was thought to be a sign of good luck if white or silver leaves appeared on the corn stalks when they were about two feet high.

If a pregnant woman or a menstruating woman "with the blood of the underworld" entered a field, it was thought the crop would spoil and turn "just like mash and rotten inside." Copulation within a field was believed to injure the crops.

Some shamans had evil reputations and were said to use their power to ruin crops. They did this, not for pay, but for spite. Such men prayed for wind or frost. Later, if accused, they merely laughed and said, "No, I never did that." These men were not punished. One informant related how a medicine man had come and looked at a fine patch of watermelons. When he left, it rained on nearby fields but hailed on·this patch of melons and ruined them. Another informant found four stalks of corn pulled from the center of his field and placed along its edge with roots toward the sun. He tracked the suspected shaman from the field to his camp. The plucking and placing of four stalks, when accompanied with the proper spell, was believed to cause a field to dry up. The victim did nothing to the shaman but returned feeling downcast. He had nothing but poor crops afterward.

The Cibecue believed that corn pollen would turn into or attract worms if it were not shaken off. The White Mountain denied this. Rattlesnakes were believed to come into the corn to collect and use the yellow pollen, and children would not run in the corn during pollination for fear of being bitten.

In the early-day girls' puberty ceremony, the girl ground corn four times. This was cooked and distributed. Goddard[129] recorded an account of the ceremony in which a basket of corn played a part.

Fig. 17. *When someone died in an Apache camp, wickiups and other structures were burned, and the site was abandoned. This abandoned site was at Cibecue.*

The corn was poured over the crown of the girl's head. The spectators attempted to obtain a handful of this to plant, for it was reputed to increase crop yield. Curtis[130] provided much the same account, saying the act of pouring corn over the girl's head was an invocation to the gods that the girl be blessed with fruitfulness. Cummings,[131] who observed the ceremony in the early 1930s, did not mention the pouring, although his account is the most complete in the literature. I did not observe it in ceremonies at Whiteriver in 1941 and 1947.

The crops and stored or cached food of a deceased person were destroyed or abandoned, although in the case of family crops or food, only part might be destroyed and part left for the deceased's children. The farm of a dead person would be abandoned for two years or more. Among the Cibecue, crops were burned, and a horse would not be turned in to use them. The White Mountain, however, thought it proper to turn a horse onto a dead person's corn. The White Mountain also stated that they could plant over the spot once occupied by a camp in which death had occurred, which the Cibecue would not knowingly do.

A kindly supernatural, Changing Woman, the mother of Slayer of Monsters, had control over fertility and fruition of plants.[132]

Summary and Conclusions

I determined in 1949 that the Apache had been practicing agriculture for at least two hundred years. Its antiquity was attested by oral traditions and by historical evidence.

While they were traveling south from El Morro, New Mexico, an Indian guide pointed out to Diego de Vargas the mountain "Peña Larga, in which, he said, the Apaches Colorados had their rancheria, and that they plant maize; and it was skirted by a river or arroyo." This was December 2, 1692.[133] The Apache mentioned may have been Navajo or Eastern Chiricahua, for both groups have occupied territory south of El Morro within historic times; or they might have been the Western Apache north of the Mogollon Rim, a group intermediate to or distinct from all these.

In "Descripcion Geográfica, Natural, y Curiosa de la Provincia de Sonora"[134] the Apache from the frontier of Sonora to the Gila are described as gatherers of wild food with the exception of some areas up the Gila and San Francisco rivers and around the springs in the Florida and other mountains, where the women planted corn. In the same work[135] the discovery in 1737 of Apache rock graneries containing "semillas" (seeds, which nearly always refers to Indian corn on the northern frontier) was ascribed to a Spanish army. Another edition of this work[136] is translated by Guiteras to read that corn was found in the granaries in the year 1747. The Apache referred to here were probably Eastern Chiricahua if that group occupied the San Francisco and upper Gila in the eighteenth century as it did during the mid-nineteenth. However, it is possible that the Western Apache, or an intermediate group, was in this area in the eighteenth century.

Zarate Salmeron[137] stated that in the Sierra Florida the heathen Apache planted a lot of "maiz, frijol, calabazas, sandias, melones, beregenas y pepinos." These may be translated literally as corn, kidney beans, pumpkins, watermelons, muskmelons, eggplants, and cucumbers. I have doubts about the last two, which may possibly have been mis-identified varieties of pumpkins.

It is difficult to place the Sierra Florida of Zarate Salmeron. Bolton[138] identifies the Spanish Sierra Florida, in parentheses and with a question mark after it, with the Santa Teresa Mountains, the northern part of the Pinaleño Mountains. There was a region called Florida by the Spanish which lay in the vicinity of the central Gila River,[139] but there was also a Sierra Florida southeast of Deming, New Mexico,[140] and possibly other Sierra Floridas in New Mexico. In this case the Sierra Florida referred to was probably in southern Arizona and the Apache were the Western Apache (San Carlos?). If the information of Zarate Salmeron is reliable, then the earliest date for Apache agriculture is established as preceding 1626 and the number of crop plants used before the American occupation is much larger. Possibly Zarate Salmeron's Apache are the practically unknown Apaches Mansos, who eventually affiliated with the Spanish and Mexicans.

Father Bartolome Sanches[141] wrote in 1757 that the Apache planted cornfields along all the Gila River and in the Santa Lucía Valley. This would apply to the Western Apache and also, possibly, to the Chiricahua. In another letter[142] in 1758, Father Bartolome described a Spanish expedition that, with a captive Apache guide, penetrated north of the Gila. In an arroyo they saw some corn fields and captured some nomads ("gandules") who said that behind the continuous mountains was a river valley where a lot of corn in rows and spirals had been planted by the Apache. This expedition entered Western Apache country, and it is not unlikely that the river valley referred to was some tributary of the Salt.

A letter written by Father Escalante[143] narrates details of a 1747 military expedition in which, on the San Francisco River four days south of Zuñi, there were "various rancherias of Apaches who cultivate the valley and with the aid of irrigation, harvest much yellow corn." These Apache were Eastern Chiricahua unless Western Apache or an unidentified group held the region at this time.

The same letter[144] included information of a pursuit of raiding Apache from Zuñi in 1754. Three days south of Zuñi an Apache rancheria was attacked, near which "is a little river and on its banks various Apaches who do not roam about or have horses but much yellow corn." Escalante thought the river might be the San Francisco. If so, the Eastern Chiricahua are again indicated as the Apache probably encountered.

According to their traditions, the Apache acquired their crop plants from various peoples, both friends and enemies. Neighbors specifically named were the Hopi, Zuñi, Pima, and Mexicans. Bourke[145] was told of traditional relations with Pueblo peoples on the Sierra Ancha, the Sierra Mazatzal, and the Rio Tonto. A Mexican who had been a captive of the Western Apache in the eighteenth century stated that these people were hereditary friends of the Zuñi and occasionally bought a Zuñi wife.[146] Before the Pueblo Revolt of 1680 the New Mexico Spaniards traveled through the Apache country to the Pimas,[147] and Cooke,[148] during the war with Mexico, met parties of New Mexicans trading among the Apache. Gregg[149] also noted the New Mexico trade with the Apache in 1840. Old Apache told an informant, when he was a boy, of Mexicans who had traded or given seeds to the Apache in former times.

Although the Apache long had contact with the Navajo, sometimes friendly but often not, no informant mentioned to me that corn or other plants were obtained from them. The Western Apache word for corn was similar to the Navajo word for corn that was analyzed by Sapir[150] as probably meaning "food of the enemy." The earliest crop plants, on the testimony of Apache informants and on the evidence of associated ritual, were corn and pumpkins. Beans were much more recent, judging again from the testimony of informants and the lack of ritual associated with them. However, beans have been cultivated by the Apache since at least 1700, wheat since at least 1860. Cotton was probably grown sporadically, if at all. Gourds were cultivated, and tobacco and devil's claw were semi-cultivated. The sunflower was probably cultivated only after the 1860s and then only marginally among the Tonto and the Canyon Creek band of the Cibecue, although the evidence was not abundant. Minor plants such as watermelons, muskmelons, and possibly others were said by Zarate Salmeron to be cultivated during the early 1600s.

No crop approached corn in importance. All who farmed planted more corn than any other crop. Pumpkins were not planted by all people, and those who raised them did not plant them every season. They could be used only during the harvest season and before heavy frost, and they appear to have been considered a luxurious addition to the diet rather than a staple. Beans were not highly regarded and were not planted by all. At a time shortly before the American occupation, wheat apparently was a more important crop than beans, although it was not planted by all and in no way rivaled corn.

Before the reservation was established, agriculture was not as important to the Western Apache as either hunting or the gathering of wild plant foods. Its importance varied from group to group. Among the Northern Tonto, only the Fossil Creek band farmed a little. Many bands among the Southern Tonto and the San Carlos groups did not farm. Perhaps 60 percent of the White Mountain farmed and 80 percent of the Cibecue, although the extent of farming varied greatly from one local group to another and from family to family. Among the Cibecue the farming population varied from nearly 100 percent in the Cibecue band to about 50 percent in the Canyon Creek band.

The proportion of agricultural products in the diet not only varied with the extent of farming but differed from year to year and from season to season. Before the American occupation, agricultural foods, principally corn, constituted perhaps 25 percent of the foods used by the White Mountain and Cibecue groups. Perhaps 30 percent of the food of the Cibecue band was agricultural, while at upper Canyon Creek such food made up only about 10 percent of the diet. It was impossible to establish estimates for the other groups. Goodwin[151] said the White Mountain diet once contained 20 to 25 percent domestic plant foods.

Informants generally rated meat (both wild game and livestock obtained in raids on Mexican settlements) as more important in their diet than corn. With some, corn formed a greater part of the diet than wild plants; with others it was used less extensively.

Although not the primary base of economic life as it was among the Pueblo, agriculture played a significant role in the social values and attitudes of the Western Apache. There was a feeling of attachment to the agricultural home sites, which were always regarded as headquarters. The ownership of farming sites conferred a certain prestige, and the products of the farm enabled an owner to play the highly respected role of the generous donor of food.

The ownership of farm lands often was identified with chiefs, rich men, or big men. Frequently, owners were assisted in cultivating their farms by those without farms, such assistance being rewarded with food during the working day and later usually with a small part of the crop. Others who had not helped were often given farm products for the asking. In this way owners acquired the admiration and gratitude of those to whom food was paid or given, and a patron-client relationship was created. Agricultural products, which could be readily stored, added to the economic security and independence of farm owners. The owners were able to maintain a higher standard of living and to offer better entertainment, further increasing their prestige and status in the community.

Attitudes toward farming differed from group to group and family to family. Some did not care to farm. Among the White Mountain and Cibecue most people liked to farm, even though not all were farm owners. A good farmer, usually a woman, was respected for ability and industry.

Because men were primarily engaged in the hunting quest and in raids, women did most of the farming and were generally regarded as the better farmers. Nevertheless, there was nothing degrading or demeaning in farm labor for a man, and many men participated actively in farming.

Agriculture did not force a sedentary form of life upon the Apache. These Indians frequently left their fields unattended while they moved to gathering or hunting grounds. Planting and harvest times were the only seasons that absolutely required residence at the farm sites.

Possibly the tendency of the Apache to live and operate economically in small extended matrilineal family units was reinforced by the possession of farm lands in the lineage. The labors of a son-in-law on the family farms were often needed, and his affinal relatives felt themselves entitled to his services.

Chieftainship was usually reinforced by the possession of farm lands, for it was highly desirable, if not essential, for a leader to be above the average in economic status. A chief's economic independence and ability to help dependents with gifts of food were increased a great deal by the ownership of farm lands.

The evidence does not indicate that before the American occupation there was in progress any shift from hunting and gathering to more dependence on agriculture. Although new farming areas were developed, they were opened not as additional agricultural lands but as replacements for lands that, for one reason or another, had been abandoned elsewhere. Such displacement was recorded for the Bear Springs district, where the ground water failed, and at Carrizo Creek, where a quarreling clan fled from its enemies.

With the advent of U.S. military occupation, agricultural activities diminished until pacification had been completed. The Apache were often too harassed and fearful to plant or to linger in the vicinity of their fields to tend them. The military practice of destroying Apache crops discouraged planting.

After military posts were established on a permanent basis in the Apache country, an effort was made to concentrate the Indians around these centers of American administration. Hunting and gathering excursions were discouraged or forbidden. The military

and civilian agents attempted to encourage agricultural development to occupy the time and energies of the Indians and to make
them at least partly independent of government rations.

Agricultural activity at first was made more difficult under military supervision by enforced concentrations, for it was forbidden
to leave the vicinity of the agency to cultivate the old planting
grounds.[152] On the basis of estimates supplied by military agents,
Frazer[153] wrote that in 1883 on the Fort Apache Reservation, 875
acres were in cultivation, but he included no estimates for the
White River and Cedar Creek areas. For 1884, with estimates on
all farming areas included, he stated that approximately 3,000
acres were cultivated by 1,600 Indians (the Chiricahua on the reservation at this time were excluded from the estimates). Estimated
crop yields for 1884[154] were 40,000 pounds of barley, 2,000,000
pounds of hay (1883 figures), and 2,000,000 pounds of corn, in addition to which there were 300 acres of cabbage, beans, melons,
and pumpkins. In 1886 an estimated 1,469 White Mountain Apache
were reported to have raised "no wheat this year," 70,000 pounds
of barley, and 120,000 pounds of corn.[155] In 1892, 1,200 acres were
cultivated in the White Mountain division of the Apache reservation. On this land 7,143 bushels of corn were raised, no barley, no
wheat.[156] In 1899 an estimated 1,849 Indians cultivated 1,240 acres,
raising 321 bushels of barley, 2,275 bushels of corn, and 10 bushels
of vegetables.[157]

In the official annual report for 1947 compiled by the Extension
Division of the Whiteriver Agency, the following agricultural figures were provided: Of 1,019 acres harvested, 216 were in forage
crops, 788 in corn, and 15 in beans. An additional 16 acres of garden crops and the yield from 1,648 fruit trees were harvested.
Field crops yielded 397 tons of forage, 4,707 bushels of corn, and
6,300 pounds of beans. The unofficial census estimate of population
on the Fort Apache Reservation in 1947 was 3,350.

The foregoing figures are far from satisfactory. Earliest official
statistics on acreages and crop yields were but estimates at best.
For years the official reports of the Commissioner of Indian Affairs
gave only consolidated figures on the Fort Apache and San Carlos
reservations, which included at various times Yavapai and Chiricahua as well as various badly scrambled groups of Western

Apache. Nevertheless, it will be noted from the figures above that agriculture on the Fort Apache Reservation fluctuated greatly during the American occupation. Traders and missionaries long resident on the reservation, as well as the Apache, confirmed this. The reasons were varied. Successive agents alternately encouraged agriculture and attempted to divert Apache energies and resources into stock breeding. Irrigation projects did not withstand the effects of flooding or failed to supply the expected amount of water. Cash income from off-reservation employment, from government make-work and relief activities, and in the 1940s from military allotment checks varied; as such income increased, agricultural activities declined, and vice versa.

The Indians never took full advantage of the agricultural opportunities offered by the Fort Apache Reservation. In the 1940s, especially in view of the improved agricultural tools and techniques that had accrued through white acculturation, the Apache were making proportionately less use of such opportunities than at the time of American contact.

Chapter 3

HUNTING

ONLY adult males hunted large game. Often, individuals hunted deer alone; other game usually required the cooperative efforts of several men. Hunting parties might consist of up to twenty men, but the usual party was made up of three to five except in an antelope hunt, for which more were needed. Old men not sufficiently active to accompany the young on forays hunted in the vicinity of the camps.

All men participated to some extent in hunting as a matter of necessity, and every man knew the customary hunting methods and ritual. However, there were a few with special hunting powers obtained by vision or through tutelage. These were specialists in one or more of the hunting fields, and they were sought as leaders or advisers. Chiefs or headmen were often skilled hunters who led hunting parties. The White Mountain stated that only religious practitioners with "bear power" could hunt that animal; this was probably true also of other Western Apache.

Girls accompanied adolescent boys at times on nocturnal hunts for birds. Other participation by women occurred in occasional quail drives in which young and old of both sexes joined.[1] Women did not take part in rabbit surrounds and drives. Although women did not often accompany a hunting party, Goodwin[2] recorded one incident when this occurred.

Areas and Migrations

Western Apache informants denied that there were individually or family owned hunting tracts. However, the Eastern White Moun-
116

tain chief Diablo claimed an unmarked tract adjacent to his farm as his private hunting area and it was not trespassed upon.[3] It was customary for strangers who wished to hunt near a farm settlement to ask permission of a local chief or influential man.[4]

Goodwin[5] delimited the general territories hunted over by some of the Western Apache bands. In general the favored spots were timbered or mountainous. Although hunters went north of the Mogollon Rim, they usually hurried southward again for fear of the Navajo. To the southeast parties sometimes journeyed as far as the San Francisco River in New Mexico. The eastern limits were the east slopes of the White Mountains and the top of the Blue Mountains, fear of the Navajo keeping them from going farther. To the northwest some of the Tonto ranged to the San Francisco Mountains. They hunted in the Mazatzals on the west and as far as the Hayes Mountains to the south. Eastman[6] mentioned a small White Mountain party that penetrated Mescalero territory on a buffalo hunt, but this was far outside the usual range.

Informants indicated that a majority of the Canyon Creek, Cibecue, and Western White Mountain bands wintered south of the Black-Salt rivers. Normally, four to six months were spent in these areas. Winter camps were moved every fifteen days or so, and the men spent their time, when not "just sitting around," hunting deer. According to Goodwin,[7] favorite winter locations for migrating Western Apache groups or families were along the foot of Natanes Rim or at places in the Gila Range, as well as on lower slopes of the Graham, Santa Teresa, and Turnbull Mountains below the piñon-juniper belt.

Goodwin[8] stated that hunting parties never stayed out more than a few days, did not range far from home, and women did not usually accompany such parties.

Seasons

Men spent much of their time hunting but were particularly active during late spring and fall. In the spring, food supplies were low and the first wild food crops of the season were not yet available. Autumn was considered the best time for hunting, since meat and hides were then prime.[9] From the end of November until April, hunting and raiding were practically the only economic pursuits.[10] Informants said the best time to hunt was when animals could be tracked in the snow.

Boys' Training

A boy was encouraged to hunt small game as soon as he was old enough to leave camp by himself, usually around the age of eight. He was taught to shoot by his father or some older person. Boys' hunting parties set forth with slings and miniature bows and arrows. At twelve, a boy hunted quail, rabbits, squirrels, and wood rats. By the time he reached puberty, he was an accurate shot and adept at hunting small game.[11]

At the age of fifteen or sixteen a boy was taken on his first deer hunt by his father, uncle, maternal grandfather, or other near relative. Occasionally, several grown boys accompanied a party hunting large game, performing the camp chores while obtaining experience. They were given the less desirable portions of meat when it was divided. Knowledge was acquired more through observation than from direct instruction.[12]

Many youths did not hunt deer until they were married, and probably none hunted alone until marriage. Some ritual hunting practices, such as the method of skinning and part of the songs, were learned early in the apprenticeship. However, actual hunting power was not gained before the age of twenty. "Hunting power was dangerous and not a thing for a bungling youth to meddle with; his heart would not be strong enough to stand it; it could make him ill or even kill him."[13]

Pride and the fear of ridicule spurred a boy's efforts. Goodwin[14] told of rat hunts in which it was a rule not to quit once a boy had started after a rat; the older boys laughed if a rat were permitted to get away.

A Canyon Creek informant told me how, in the mid-1880s, his San Carlos father took him on hunts. He was only five or six when these trips began, and he was taken on successful deer hunts over a period of three years. As he rode behind his father on the horse or trudged behind him when he stalked, his "father talked, 'This is the way they hunt,'" The boy was allowed to help carry the meat to the horse and was taught how to pit-bake meat. At times his father would exhort, "Hunt. Don't be afraid of horses. Exercise every morning and make yourself strong or sometime you'll get a hard job and give up right away. If you exercise all the time, then you'll be a man. Some people just look at their wife—wonder what their wife is going to do. You help your wife; you go a long ways and hunt deer pretty good and carry it home. That's the way to help."

Later in his childhood the informant hunted small game with other boys. Rabbits, birds, squirrels, rats, and mice were all hunted with the bow and arrow. Birds' nests were raided. Some boys made fires and cooked and ate their game, but this informant always dutifully took his home.

He was shown how to make bird blinds by his father. An old man carefully taught him how to make a rock deadfall trap. Boys listened raptly to the tales of an old hunter.

A White Mountain man told of being sent to hunt by his foster mother at the age of eleven when the family was in dire need of meat. The woman, a maternal aunt, was exceedingly proud of him when he brought back a wild pig. She distributed a portion of the kill to every household in camp, as was customary with the first of each species of animal a youth killed. Recipients of meat so distributed said a prayer for the young hunter's future success: "May he always be luckly." Among the White Mountain there was no taboo against a boy's eating his first kill. However, Gifford[15] reported that Northern Tonto boys were not allowed to eat their first four kills.

Weapons

The bow and arrow were the most important hunting weapons. The White Mountain bow was described by one informant as a flat self-bow about three and a half feet long (the same length as the arrow) with a very strong pull. Some Indians wrapped sinew around the bow to increase its strength, but this varied with individual taste. The White Mountain bow was said not to be backed with sinew, only wrapped. (Gifford[16] stated that the White Mountain used a "trussed" bow with sinew cord down the back.) Buckskin was also wrapped about the bow by some Apache.

The Tonto groups used a recurved bow, but among all others it was nearly straight.[17]

Informants stated that the bow was made of mulberry wood. From the literature it would appear that Apache bows were also made of ash,[18] juniper,[19] willow, walnut, black locust, and other wood.[20]

Gifford's[21] description of bow lengths in terms of distance "to armpit" and so forth may be roughly interpreted to mean that lengths varied from three and a half to four and a half feet, with the Northern Tonto bows shortest, followed by the White Mountain and San Carlos, Cibecue, and Southern Tonto in ascending order. The Tonto (Northern or Southern undifferentiated) bow was described by both Möllhausen[22] and Smart[23] as about five feet in length, the arrows being three feet.

All groups used sinew from the back and leg of the deer and two-ply vegetable fiber for bowstrings, according to Gifford.[24] Informants stated that rawhide was also used by the Cibecue and White Mountain.

To make a bow, the Northern Tonto first removed the bark, then allowed the wood to season before shaping it with a stone knife and filing stone. They and the Southern Tonto heated the wood and bent it to the desired shape in a tree crotch. The San Carlos placed pitch on their bows to ensure that they kept their shape, while the Cibecue painted the bow with creosote gum to straighten it. The White Mountain put mescal juice on the concave side of the bow to straighten it.[25] (Gifford did not comment on the effectiveness of such applications.)

According to Gifford,[26] the bow was held horizontally, obliquely, or vertically by the Southern Tonto; vertically or obliquely by the Cibecue; vertically by the San Carlos; horizontally or vertically by the White Mountain. All groups used a hide wrist guard, and all used the Mediterranean arrow release.[27] Cibecue and White Mountain informants indicated to me that the bow was held vertically, while the position of the arrow release might vary with the individual. Some Apache used a three-fingered pull on the bowstring, with the arrow between the index and middle fingers (Mediterranean);

others used a two-fingered pull with the thumb and index fingers steadying the arrow; others pinched the arrow between thumb and index finger and pulled it back against the string.

Mason[28] wrote that the range was "not much over 150 yards" but that the penetrative power of the bow was great.

Apache arrows were made of reed, with a wooden foreshaft. The reed used was called arrow grass by the Apache.[29] The Western Apache also used one-piece wooden arrows made of willow or other woods.[30] Hands, teeth, and wrenches of stone, pottery, wood, and horn were used for straightening arrows.[31] Headless arrows were used for practice and for birds and small game.[32] Arrows with four cross-sticks lashed to the point were also used for hunting birds.[33]

Radial feathering with three feathers was used by all Western Apache, according to Gifford.[34] Smart[35] stated that four strips of feather placed six or seven inches up the shaft from the butt were used by the Tonto. Tangential double feathering was used by the Northern Tonto, Southern Tonto, and San Carlos. All Western Apache groups used hawk and turkey feathers. Eagle feathers were used by the Southern Tonto, crow feathers by the Southern Tonto and to some extent by the Northern. Beside sinew wrapping, the Cibecue also used piñon pitch to fix the feathers.[36]

The fletched part of the shaft was painted in distinctive patterns by each group. Northern Tonto colors were blue and red, Southern Tonto black and red encircling bands on a yellow ground color, Cibecue red and black. The White Mountain used a black band at the base of the cane arrow, with a red band, made from red clay and piñon gum, adjoining. The San Carlos used a lightning design.[37] Tonto foreshafts were colored as if with the blood of some animal.[38]

Foreshafts were attached to the canes by gum. Smart[39] stated that in some cases the foreshaft was also withed into position firmly, in others only lightly attached.

Mason[40] wrote that arrowheads were fashioned from obsidian, sheet iron, hardwood, and beer bottles. He noted many varieties in shape, often in the same quiver. The Apache produced a flint (chert?) or obsidian point in five to eight minutes.[41] Gifford[42] stated that stone arrowheads with a tanged base were used by the Southern Tonto and San Carlos; with a stemmed base by Southern

Tonto, San Carlos, Cibecue, and White Mountain; with a concave base by Northern Tonto, Southern Tonto, and San Carlos; with a side-notched base by the Southern Tonto; with a convex base by the White Mountain (no other group being asked); with serrate sides by the Northern Tonto and Southern Tonto. The serrate head was used by the Northern Tonto for the hunt only, especially for deer and bear; it was reputed to hasten death by lacerating the animal's internal organs. Detachable heads were used by Southern Tonto and White Mountain.[43] The Cibecue hollowed out the tips of mountain-sheep horns with a heated stone point, sharpened them, and attached them to arrow shafts with piñon gum and sinew. Mountain-sheep horn was said to be used for no other purpose. (However, Gifford[44] said arrow wrenches of perforated female mountain-sheep horn were used by the Northern Tonto, San Carlos, and Cibecue, the latter obtaining it by trade.)

Quivers were fashioned with separate compartments for bow and arrows by the Cibecue and White Mountain and also[45] by the Northern Tonto and Southern Tonto. The San Carlos and Cibecue also strapped the bow to the outside of the quiver with buckskin.[46]

The most highly prized material for quivers was the skin of the mountain lion, which was reputed to keep the arrows dry and also, undoubtedly, was believed to have ritual significance. It was valued so highly that a horse was given in exchange for a pelt. Gifford[47] also mentioned the use of wildcat skin by the Southern Tonto, coyote skin by the San Carlos, Cibecue, and White Mountain.

Gifford[48] reported that a cased skin quiver was made by the San Carlos of coyote hide; that all groups made open-skinned, sewn hide quivers. In the latter type the Tonto groups left the mountain-lion tail on the quiver, the Southern Tonto cutting it open and painting the interior yellow. The Southern Tonto fashioned the quiver from a rectangular piece of buckskin. The bottom consisted of a leftover piece of hide. To ensure rigidity, a stick was sewn along one side. The diameter at the top was slightly larger than that at the bottom.[49]

Quivers were carried on the back so that an arrow could be jerked out over the shoulder.

Spears were used in hunting hibernating bears and also, at least by the White Mountain, occasionally in hunting elk and antelope. A

Cibecue informant who, as a boy, had traveled in White Mountain and San Carlos country stated that as late as the mid-1880s most of the elderly people carried five- or six-foot spears with iron points. The points were a foot long and two inches wide. He had seen horses and cattle killed with them but thought they had been used primarily for bear and in war.

Smart[50] stated that the Tonto used lances with a knife or bayonet socketed on the end of a long pole. Ogle[51] had been told by Barnes, a soldier at Fort Apache about 1880, that the Apache lance was fourteen feet long, made of agave stalk, reinforced at points of strain with deer sinew, and pointed with a bayonet head.

Gifford[52] reported that the San Carlos used a one-piece spear of ash eight feet long; that the Cibecue had a sotol stalk with an inserted two-bladed hardwood point; and that some groups used stone and iron points.

Several White Mountain and Cibecue informants denied that throwing sticks were used, although one Canyon Creek man stated that long (six-foot) sticks (clubs used in drives) were occasionally thrown at rabbits. However, Gifford[53] said straight throwing sticks were used for hunting rabbits and small game by the Northern Tonto, Southern Tonto, San Carlos, and White Mountain.

A club was made by removing the bone from the upper end of a cow's tail, inserting a round stone, and sewing the skin over this. A White Mountain man stated that this club was used for dispatching an animal after it had been run down; Cibecue informants denied its use.

Gifford[54] noted that all the Western Apache used a wetted stick twisted in the fur to pull rodents from their holes, that all except the Southern Tonto used a notched stick, and that none used a hooked stick. Bourke[55] observed that Apache boys used curved "rat-sticks." Some of my informants had used the notched stick, which was moistened with spittle. One had seen an old Apache man use a long stick with a sharpened hook on the end to draw rats and rabbits from their burrows.

Cibecue boys used the sling as a toy and for battles among themselves, not for hunting. White Mountain boys used it in hunting birds and small game, although not as frequently as the bow and arrow. The sling consisted of a diamond-shaped section of hide to which thongs were attached. The patch was cut from the neck of the deer "where thick," and the corners of the diamond were squared. The dimensions were about three to four inches by six to seven inches. Thongs were twenty-four to thirty inches in length. One thong terminated in a loop that was placed over the middle finger. The other thong was held between the thumb and index finger until time for its release. The sling was twirled around the head, sometimes once, sometimes several times. No knot or stick was used in the thongs to improve the grip. Gifford[56] stated that all Western Apache used the sling for killing birds. The Northern Tonto sling was of yucca-leaf fiber.[57] Informants believed the sling to be an old Apache implement. While rocks were usually obtained on the spot where used, they were sometimes carried in a sack. Cibecue boys used to carry four slings, one in the hand, an extra over the shoulder, and one or two tied to the legs.

A White Mountain informant claimed that antelope were once taken with the lasso, used from horseback.

Arrow Poison

Arrow poison was used to some extent by all Western Apache. Gifford[58] said the Northern Tonto and San Carlos used it for war only and that it was used for both war and hunting by the Southern Tonto, Cibecue, and White Mountain. A Canyon Creek informant stated that "a long time ago" all the Apache used arrow poison but that in more recent times (during the hostilities with the Americans) not all individuals had continued to use it.

It appeared that the making of arrow poison varied not only from group to group but with the individual concocters. A Canyon Creek informant described the process as follows: A small internal organ "like a stocking" from the top of a cow's stomach was hung until it rotted. Wasps were caught and held against this rotted organ until they stung it. Then pigeon blood was added. The material was kept about two weeks, then mixed with burnt cactus spines. The substance was then placed on arrows and spears, both point and shaft, to a total length of four or five inches. It was used both in war and in the chase. A mere scratch by an arrow so treated was reputed to cause a deer to swell up and die.

An old White Mountain scout stated that only a few of his people could make arrow poison and that these kept their processes secret. His tutor had instructed him never to tell anybody how to make it. His poison was made from fixed proportions of different kinds of bitter roots, which were pounded, moistened, ground fine, and mixed with deer blood. The substance dried like a powder. When used, the powder was moistened and rubbed on an arrowhead with two sticks. It was highly prized and closely guarded. The poison was said to be effective only on animals, not on human beings, and it could be swallowed without harm. A small scratch was said to be fatal to a deer.

Mason,[59] Palmer,[60] and Gifford[61] described some of the ingredients and processes used in the making of arrow poison by various Apache groups. All involved the putrefied inner organ of some animal; into this organ, rattlesnake and insect venom and various plant substances were introduced.

Bourke,[62] who had an opportunity to observe the effects of poisoned arrows on men and animals struck by them, expressed disbelief in their virulence. Mason[63] said wounds showed symptoms of septicemia rather than rattlesnake (*Crotalus* sp.) venom, the poison supposedly used.

Pets

Information on pets was contradictory. Some informants, both White Mountain and Cibecue, denied that the young of any animals or birds had ever been kept. Others from both groups stated that before the arrival of the Americans, young turkeys were occasionally raised. Goodwin[64] stated that young turkeys were occasionally put in a "turkey basket" and kept as pets. Turkeys were fed grasshoppers and corn and became so tame that they "followed the people just like a dog." However, they nested away from camp and, after their young were hatched, disappeared. For this reason, and because the Apache were nomadic, turkeys were usually killed as soon as they attained full growth. Small feathers of the turkey were used for arrows, but the birds were always killed before being plucked. One man stated that wild turkeys could not be tamed, although his people had tried; only "those that came from white people" would not wander off.

Several informants said fawns were not captured alive because it was "bad luck" or "the gods didn't like it." Only one man, who had spent part of his boyhood with his father's San Carlos relatives, told of taming deer. He had been told that young deer were kept both before and after the Americans came. They were fed a milky liquid made from hot water, dried mescal juice, and crushed walnuts until they were old enough to graze. They were killed and eaten when a distant trip or change of residence was contemplated.

The same informant stated that in prereservation times people raised coyote whelps but these ran off as soon as they were large. Small rabbits, gophers, and squirrels occasionally were kept. Quail were also kept at times; these would run in and out the wickiup. The young of mountain lions, bobcats, and skunks were not tamed. The young of raccoons were not kept to maturity, for they "grew up too wild." In the late 1870s a San Carlos man brought home a small owl and kept and fed it until it died, thereby frightening others because of the Apache belief that the spirits of the departed take the form of owls.

Goodwin[65] related that one of his informants claimed only members of clans related to eagles had the right to tie young eagles in their nests, allow them to mature, then pluck and release them. Apparently this was the only Goodwin informant who knew of this method. My informants denied this and stated that an eagle was always killed before plucking.

Dogs

There were few dogs among the Apache during the period of hostilities with the Americans, since it was feared their barking would disclose the location of camps to the soldiers. Before this time, Apache exposed to raids from Indian enemies often took the same precaution.

One instance was told of a Canyon Creek man whose dog was so well trained that he would not bark when both dog and owner hid from American soldiers. A few dogs were trained to catch and retrieve rabbits or other small game. Dogs were not trained to retrieve from the water.

Aside from the occasional running down of small game or quail or the treeing of squirrels, dogs were not much used in the hunt. The White Mountain stated that dogs were used to run down deer only if the hunter had shot all his arrows. A Canyon Creek informant stated that dogs were occasionally used to trail and hold deer at bay until the arrival of the hunter. They were especially useful in tracking a wounded deer. To train a puppy for this purpose, the feet of a deer were split, heated over a fire, and then held forcibly to the nose of the "crying" animal. Gifford[66] recorded that the Cibecue also placed the feet of turkeys and rabbits over a dog's nose for the same reason.

Instances of castration of dogs were remembered by two Canyon Creek informants, but the practice was never general and was not held to be of value. (Only one other instance of animal castration was recorded. In this case a San Carlos great-grandfather of the informant had castrated and raised a fawn until "big and fat" for butchering.)

Informants did not believe the dog was ever eaten. However, the Cibecue at one time ate the wolf and coyote, although the White Mountain did not. Neither group ate the fox.

Herbivores

Deer (*Odocoileus* spp.), antelope (*Antilocapra americana*), elk (*Cervus merriami*), and mountain sheep (*Ovis canadensis*) were important food animals, particularly the first. Hunting methods were usually confined to individual stalking or to small drives, although large parties among some groups are recorded as using the surround and fire drives.

Mountain-sheep hunters habitually worked in pairs among the Canyon Creek group, one in ambush while another drove the animals. The sheep were once numerous in the mouth of Canyon

Creek and were also at Tortilla Flat and in a canyon near Roosevelt. They are still to be found in the latter place. The White Mountain used blinds of brush or rock in the Salt River Canyon when hunting sheep. There appeared to be no taboos connected with the use of mountain-sheep horn or skins, but the horn was used only for arrow points and the skin only for breechclouts. Goodwin[67] recorded a tale that purported to account for the fact that mountain sheep must never be pursued or "buckskin" made out of its hide, but my informants did not mention such restrictions.

The antelope was said to have been numerous at one time in the vicinity of Cedar Creek and Fort Apache. Antelope were driven toward hidden hunters by horsemen waving hide robes. At other times, relays of men would run them down on horseback. When hunted by horseback, they were killed with bow and arrow and spear and even lassoed, according to a White Mountain informant.

White Mountain stalkers used the whole headskin of the antelope and painted their bodies with a mixture of yellow clay and white lime. When close to the game, the man held his weapons against his chest. Another hunter attracted the attention of the antelope while the masked man crept within range. No game calls were used for antelope, but the antelope was said to stop at the sound of a loud yell.

Brush or rock blinds were occasionally used in hunting antelope, as they were for mountain sheep and deer. Antelope were said not to be hunted with dogs or to be driven over cliffs. Gifford[68] reported the circle surround and corral drive for antelope among the two Tonto groups. The Southern Tonto were said to surround only young antelope, which were caught by hand and killed by pressing the foot over the heart. The Northern Tonto appointed an antelope-hunt leader.[69] Their antelope corral was an enclosure about one hundred yards in diameter, built of juniper branches and trunks laid horizontally. The wing of the chute extended one-eighth of a mile and was built over a ridge. Two men were stationed at the juncture of the chute and the pound. Six or eight men howling like wolves drove the antelope toward the chute area. When the animals were impounded, four men went to the center of the corral and shot the animals, each shooting in one of the cardinal directions. One beast was released for good luck.[70]

Cremony[71] stated that Chiricahua hunters dressed in the skin, head, and horns of the antelope and imitated the actions of the animal as they approached them. He also described the Mescalero stalking of antelope by waving a red rag on a yucca stalk.[72] My Western Apache informants denied the waving of flags or of legs to hold the attention of antelope. A Mescalero surround consisting of a double circle of ninety-six horsemen killed eighty-seven antelope.[73]

With the exceptions noted above, antelope were hunted in the same manner as were deer.

The elk once was eaten by all people. In the 1940s the White Mountain or Cibecue would not hunt or eat the animal. This aversion to elk dated to a time, subsequent to 1912, when a number of people became ill after eating elk flesh, a concrete illustration of one manner in which a food might become taboo.

Among the White Mountain, groups of three, four, or five men hunted elk by circling and driving them toward one or two of their number in ambush. The antlers were never kept but placed in a tree. The bones were not disposed of with any ritual. In general, elk were hunted the same way deer were hunted. To avoid an itch thought to be caused by eating elk meat, the fat of the animal was rubbed over the body.

The most important game animal of the Western Apache was the deer. Its flesh was the most prized meat, although not always mentioned as the tastiest. The hide and sinews were used in the manufacture of clothing and containers of all kinds. Supernatural powers were attributed to the deer, and considerable ritual was involved in hunting it.

In the mid–twentieth century there were black-tailed (*O. hemionus hemionus*), white-tailed (*O. couesi*), and small Mexican deer (*O. hemionus canus*) on the Fort Apache Reservation, the first-named being the most numerous.[74] Comparatively few were killed, as there was only a short hunting season in autumn. The old hunting songs and ritual had been forgotten by the current generation of hunters. Young men might stop at the sight of deer track and blow smoke ritually in the four directions, but they did not know the accompanying songs and prayers.

In early times adult males spent much of their time hunting deer. Hunting was done singly and in groups. If a group of men were involved, they spread out upon reaching the hunting area. Hunters left before sunup, usually on foot. Equipment consisted of weapons and some yucca string to tie the meat. An ear of corn or a piece of mescal the size of the hand, or both, was carried for food. This was tied to the belt by grass string, not yucca. When the hunters were ready to eat, a fire was built and the corn cob spitted on the end of a stick and roasted. The burned parts were scraped and the corn eaten from the cob or shelled into the hand.

The hunter remained in the field for the full day unless successful in his quest, but he never remained out overnight. He walked most of the time, with occasional interludes of sitting and resting. When a deer was killed, it was hung in a tree until the slayer could return for it, the same day or the next, with a pack horse.

Stalkers preferred to conceal themselves behind grass, as it was believed deer and antelope could see through trees and brush. The disguise consisted of the headskin and antlers of the deer. Occasionally the hide of the deer was also draped over the shoulders. Goddard[75] said antler masks in the condition of the season were used. The user of a deer or antelope mask had to be a man with a knowledge of special songs and prayers. According to Goodwin,[76] insanity or some other misfortune was expected to befall one who, without the power and knowledge of stalking heads, put one on or handled one.

Gifford[77] indicated that all the Western Apache used deer calls and[78] that the Northern Tonto lured the doe by imitating, by means of a leaf in the mouth, the cry of a fawn attacked by a coyote.

Informants stated that deer formerly were run down, in the heat of summer or in the heavy snow of winter, by strong, fleet-footed men. The animals were dispatched with an arrow or club.

Several hunters frequently worked together as a team. In such cases, part attempted to drive the deer to the ambushed archers. In the lower and more open country they sometimes concealed themselves behind brush or rock blinds. Gifford[79] stated that the Cibecue hid in stone-and-brush blinds in the saddle between two hills. At times, while three or four men drove, two archers were stationed on knolls between which ran a deer trail.[80] Archers were also stationed in narrow or box canyons up which deer were driven.

Gifford[81] stated that stick-covered pitfalls were used in narrow trails by the Southern Tonto and the Cibecue. The Cibecue used a straddling bar and a fence hurdle in the front portion of the pit. The Southern Tonto used pits in series; these were six to nine feet deep. My informants denied the use of any type of pitfall or snare for deer; two, however, said the Chiricahua used pitfalls with impaling stakes.

Deer were tracked when there was snow on the ground. At such time two men would circle far to the front while others followed a straight course, causing the deer to run from the trackers to the hunters ahead.

Dogs at times were used to trail deer and bring them to bay, usually when the deer had been wounded.

In early times deer were driven over a cliff in a canyon below Cibecue. In the summer, deer were sometimes encircled and driven toward waiting archers with the aid of fire. Gifford[82] reported the surrounding of deer among the Cibecue, White Mountain, and Northern Tonto.

Parties of men went out for several days under the direction of a leader with hunting powers. This man might be a chief or head man, but not necessarily. Special ritual preceded and accompanied these hunts. Youths accompanied such parties as novitiates, doing camp chores as they learned hunting skills and ritual.

Carnivores

The flesh of wolves (*Canis occidentalis*), coyotes (*Canis mearnsi*), or foxes (*Urocyon* sp. and *Vulpes macrotis neomexicana*) was taboo among the White Mountain, but they did eat mountain lions (*Felis concolor*) and bobcats (*Lynx rufus*). To what extent the latter animals were eaten was not learned. The Cibecue, on the other hand, could all partake of wolf or coyote flesh, but only a few shamans ate mountain lion or bobcat meat. The use of the skins of carnivores has been described elsewhere.

People once salvaged the carcasses of animals slain by carnivores and brought them home. Among the White Mountain, such meat was eaten only by people who were past child-bearing age for it was believed that if young people ate it, they would become sterile.

The mountain lion was looked upon as a hunting deity.[83] The Western Apache prayed for luck to this animal when deer hunting. A White Mountain man stated that the hunter prayed to it because the lion could run swiftly like the deer. The lion itself was killed wherever encountered. Occasionally, hunters ambushed the beast at the spot where it had left a carcass.

Bobcats were not hunted but were killed if encountered.

Gifford[84] stated that the Northern Tonto and Cibecue prayed to the wolf when deer hunting, but the White Mountain did not.

The Cibecue believed that if a coyote barked near the hunting camp, it was an omen of good luck. They said, "Hurry, hurry, coyote, let's show up the deer first thing early in the morning and you can use the blood and guts." A heavy rock deadfall baited with a mouse or rat was used for trapping the coyote. This was placed in trails not too close to camp, as it was feared young children might be injured by it. Coyotes were also shot.

Gifford[85] described three types of deadfall traps used by the San Carlos for coyotes. One was a heavily weighted stone or log deadfall held up by three sticks in unstable equilibrium. Another, used also by other groups for all carnivores, was made with collapsible log side walls. Another was a type in which the coyote's neck was broken by a falling stone as the animal grasped the bait.

Bears

Bears (*Ursus* sp.) were treated by the Western Apache with considerable ritual respect. The animals were feared because they were known to attack and maul humans when suddenly encountered. On winding trails, travelers sometimes shouted or sang in order to warn bears of their approach. Contact with the animal was also thought to cause illness. Springs contaminated by bears or around which bear tracks were found were left unused until all traces had been washed away by rains.

Bears were hunted only by religious practitioners with the necessary "bear powers." Most informants stated that they were eaten, although it was evident that not everyone ate bear flesh. It was not determined definitely whether the use of bear meat was restricted to those with supernatural powers, but probably it was not. One old bear hunter had told an informant in the 1890s that his crippled, clenched, and stiffened fingers, resembling a bearlike claw, were the result of eating bear in his youth.

Bears were said to have been the brown and black varieties. One old man, who apparently was not given to understatement in his yarns, claimed in the last century to have seen a white bear in the White Mountains, possibly an albino.

A White Mountain informant with bear powers stated that because bears were dangerous they were hunted by a group of four or five men, either on foot or horseback. The hunters had to be medicine men. Gifford[86] said of the Northern Tonto that bears were killed with a single arrow if the hunter knew the medicine for killing; another hunter without such power might use a hundred arrows without mortal effect. Bears were shot with the bow and might be dispatched with the spear if necessary.

When hibernating bears were hunted, one man was stationed in front of the den, others took positions on either side, and another, if possible, would stand above the den. The bear would be aroused by poking it on the nose with a stick. As the beast emerged, it was shot or speared in the heart.

A White Mountain hunter denied that the dens of hibernating bear were entered. However, a Cibecue informant had been told that hunters went into the den with a spear, and one old hunter even claimed to have dragged a bear from its lair by the paw. A Cibecue informant who had himself hunted bears said that people were afraid to attack bears with arrows because the wounded beasts were dangerous, but he said that people would hunt them with a flintlock gun, shooting for the chest, not the head.

The White Mountain referred to a bear as "grandfather" (mother's father), and if one was encountered by chance, it was told to "go away, grandpa." However, informants stated that in hunting no words were said to the bear either before or after it was killed. Gifford[87] stated that the Southern Tonto, Cibecue, and White Mountain addressed the live bear and that the Northern Tonto addressed the dead bear. His inquiries were limited to those groups, and the Northern Tonto were the only group asked about addressing the dead bear. According to Gifford,[88] the Cibecue hunter said,

"I am going to shoot you. I want you to die with the first arrow."
Bourke[89] stated that the Apache prefixed the respectful term *old
man* to the word for bear. The Mescalero used circumlocutory
phrases for the bear, believing that use of the regular word would
cause the animal to appear and communicate a painful disease.[90]

There were ritual songs and prayers for hunting bear among the
White Mountain. A set of curing songs addressed to the bear was
used for people who were constipated. The old man who knew this
rite would not sing them for me, as he believed that if they were
sung when no one was ill it would bring back luck to the well—that
perhaps some of his children would become constipated.

Bourke[91] stated that the killing of a bear was the occasion for a
war dance in which the pelt was carried around a circle, first on the
shoulders of the slayer, then on those of other warriors. Elsewhere[92] he noted that much pollen, usually tule pollen, was thrown
on these occasions and that the dancing was frenzied. One such
dance that he observed in the Sierra Madre in 1883 lasted all night,
with no cessation in singing and dancing.

Bear flesh was boiled alone or with pitbaked corn.

Small Game

Cottontail rabbits (*Lepus sylvaticus*), jackrabbits (*Lepus* sp.), prairie dogs (*Cynomys ludovicianus*), wood rats (*Neotoma* sp.), field
mice (*Microtus* sp.), ground squirrels (*Citellus* sp.), and tree squirrels (*Sciurus* sp.) were hunted by boys. Although men killed such
game on chance encounter, they did not usually hunt it systematically except for occasional rabbit drives.

The jackrabbit was not considered choice meat because it was
tough, but the cottontail was esteemed. Bourke[93] said tule pollen
was offered to the jackrabbit. Rabbits were run down by swift
youths, especially when heavy snow covered the ground. Dogs occasionally were used to run them down. When rabbits hid in their
burrows or in hollow logs, they were pulled out with a wetted
notched stick twisted in the fur or were smoked out. Gifford[94] reported that the San Carlos plugged rabbit burrows a short distance
from the opening and extracted the animals by hand when they

sought refuge therein. Occasionally in a field rabbits were flooded out, as were rats and gophers. Deadfall traps were used for rabbits, as for other small to medium-size game, but there were no snares.

In stalking rabbits, boys often worked in pairs, one behind the other. The first boy would continue straight ahead and thereby hold the attention of the rabbit as the second approached within shooting distance of the animal. Rabbits were killed with bow and arrow and, by the White Mountain, sometimes with the sling. Throwing sticks were not used. Clubs (not throwing clubs) were used only when game was run down or encircled. Gifford[95] referred to game calls used for rabbits by all Western Apache except the San Carlos.

Rabbits were sometimes hunted by large parties of males of all ages, who surrounded an area and closed in or spread out and beat through an area. In summer on suitable terrain, fire was used as an

Fig. 18. *This young hunter had knocked the squirrel out of a tree with a rock, after his dog treed it.*

aid, a large segment of a circle being fired while a line of men closed off the unfired gap. Rabbits were killed with arrows or with yucca-stalk clubs about six feet long. One informant stated that a fire circle might be a mile in diameter; another had seen brushy level areas one-half by one-quarter of a mile in size fired. Women did not participate in rabbit drives. Gifford[96] reported that rabbit hunt masters were appointed by the Northern and Southern Tonto; for the Southern Tonto, these were temporary.

Gophers and ground squirrels were not eaten except in times of food scarcity. Squirrels were shot from trees, where they were sometimes treed by dogs. I saw one killed with rocks by a boy of fifteen whose dog had treed the creature. Some groups were re-ported by Gifford[97] to smoke squirrels out. Prairie dogs were eaten but were reputed to be "all fat, no meat."

Of all small rodents, the wood rat was considered the greatest delicacy. Rats were trapped with rock deadfalls, flooded or smoked out of their nests, occasionally pulled out of holes with wetted notched sticks or dug out. One case of the use of a hooked stick was reported. An informant stated that brush nests were sur-rounded while one boy or man removed the sticks on the nest until the rats ran out. They were then stepped on, stoned, clubbed, or shot with arrows. Bourke[98] observed that where rats burrowed under mesquite or other brush and had made several entrances to their nests, one boy would lay the curved end of a rat-stick across the mouth of one hole. Others would poke sticks into the other en-trances. When a rat peered out of the one unobstructed hole, the rat-stick was pulled toward the holder, breaking the rat's back. Davis[99] described the firing of a brush-pile nest. The surrounding Indians killed the rats as they ran out with long, limber sticks.

Rats were prepared in several ways. They were roasted on hot coals and ashes. Soups were made from them. Boiled rats were mashed except for the heads, teeth, and vertebrae. Sometimes they were placed in the fire whole and singed, after which the hair and hide were scraped with a stick, the body broken open with the hand, and the entrails removed with the fingers or shaken out. Liver, heart, brains, tail, "everthing" was eaten except the intestines.

The White Mountain encouraged boys to hunt by telling them that the boy who brought in the most rats would get a wife. "One who filled a long pole with rats would get one, while lazy boys would not."

A story of the development of Apache culture was recorded by Goddard;[100] in it the condition of the people was depicted as originally so poor that they obtained food by setting fire to the nests of field mice at the base of sotol stalks and eating the singed mice that were left; only later did they learn of wood rats, rabbits, and deer.

Porcupine (*Erethizon epixanthum couesi*) flesh was highly esteemed. The quills were removed with stick tweezers, in later times with tin tweezers. Goddard[101] recounted a tale in which a porcupine was pulled from its burrow with a stick twisted into its quills, then pit-baked.

Beaver (*Castor canadensis*) meat was said by one informant to be the best he had ever tasted. The animals were shot or taken with deadfalls. Raccoons (*Procyon lotor*) were also eaten. Mink (*Lutreola vison*) were not eaten. Skunks (*Mephitis*) were said by the White Mountain and Cibecue not to be eaten. Gifford,[102] however, said the Southern Tonto ate skunks.

Information on eating badgers (*Taxidea taxus*) was contradictory, but old Cibecue and White Mountain informants stated that they were once eaten and even considered good. They were shot, clubbed, and trapped. At times they were dug out with digging sticks.

In the 1940s the White Mountain and Cibecue Apache did not eat or hunt the wild pig (*Tayassu tajacu*), although these were numerous in parts of their reservation. As the animal was known to attack humans, it was feared. Formerly it was hunted. On one occasion a wild pig was killed by a boy who encountered it by chance. He sold it at a Cibecue trading post. Observers of the 1870s and later times reported that the Apache detested pork and were only with difficulty educated to the idea of eating issue bacon.[103] Bacon, ham, and occasionally fresh pork were purchased by the Apache from the reservation stores in the 1940s.

Birds and Eggs

Turkey, quail, pigeon, and dove were hunted and eaten by all Western Apache. Water fowl were also eaten, although perhaps not all species. The White Mountain stated that geese and ducks were eaten, while two Canyon Creek informants stated that geese were eaten but not ducks. Ducks were said by one of these men to be shot for their feathers but not to be eaten, even when people were hungry. Hunting on the water with the aid of gourd head masks, as described by Cremony[104] for the Eastern Chiricahua about 1850, was denied. Although the White Mountain ate ducks, these were avoided by pregnant women, for it was thought that if ducks were eaten the child would be born with webbed feet.

Eagles, hawks, turkey buzzards, cranes, crows, and owls were not eaten, nor were their eggs used. The blue jay (*Cyanocitta* sp.) was not eaten because it was thought to give warning of approaching enemies. Other birds besides those named were eaten, but these were not identified. Birds' eggs, except those of the tabooed species listed above, were eaten when found.

In 1879 turkey (*Meleagris gallopano*) in the vicinity of the Black River were reported[105] to be "so numerous they seemed to cover a five acre lot." The birds weighed up to twenty-five pounds.

Turkeys were hunted during the day and also at night. In the daytime a "gobbler tail" was sometimes held as a mask before the hunter's face. This was said to attract pugnacious turkey gobblers. The favored hunting technique for turkeys was to locate a roosting place and return at night to kill the birds. On moonlit nights, especially when the ground was covered with snow, they were shot from the tree with arrows. At other times they were shot immediately after sunset while there was still light enough to see. Others, but not all, among the Cibecue and White Mountain (and Northern Tonto and San Carlos also, according to Gifford[106]) hunted turkeys by the light of grass torches. Toward the desert the White Mountain at times built fires under the roosts. The smoke was said to blind and stupefy them and they would not fly away. Boys and girls went out together on such night hunts, the girls building the fires while the boys shot the birds. Sometimes a pole might be leaned against a tree before the birds went to roost. That night the hunter would return, climb into the tree, and attempt to kill turkeys with a stick or grab them by the legs or neck.

Dove and quail (*Lophortyx gambeli?*) were also hunted at night, with or without the aid of flares, and among the White Mountain by building fires under the roosts. A very few hunters used dogs to flush quail in order to make them take refuge in trees. Gifford[107] stated that the San Carlos ran down quail when they were wet. Goodwin[108] mentioned occasional quail drives in which the young and old of both sexes joined.

The Cibecue hunted dove and other birds from blinds. A tree near a spring was chosen, or an old dry tree was erected. Around these brush was piled after the manner of a wickiup. The hunters hid in them. As the birds alighted in the tree, the hunter shot them. An informant's father had helped him build such blinds when he was a boy, and a number of boys together often put up several blinds.

Turkeys and quail were sometimes run down.[109] Frequently they were killed by accurately thrown stones.[110]

Traps, baited with seeds, were sometimes used for quail. One was a rock propped up by a stick to which a string was attached, the hunter hiding behind nearby shrubs to pull the other end of the string when the birds were under the deadfall.

A more elaborate deadfall was a rock propped up by a step-jointed stick. Slightly above ground level a cord was strung from the stick to the lower part of the rock. Another stick laid horizontally across the string destabilized the prop stick when a bird or rodent stepped on it. A box could be used instead of a rock.

Still another device was a long stick laid horizontally against a tree or peg fulcrum. From the short end of the stick a cord led to a concealed hunter who, with a quick jerk, snapped the long part of the stick around and against the feeding birds.

When eggs were found, they were eaten, even if partly incubated. They were boiled and roasted in hot ashes, never eaten raw. Gifford[111] reported that Northern Tonto and Cibecue children did not eat quail eggs lest they have freckles; among the Cibecue this taboo was attributed to the greed of the elders.

Feathers from many species of birds were used for fletching arrows, ornamenting caps, or for ceremonial purposes. Turkey feathers were easily procured and were perhaps most used for arrows and caps. Eagle (*Aquila* sp.) and hawk feathers were used ceremonially and were usually handled, at least initially, by men with "eagle power."

A White Mountain informant stated that eagle feathers were

Fig. 19. *An Apache maiden, Evelyn Ethelbah, and her sponsor after they were sprinkled with pollen by a medicine man during the girls' puberty rite at White- river in July, 1947.*

Fig. 20. *The sunrise ceremony concluded the four-day girls' puberty rite. At dawn the maidens grasped the ends of eagle feathers held by their sponsors and were led east toward the rising sun through a pole tipi.*

Fig. 21. *The girls, grasping eagle feathers, are drawn forward by their sponsors in the conclusion of their puberty rite.*

desired for "holy" things. The birds were killed by anyone, but only members of clans related to the eagle could safely pluck the feathers. The plucker was obliged to leave some feathers on the bird. When pulling the feathers, the plucker faced to the west, then threw the first feather over his back toward the east. The next three feathers were thrown successively to the south, west, and north. Thereafter the feathers were thrown first to one side, then to the other, but none to the front. When the plucking was completed, except for the feathers to be left on the bird, the Eagle Clan member turned his back while the owner of the eagle picked up the feathers. Then the body of the eagle was placed on the top of a tree. Feathers of poisoned eagles were not used.

A hunter who acquired eagle feathers was expected to share them. Before anyone could use them or wear them, they were "fixed" by a medicine man, one with eagle power. Thereafter they were used in various "secret" dances, worn in pairs on caps, or worn around the neck or under the shirt. In the 1940s, men still could be seen on the Fort Apache Reservation with a downy feather protruding from the shirt, and a cap decorated with eagle feathers was worn by an old man at a social dance in 1947. During the girls' puberty rite, a down feather was worn on the forehead of the "debutante"; other feathers were suspended from the staff used in the ceremony. Feathers were used in applying pollen to her face, and in the final morning sunrise ceremony she was drawn to the east by her male sponsor, who held an eagle feather with each hand for her to grasp. Eagle feathers were suspended from the four-pole open lodge in which the sunrise ceremony was conducted and from the elbows and wrists of the gan dancers who performed during the preceding nights. It was of interest that stones, blue (turquoise) for men and white (crystal) for women, the most efficacious of which were obtained from Pueblo ruins, could be used or worn in the same way as eagle feathers.

Reptiles, Fish, and Insects

With one exception, the Apache denied that they had ever eaten snakes or lizards. A Canyon Creek informant stated that the Tonto formerly ate a large lizard (probably the chuckwalla, *Sauromalus obesus*) but that no other Western Apache ate it; he did not know whether the Chiricahua or other surrounding Indians ate it.

Until modern times the Apache were afraid to kill snakes, but in the 1940s they tried to kill rattlesnakes (*Crotalus* sp.). Snakes other than rattlesnakes were never molested. In the days when poisonous snakes were unharmed, a gray rattlesnake with black spots "the same color as the earth" bit many San Carlos Indians living in the Salt River Valley.

When snakes were killed, accidentally or otherwise, they were buried to prevent contact with snake blood or a dead snake, for if such occurred it was believed that the unfortunate person would become crippled.

It was also believed by the Apache that contact with lizard blood was dangerous. Persons stepping on a lizard were thought to get sore feet, rheumatism, or "black poison and cracked body." Cibecue boys used to kill lizards with rocks or sticks. A White Mountain informant stated that if one killed a lizard, bad luck followed unless something were given the creature to cover its body. A rag or a handkerchief would be placed over it with the words, "This is for you."

Ritual also followed the killing of a spider or scorpion by a White Mountain. On such occasions it was necessary to say, "Go bite my cousin (name of cousin)." Any paternal or cross-cousin would do. No likes or dislikes were involved in the choice of the cousin named.

The Western Apache did not use fish until after contact with the Anglo-Americans modified the prejudice against such food. Even in the 1940s only the younger men fished or made use of fish for food. Older people and women were said not to like them.

With one exception, informants denied the use of insects as food. A Canyon Creek man stated that a green worm seven inches long with a "horn on its tail" was gathered from the ground and "boiled with spinach." When dead, the dried insect was also rolled up in the hands and smoked in cigarettes. The surviving Oatman girl, a captive of the Tontos, stated that her captors ate worms, grasshoppers, reptiles, and all flesh.[112]

As late as the 1920s the White Mountain children chased "big black bees" with a fan made from yucca leaves. When knocked down, the stinger was removed from the insect and the "sweet stuff" sucked out. This was said to be very good.

In 1948 small boys of the age of six or seven were observed shooting grasshoppers and other insects with cactus-spine darts fired from homemade spring guns.

Butchering

Skinning and butchering of animals was considered to be men's work, while the care and preparation of meat and skins was the work of the women.[113]

Large animals were usually skinned and butchered where killed for greater ease and convenience in transporting home. However, the whole carcass was sometimes carried home before butchering. Gifford[114] reported this as the usual Northern Tonto method.

The White Mountain preferred to skin deer on scrub-oak branches. If these were not available, grass and leaves were put under the animal. Juniper branches were not used because they made the meat bitter, and piñon branches were said to give it an unpleasant odor. The animal was never skinned on the ground or hanging. The usual skinning procedure was to make an incision on the ventral side of the animal from chin to tail. Other incisions were made up the inside of the legs and around the legs just above the feet. The pelt, when removed, included the face and ears and tail. Occasionally a small animal was skinned by cutting off the head and casing the hide. Gifford[115] reported that some San Carlos quivers were made of the cased skin of the coyote. The ritual of skinning required that the hide be laid four times in one direction by the Northern Tonto, one time by the San Carlos, Cibecue, and White Mountain.[116]

The entrails of a deer were wrapped in the hide and carried home. These were considered the best parts of the animal, the cleaned intestines being a particular delicacy. Unwanted parts were not scattered but were carefully piled on top of a nearby bush. Deer blood was preserved when possible and transported in the animal's stomach. Meat other than the entrails was wrapped into bundles and tied with yucca, yucca cord being carried by hunters for this purpose. The udders of does with young were saved and the milk preserved if possible.

At camp the meat was pounded and squeezed to extract the blood. Blood so squeezed, with that salvaged at the kill, was cooked about half a day in the animal's stomach or boiled with fat, corn meal, and wild onions. This "blood sausage" was said to be "stiff, just like ginger bread" and was sliced "like a chocolate cake." Doe udders and milk were cooked over coals. The milk was reputed to taste like cottage cheese.

An old Cibecue hunter claimed that looking through the stomach fat of a deer caused trachoma, a belief not known to White Mountain informants. The feet were cut from the animal by the White Mountain as soon as they arrived home and were thrown in any direction because it was feared children would find and play with them, thereby incurring bad luck.

During the period when elk were still hunted, the Cibecue cut out and threw away a gland under the tail. It was reputed to impart an odor to the meat if not quickly removed. It was thrown in the direction the wind was blowing.

Among the White Mountain, when turkey were killed, the "red

bag" under the neck was never cut or opened but thrown away, lest a snake be found inside.

Skins

Skins were dressed by both men and women.[117] Women, however, more commonly cared for them.[118]

Goodwin[119] described the dressing of deer hide. The hide was first soaked in a grass-lined, water-filled hole. The next day, the hair was removed. Then the hide was placed over a post and scraped to remove all particles of fat or meat. Fleshers were made from the cannon bone of a deer. After this the hide was placed in the hole and soaked, then removed and wrung dry. This was repeated several times. Deer brains were boiled in a pot and rubbed into the hide with dry weeds. The hide was then soaked again, this time in a basket. The process was completed by working the hide with the hands until it was soft. Goodwin[120] recounted a tale in which a woman made hoops of saplings on which to stretch hides. Hides to be used for blankets were not dehaired.

Tools used in preparing hides, in addition to the cannon-bone flesher, were oval flint blades for skinning (the same tool described as used in trimming mescal leaves) and sharp rib-bone scrapers for dehairing. A White Mountain woman stated that while dressing buckskin the worker might not drink liquids; violation of this taboo was thought to be followed by a hardening and drying of the skin.

Bear hides were difficult to dress. The "bear grease" was first rubbed off with a stone tool. Ashes were put on the inside and charcoal rubbed in with the hands. The skin was then pounded and scraped with stone tools. The scraping might consume two days, as the hide did not soften readily. Sometimes it was rubbed with deer brains to aid the softening process. After the pounding and scraping process, the hide was stretched in the sun and pinned down with about fifty wooden pegs. When it had dried, it was removed and buried in damp earth, then worked with the hands until it became soft. The hair was not removed. Hair was never removed from any hide except those of deer and occasionally elk.

The Apache considered buckskin the most valuable hide, making from it all articles of clothing and footwear, blankets, carrying and storage bags, and other minor articles. Buckskin was a standard article of trade.

The thick skin from the sides of a deer's jaws was used for the soles of moccasins, skin from the middle of deer legs for the uppers. Sinew was used for sewing.[121] Buckskin caps were made and ornamented with turkey, hawk, and eagle feathers. Large sleeved shirts and trousers were also made of this material. The trousers, at least, were a rather late article; prereservation dress for men consisted of moccasins, hip-length leggings, and breechclout.

An unornamented deerskin bag, used in the same manner and for some of the same purposes as the burden basket, was said to be ancient. It was about eighteen by eighteen inches in size and was round when full. The bottom and sides were sewn with sinew. A carrying strap one inch wide was slung across one shoulder and under the opposite arm by men. Men also might use a back pack with the strap around the neck and secured with a hand clutch. Women supported the bag on the back with the carrying strap across the forehead.

Another type of buckskin bag, similar to the 1940s Apache saddle-bag, had a cross slit opening in the center of one side, the load being distributed at both ends. The antiquity of this bag was not determined, but it probably dated from the time of the acquisition of the horse.

A White Mountain informant claimed that on occasion deerskin water bags with a carrying strap were used on trips, but these were not used in permanent camps. Before using them it was necessary to soak them overnight. A Canyon Creek man stated that while water bags might be made from the paunch of a deer, the hide was never so used.

Buckskin had a variety of minor uses. Flour was stored in cased fawn skins. Buckskin thongs were used to wrap a bow, to secure the top edges of the burden baskets, and to bind women's hair. For the last-named purpose a buckskin square ornamented with painted pink or yellow dots, or later with brass knobs, was tied around the hair at the base of the neck, with the hair below the binding hanging loose.

Whole deer hides were used as blankets, usually with the hair on, and at times as weatherproofing on the outside of the wickiup.

The hides of unwounded animals were used for ceremonial purposes. Animals were run down, not shot. Such unblemished hides were given, with turquoise and downy eagle feathers tied to the forehead, to religious practitioners as a ceremonial gift.[122] Bourke,[123] who had seen attempts to capture a fawn alive, believed that buckskin for sacred purposes must be that of a strangled animal when possible. The Southern Tonto practice of surrounding young antelope, catching them by hand, and killing them by pressing the foot over the heart, as described by Gifford,[124] suggested a possible ceremonial use for these hides also. A White Mountain woman stated that the skin of a deer fetus stuffed with grass was carried over the shoulders of the clown dancer. The clown might also dance with fir branches over the shoulders if such a skin were not available. This informant had been attempting to purchase a fetus hide for use in her daughter's puberty ceremony and first had bid five dollars, then ten, for one, but the owner had refused to sell.

Elk hide was used principally for beds, blankets, moccasins (including the whole feet and leggings), and pack sacks. It also was tied on the exterior of the wickiup to break the wind. Elk hide was said to be good for nothing except the above-mentioned uses. Occasionally the hair was removed from elk skins in the dressing process, as it was "too coarse—too thick."

A White Mountain myth, "The Man Who Pursued Mountain Sheep," was said by Goodwin[125] to account for the fact that one must never pursue a mountain sheep and never make a "buckskin" of its hide but restrict oneself to killing and eating the animal. A Canyon Creek informant stated that mountain-sheep skin was used for clouts, a two-foot strip being passed between the legs and under a belt, front and back. The skin was considered good for nothing else, as it was "too thin—just like calico."

Buffalo skins were an expensive import well liked for robes and blankets. Two were sewn together to make a blanket.

Buffalo cowhide was used for blankets and moccasins. The thin skin from the area of the udder was used to make pack sacks.

Bear skins were usually used only for robes and blankets. They might also be placed around the outside of the wickiup, and one Cibecue informant said they might be used for shirts. Bourke[126] stated that the pelt of a slain bear was carried around in a circle in a dance, first on the shoulders of the slayer, then on those of other warriors.

Coyote hides were made into blankets and articles of clothing, including shirts, caps, and moccasins. A hip-length sleeveless shirt, said to date from pre-Anglo-American times, was made from two hides. Such shirts were worn by both sexes and all ages. Before the advent of the whites, it was undecorated; after the whites came, dyes were used to color the hair on the hide.

As mentioned in the section on weapons, the mountain-lion hide was in great demand for use in quivers. Bourke[127] stated that it was considered medicine by deer and elk hunters.

Bobcat skins were made into blankets, if enough could be obtained, or fashioned into small sacks, an everyday cap, or used like a scarf to wind around the neck.

Badger skins were used in making blankets, shirts, and caps. In the last-named, parts were left hanging down the cheeks.

Fox skins were made into caps with cheek flaps. Goodwin[128] reported that White Mountain Chief Diablo hunted gray foxes for blanket skins.

Skunk skins were made into blankets, shirts, caps, and moccasins. The tail was used for a head band.

The tails of raccoons and other tails were left hanging from caps or detached and wrapped about the neck.

Beaver skin was considered good material for sacks or clothing or "anything." It also was made into a cap with the tail left hanging at the back of the head.

Squirrel skins were sewn together to produce blankets, the tails left "sticking out." Blankets were also made from rat and gopher hides. Skins of different animals might be used together in the same blanket. When using the blanket, it was spread flat if shared by more than one individual; otherwise an Apache rolled up in it.

Rabbit skins had various minor uses. They were used for baby blankets. In winter, they were wrapped around the feet inside the moccasins, the skin side next to the foot, fur side out. Occasionally they were made into caps. Their principal use, however, was for small sacks. Such a bag was fashioned by cutting off the head of the rabbit and casing the skin. This skin was rubbed with grease, reversed, and a strip of buckskin then added for a handle. It was not ornamented. It was held in the hand or attached to a belt at the hip and was used for tobacco, corn, or small personal items. No large blankets were made of rabbit skins.

Meat Recipes

The choicest parts of venison were broiled over the fire or hot coals. Usually, the select portions were cooked rare, although some Apache preferred their meat well done. Meat was cooked by placing it directly upon hot coals, on a flat rock over the coals, or by spitting it on a stick. Other parts of venison were boiled, alone or with "pepper" leaf. Meat was not boiled solely for the purpose of softening tough cuts, for the Apache were very fond of boiled meat and of meat soups.

The favorite recipe consisted of boiled, macerated venison into which acorn meal had been pounded. A gruel was made of meat, soup stock, and acorn meal. *Butter soup* was the term applied to this dish by the whites because of its yellowish color.

Venison was boiled with corn and beans, also at times with wheat.

The recipes mentioned apply also to the meat of animals other than deer.

Pit baking was a favored method for cooking some cuts of meat, some kinds of animals, and any meat while on the hunt or raid. Deer heads were wrapped in bear grass (in modern times in a wet gunnysack) and cooked overnight. Porcupine was invariably cooked whole in this way after the quills were burned off. Gifford[129] said the Northern Tonto cooked wildcat meat and the Southern Tonto cooked coyote, wolf, wildcat, and horse and cow heads in this manner. For pit-baking meat, a hole no larger than necessary was scooped out, a fire built, and a small rock placed on the fire. The animal or bird to be baked was placed, usually with the hide or feathers on, upon the rock, then quickly covered with wet or green grass and earth. The Northern Tonto, according to Gifford,[130] covered their wildcat meat with pine needles and earth.

Entrails were the first part of the meat eaten. Reagan[131] stated that beef intestines were washed inside and out and broiled over the fire, while the stomachs of edible animals were washed and cut into sections for broiling. Reagan added that in early times the intestines were eaten raw without cleansing. This was denied by my informants. Bloom[132] recounted a scene on the Gila in which Apache were purported to have roasted the entrails of a dead horse, containing all the filth, in ashes, then eating pieces, with the "seasoning" running down their faces. Intestines were usually stripped.

Blood saved or pounded out of an animal's flesh was made into sausage. It was encased in the animal's stomach or intestines. Such blood, mixed with salt and fat, was either boiled or roasted over the fire.

Vertebrae and other bones were kept to make soup. If not used immediately, they were cut or broken and dried. Such stored bones were placed in saddlebags by the wickiup or in a tree and would keep all winter. Gifford[133] reported that the Cibecue, after first extracting the marrow, boiled bones four or five times for soup and that they also pounded vertebrae and other bones with mescal juice and ate them without further cooking.

Bourke[134] noted that the Apache scouts spitted heads, hearts, and livers of game and broiled them before the fire.

Live turtles were placed upon hot coals and roasted, after which they were parceled out to all in the camp to eat as "medicine."

Turkeys were roasted or boiled. A Cibecue informant stated that the feathers were always removed before cooking, as was sometimes the skin. The intestines were removed and the gall bladder thrown away; the rest of the fowl was eaten. Other birds were cooked in the same manner or were pit-baked.

According to Goodwin,[135] rats were placed in the fire and the hair singed off, then skinned, and either roasted or boiled. Santee[136] stated that wood rats were strung together on a string and lowered into a can of boiling water without skinning or cleaning.

A method of preparing meat for boiling was to compress a lump of it in each hand simultaneously, forming balls. The use of one hand only was tabooed, but the informant did not know why. A Mexican-style tamale of corn with deer or horse meat was boiled in corn husks.

After the introduction of frying pans, meat was frequently fried, often with potatoes. Potatoes also were often boiled with meat, but, according to Palmer,[137] green vegetables were never cooked with meat.

Meat was stored for future use by cutting it into strips, sun-drying it, then pounding it.

Chili was occasionally brought from Mexico. When available, crushed chili powder was sprinkled over meat that had been broiled and was also eaten with corn mush and beef jerky.

Storage

Venison was stored by hanging it under or placing it on ramada-type platforms. One instance of a tree platform was reported. Meat tied between pieces of cedar bark for protection from moisture or tied in a tree was said to keep for three to four months. Meat was cached in this way when a family left its permanent home. Ground caches were not used for storing meat.

Pemmican was made as follows: After being cut into thin strips about one foot long, meat was dried two days on a shrub. It was then pounded on a flat rock with a cylindrical hammer stone. The pounded meat was put loosely in a deerskin sack or a carrying basket and covered with anything available. If hung in a cool place in the wickiup, it would keep for about a year. Meat was never packed with grease or berries.

Division and Trade

Among the Apache, generosity was an ideal. Successful hunters were expected to share their kill. All neighbors might be included in a division of meat; however, the "poor" (meaning, in this case, those in need, or families without adult men to provide for them) were especially favored. There were also conventions under which others might share part of a hunter's kill. A hunter's relatives by marriage had strong claims on his game.

All informants insisted that in prereservation times everyone shared a kill or catch. The Apache were taught to divide and were never selfish. If people did not stop a hunter as he carried his carcass home, the hunter would later cut it up and take portions to them. He might give away all the meat at once or wait and give some every day until it was consumed. Frequent contrast was made between this ideal condition of old and the ungenerous individualism of later times.

There were reported incidents that deviated from the ideal of dividing meat. Although some people—"big men," "chiefs," "good men"—always shared their meat with others, there were some "poor" people who would attempt to hide food. Such men would conceal their venison by hiding it in a tree and go out at night to bring it in for their children. "Too many people tried to hide."

A twentieth-century hunting episode will illustrate the differing attitudes of the ideally generous Apache and the deviant. Two men went hunting together, one killing five deer and the other four. The more successful hunter hid two of his deer and brought in only three, while the other brought in all four of his. The kill was divided equally between the two hunters and the meat was later apportioned to relatives and friends. When the killer of four deer later heard that his hunting partner had hidden and kept for his individual use two-fifths of his kill, he said he was so angry that he would like to kill him. An old informant, survivor of pre-American days, stated that some people had always behaved in such a selfish manner.

Among the White Mountain a skillful hunter was frequently followed at a distance by those who were less adept or energetic. Although such men knew they were being followed, they seem to have made no effort to elude their trackers or throw them off the trail. The followers approached if the hunter was successful, and the kill was divided. In such a case the slayer had several options. He could tell them he was going to keep the hide and allow others to help him with the skinning, or he could tell one individual to skin the carcass and this man would then receive only the skin and head of the animal, no meat.

Goodwin[138] said it was the custom for a companion, not the killer, to claim a deer. An anecdote in which a deer was claimed by people other than the killer and the hide was slashed so as to make it unusable indicates that hunters did not invariably accede with

good humor to others' claims. Gifford[139] noted that among the
Northern Tonto and Cibecue a killer's companions obtained the
hide. Gifford's information on the other groups concerning this
point was apparently inconclusive. It would appear that whoever
obtained the hide received also the head and brains and perhaps the
spinal cord. According to Gifford[140] a Southern Tonto hunter divided all the meat he killed among his companions; only if another
made a kill would he receive any meat.

Some chiefs among both the Cibecue and the White Mountain
sent out hunting parties. Although a portion of the meat would usually be given the chief and he would be glad to have it, it was stated
that "he would not care" if he received none, as the hunters were
sent primarily to procure food for their own families. In a local
group at Cedar Creek a division of the kill of such hunting parties
was made by a man temporarily appointed for that purpose. This
would not be the chief and would not be the same man in every
case. Of those who exercised this function, "some were good men;
some bad—not to be trusted." The most important item in the division was the skin.

Relatives by marriage received special consideration from a
hunter in the distribution of his game. Even while courting a hunter
often brought small game as a gift to his sweetheart.[141] According
to Goodwin,[142] a man was expected to hunt and to share the kill
with his in-laws; thus a man might hunt deer especially for a new
sister-in-law (brother's wife). A man's wife's sisters helped themselves to the meat he killed. Game, when killed, was expected to
be divided also with the wife's brothers, and they might even help
themselves to it without asking.[143]

The small game hunted by boys was divided equally among the
participants after a hunt.[144] When boys accompanied adults on a
hunting party, they received some of the less choice portions of the
kill when the meat was divided.[145]

A hunting partnership was sometimes formed with crows by a
hunter who would say, "All right, I go to hunt deer now. I will let
you have the guts. The deer is right close now. Where is he? You
take me over there and I'll let you have the viscera." The crow was
reputed to fly over to the deer. There the hunter would leave the
unwanted portion of the carcass (little enough) for the crow and

hide the meat in a tree, but the crow would "steal" part of the meat nevertheless.

Meat was sometimes exchanged for corn, but there were no professional hunters. Buckskins were occasionally traded to the Tonto, Navajo, and Pueblo.

A wide distribution of certain types of kills was expected. Thus, as mentioned in the section on boys' training, a youth's first kill was divided among all the camps in a group. The White Mountain divided turtles among all families, as the meat was considered a medicine for whooping cough and other ailments. A successful eagle hunter was expected to share the feathers.

Miscellaneous Ritual Associated With Hunting

There were standardized acts of hunting ritual, including prayers and song, that every man could learn. In addition, there were extra hunting powers, usually exercised through prayer and song, that were acquired through contact with the supernaturals or, as proprietary rites, were acquired from the holder. Those with proprietary rites usually taught them to a relative, although others, for a fee, might arrange to learn them. Those with extra hunting powers were often sought to lead hunting parties, and hunting skill and powers added considerably to a man's prestige.

The Cibecue offered prayers to the sun or to the gods and made an offering of yellow pollen before deer hunts. They also used colored stones and effigies from Pueblo ruins, although exactly how I did not learn.

It was believed that if an owl hooted near the camp, many deer would appear in the morning. If a fox barked near camp, someone would sicken and die. Roadrunners that walked around and around the camp in the daytime without fright betokened a death in the family of the hunter.

Strict taboos were observed on the hunt by the Cibecue. There was no joking, no talking of meat, no unnecessary conversation of any kind. In boiling meat, the cook was careful not to expose it to view and stirred it quickly. Meat was never thrown, to a dog for instance, but was handed slowly. Meat was not thrown away. Any unwanted entrails were piled carefully on top of brush. The Mescalero also thought it unlucky, apparently at all times, to throw food about or to handle it carelessly. Even bones were placed in a neat pile and disposed of at once, not thrown around. To do otherwise was thought to risk the loss of hunting skill and cause a shortage of food.[146] Hunters could not take utensils along, or any meat for food. These precautions were not followed in the 1940s.

The Cibecue sweated in the sweat house and sang hunting songs both before and after the hunt. Hunters looked at Sun and prayed, and Sun showed them where the deer were. At other times they prayed to a large, bright star at an angle of about thirty degrees above the horizon, probably the morning star.

The larger overnight hunting parties sang deer songs at night, at which time the hunters placed their guns against a tree. The medicine man in charge would sometimes predict they would be lucky. At other times he would say, "Somebody has talked way back home; somebody has talked behind you; you will not see your deer." Both Cibecue and White Mountain believed the hunter would have no luck if his female relatives or people back at camp talked about his quest. A wife, queried as to the whereabouts of her husband, would not answer that he was hunting but, with a wave of the hand, would say, "Over there." In the morning a medicine man might say that he had dreamed of blood on his hands or that his feet were bloody and continue, "I think that's lucky; how did you fellows dream?"

The White Mountain deer hunter prayed to the gan for good hunting and also to the deer and to the mountain lion because it could run swiftly like the deer. Women prayed to Changing Woman. Night and morning prayers were said by the individual before the hunt, and special deer or antelope songs were sung. The day before the hunt, deer songs were sung in the sweat house.

There were no offerings of meat or pollen or colored stones during the hunt by the White Mountain. Turquoise and other stones were left at home, for it was thought no animal would be killed if they were carried. No meat was taken along on a hunt.

Continence before the hunt was not compulsory, but if it were not observed, both man and woman were obliged to say a special prayer. Goodwin[147] implied that continence was observed in his anecdote of a young newly married couple who went into the mountains on a five-day deer hunt, sleeping together but remaining continent lest the deer be driven away by the hunter's smell.

When a White Mountain hunter first sighted a deer track, he sat on a stone in a sunny spot and smoked a pipe, watching Sun. He first puffed smoke toward Sun. This ceremony had to be performed in the morning in order that the first puff would be in an easterly direction. After puffing four clouds of smoke toward Sun, the hunter repeated his action toward the highest mountains in the cardinal directions, beginning at the east and moving clockwise. Prayers and songs accompanied this ceremony.

When a group of animals was encountered by the White Mountain, one at least was allowed to escape. A slain animal was directly addressed in prayer. After killing and butchering the deer, the meat was piled upon the hide and covered with the hide. This was patted four times for luck with this prayer: "I hope I'll be able to kill all your brothers and sisters."

White Mountain hunting parties might sing all night before the hunt. Before building a fire, a special poker about two and a half feet long had to be cut or bad luck would ensue.

Animal fetuses were considered good but were eaten only by the aged, as it was thought such flesh would cause young people to become blind before they grew old. Young people did not eat the heads of deer for fear that sores would break out on their heads.

Bourke[148] stated that sacrifices were made in sacred caves before deer, antelope, or elk were hunted. Offerings consisted of baskets, branches of pine and juniper, stones, petrified wood, and prayer plumes. Women were not present at these ceremonies, for if a pregnant woman were to observe them, it was believed her child would look like a deer. Fire was kindled by friction sticks, not with flint and steel or matches. The medicine men on these occasions attempted to propitiate the animal gods whose progeny they intended to destroy.

According to Bourke,[149] the Apache threw a pinch of tule pollen to the sun with a prayer before going out on the hunt. In one such prayer the petitioner said, "With the favor of the Sun, or permission of the Sun, I am going out to fight, hunt, or plant," as the case might be, "and I want the Sun to help me." Another went: "Be good, O Sun, make me succeed deer to kill." Another account of a prayer[150] mentioned that it was ended with a sharp, snapping syllable, *ek,* as if to call attention.

Tule pollen was offered to the bear, snake, and jackrabbit.[151]

Goddard[152] recorded in "Prayers for Hunting Deer," some Apache taboos and prayers. Menstruating women could not eat the head or heart of a deer or the hunter would lose his power to kill. A hunter represented himself as coming from an attractive house so that the deer would wish to come. The hunter might speak several prayers: "[Spirit] you are my brother. Hurry and bring me the one you like." "[Spirit] you are my brother. Hurry and bring me the one you like." "Panther Boy, there is food in your camp. Hurry and bring me the forked horn deer that you raise." "Bullsnake, bring me what you raise at your camp." Such prayers were used when large deer were desired.

Another series of prayers[153] ran as follows. "[Spirit] my father, I spoke to you. I am going after that which you look upon. You must bring it to me quickly. Bring me quickly the largest male deer upon which you look." Then, after sighting the deer: "Wind, my brother, do not warn him from me." After starting again to hunt: "I am going where my sister is walking. You must hurry, my sister. I said I would come to you before the sun is very high." Then followed a prayer to the wind, "My brother, 'Hurry,' I said to you," after which the hunter killed a female deer that came to him. After beginning to hunt, the hunter prayed several times: "[Spirit] my brother, what will you do? You have some deer for pets. Bring me one of them anyway I ask of you." "[Spirit] I am your child." "Black Whirlwind, my brother, you must hurry to help me, I say." "I am after you, I say. It shall be the largest male deer and its body shall be large. It must not be looking around, because I have prayed to you."

Goodwin[154] stated that Gan, Wolf, and Mountain Lion were all believed to have power over deer.

In a tale recounted by Goodwin,[155] two deer were laid back to back on the grass to butcher so that the hunters would continue to have good luck hunting.

Goodwin[156] mentioned a power that was used primarily for creating the love impulse in humans but that might also be used as an added hunting power for deer, antelope, and mountain sheep when the hunting power alone was insufficient.

A few ritual practices in the hunt mentioned incidentally by Goodwin[157] were the placing of shed antlers in a tree, praying to a raven flying overhead, and the setting aside of certain internal organs as an offering to Raven.

Gifford[158] stated that the night before a hunt the Northern Tonto chief assembled hunters at his house, where they smoked about nine in the evening, sang four deer songs, and the shaman predicted the number of animals to be killed and when. Among the San Carlos, five or six hunters, at the behest of the chief, discussed the hunt, sweated, smoked, and prayed to the gan spirit in charge of deer, "May I have good luck henceforth; and do thou let me have another deer." If no deer were taken after two or three days, a singing rite was held at the initiation of the hunt leader. The Cibecue, with pollen in the fingers, prayed to Sun, who owned the deer and could see where they were, and to Changing Woman, the co-owner of the deer.

Gifford[159] reported that the Southern Tonto prayed to the "father" and "mother" of the deer, asking for their "children." The burden of prayer was always for continued success, according to Gifford.[160] The Cibecue and White Mountain asked, "May I kill more." The Northern Tonto asked for the father, brother, or other relatives of the slain deer. The Southern Tonto prayed, "May I kill a deer again." The San Carlos asked, "May I have good luck everywhere."

Before leaving on a hunt, the Southern Tonto ate only mescal, no meat or salt.

The corral windbreak was used by Northern Tonto hunting parties, a fire being burned therein at night; the bows and guns were placed on a log pointing east and sung over. While the shaman sang, a gun might discharge.[161]

The Tonto groups stated that deer were the "cattle of the gan," while the White Mountain held that they were the "horses" of these spirits.[162]

After slaying a deer, the Northern Tonto oriented it toward the hunter's home. The Cibecue and White Mountain oriented it toward the east.[163]

The Northern Tonto plugged the nostrils of a slain deer so that other deer would be less wild.[164]

Gifford[165] recorded that the Northern Tonto and Cibecue prayed to the wolf when hunting deer (the Southern Tonto and San Carlos were not asked).

Summary and Conclusions

Meat from game animals made up a major portion of the Western Apache diet. The White Mountain and Cibecue, which were the most strongly agricultural of the Western Apache groups, depended less upon game than did other groups. The proportion of meat in the diet varied with the seasons (autumn to spring being the principal hunting season), with the abundance of the agricultural and wild food harvests, and with the success of raids upon the livestock of the Mexicans. Before American soldiers disrupted the hunting and raiding activities of the Apache, approximately 35 percent of the food consumed by these Indians was meat. This figure is at best an estimate based on the recollection of informants who were never accustomed to think in exact quantitative terms. Goodwin[166] estimated that meat comprised 35 to 40 percent of all White Mountain foods in prereservation times, and Opler[167] estimated that in the same period the diet of the White Mountain and Cibecue was 35 percent meat.

Venison was not only the most important meat quantitatively but also perhaps the most esteemed. Next, in the order of their quantitative importance, were other large game, antelope, elk, mountain sheep, bear; small game; and the burros, horses, and cattle taken in raids. It should be mentioned that antelope, elk, mountain sheep, and bear, particularly the last three, were not as dependable a source of meat as deer or small game and that they were not hunted as regularly; frequently, small game became more important. Wood rats were mentioned almost as often as venison as the tastiest meat food; badger meat and beaver tails also received mention (once each) as the best of traditional meat foods.

Although some were more adept than others, all Apache men participated actively in hunting. The good hunter was highly respected. Often the affinal relatives of such a man would offer him a plural wife—a sister, niece, cousin, or clan sister of his first wife—to indicate their esteem and to bind him more closely to the family. Hunting ability or supernatural hunting powers were not required for chieftainship, but such abilities or powers were frequently possessed by chiefs.

The Western Apache did not make the fullest use of the fauna available in their habitat. Carnivores and bear were not universally eaten; reptiles, with the exception of the chuckwalla among the Tonto and the tortoise used for ritual purposes, were ignored; certain predatory birds and waterfowl avoided; only the Tonto used insects (a horned caterpillar); and fish were unused.

Within the period of Anglo-American occupation there were radical changes in the Apache attitude toward and the use of foods. The elk, once an esteemed source of flesh, became a tabooed animal after 1900. Fish, once unthinkable as an article of food, were gradually making their way into the Apache diet during the 1940s. The fondness for entrails as the choicest part of an animal persisted in spite of official attempts to discourage their use and in spite of the cultural disapproval of the whites. With venison no longer available in quantity, there was a shift to beef as the chief meat in the Apache diet.

Chapter 4

GATHERING

Formation of Gathering Parties

The gathering of wild plants was often done by individual families or extended families separating temporarily from the larger group. Others might attach themselves for a time to a family party.

A local group functioned as a whole only in occasional mass movements to a gathering area. Ordinarily, the family cluster or a party made up of individuals from several families acted as the economic unit in gathering and hunting. If a family planned a trip, others, hearing of it, might join to form a party large enough to travel safely. A chief, subchief, or headman would be in charge.[1]

Parties going to the lower elevations for mescal, mesquite, or saguaro, usually a trip of ten to fourteen days, were small and worked independently. In other important midsummer food harvests nearer home, the stay was usually longer, and parties from the same or different groups often made adjacent camps. Even after the harvest they might remain in the location for a while. Although gathering parties were commonly from the same local group, a family or cluster might join a party from another group. If two local groups combined in a gathering venture, they usually remained in separate camps. The chief of a local group arriving late might direct his people to make their camps at a distance from others, and late arrivals would ask for their clusters or local groups.[2]

When courting, youths and girls often went in groups to gather seeds. The girls carried the baskets and beaters. After their return, they cooked the seeds, later taking the food to the boys' camps to be eaten.[3]

161

Children of twelve or so took an active part in the procuring of foods. Usually, the boys hunted small game while the girls gathered. Salt-gathering trips were usually made by men, though women sometimes accompanied them.

Men took practically no part in the gathering of plant foods except mescal; here they performed the heavy labor of preparing the fire pits. One old man repeated the exhortations of his grandmother and widowed mother in his youth: "'When you get big, you will marry. If you are lazy, everybody will laugh at you. You hunt. You get horses. You go with your wife and dig mescal and pick up the wood and fix it for her. You pack it where the oven is. Don't go away—you afraid to stay—come back while I talk to you.' Then when she finished, I would go play and forget everything right away."

Migrations and Camps

Goodwin[4] explained the seminomadic existence of the Western Apache on the basis of their subsistence activities. According to him, agriculture, the hunting of large game, and the use of wild plants and small game all played an important part in their mode of life. Hunting and the gathering of wild plant foods kept them moving because the food plants grew at different elevations and in different seasons. Food-gathering journeys took ten days to a month. Pack horses were used when available, but foot travel remained general. Possessions were packed on the back in burden baskets when people were afoot.

According to Goodwin,[5] most of the White Mountain left their fields when the corn was about three feet high to gather wild plants, returning in September for a month of harvest. My informants stated not only that they spent most of the summer gathering but that most of the people often spent the winter in the lower country south of the Fort Apache Reservation.

After the agricultural harvest in the fall and the local wild-plant harvest, particularly acorns, had been gathered, families migrated south across the Black or Salt rivers and remained in mescal areas until March or April. They camped at different places each year because the mescal would be exhausted in previously harvested areas.

An upper Canyon Creek man described the annual migrations of his family in the 1880s in considerable detail. The rest of this section is mostly from this man's account. The family consisted of husband, wife, the wife's mother, and a varying number of small children, of whom this informant had been one.

Three horses were taken. Small children sometimes walked, sometimes rode with a parent, sometimes rode a led horse. The grandmother walked. Observation confirmed the statement that "the oldest woman never rides a horse." The equipment carried included one mano (a flat, rectangular mulling stone), but no metate (a shallow, rectangular stone quern, always quite heavy); one burden basket, four pitched water baskets, one coffee pot, one frying pan, one bread pan, and one butcher knife. The duffle was packed in skin and cloth saddlebags. (These were rectangular bags, usually half again as large as a gunnysack; the only opening was a slit across the center of one side. They were loaded through the slit, the load was balanced equally in each end, and the bag was slung across the saddle or back of the horse.)

The order of march was man, woman, and boy. An attempt was made to be careful that the trees on the trail did not rip the pack sack; nevertheless, this frequently occurred. According to Goodwin,[6] on such marches the boys always carried the pitched torches for making fire. To make them strong and helpful, they were also made to carry other loads.

The family usually camped in order to gather wood and water and to prepare beds. Beds were made of weeds and grass and were placed near the fire. Occasionally, they were made under a tree or between trees. Santee[7] observed that the Apache always bedded under some kind of shelter, even if it was only a few bushes; the Indian would build a small individual fire, rake away the coals when the ground was warm, then curl up on the warmed spot with feet to the hot coals.

The family arose before sunrise. Breakfast was cooked and eaten and the horses found, or the father might go after the horses while the meal was being prepared.

The Salt River crossing was made with some care. Men and horses swam it, swimming diagonally to the current. Children crossed on the horses. They were not tied to the horses but were tied together with a rope that encircled all the children on a horse.

Women were helped across by means of two ropes tied at the waist, with a man on the end of each rope. The one in front swam ahead until he secured footing, then pulled the woman in, while the one in the rear paid out the other rope. Sometimes people crossed holding on to the tails of the horses.

After the winter campgrounds had been reached, mescal was prepared twice, once upon arrival and again just before returning to the agricultural sites. Camp was moved every fifteen days or so for better grounds. People led a rather leisurely, pleasant existence. The men hunted deer, the women made baskets, and the boys hunted small game, brought in the horses, and played.

The winter camps were temporary habitations. If rain threatened, a ramada could be erected by a man and wife in about two hours. If it was windy, oak or mesquite or any kind of brush was piled on the north and south sides of the camp with a fire in the middle; this brush shelter might be put up alone without the overhead protection of the ramada. Wickiups were never built. The winter camps were warm during the day but sometimes cold at night.

Implements and Techniques

Implements used in gathering included digging sticks, poles to knock off or hook down fruits and nuts, cactus tongs, seed beaters, knives, and carrying baskets or sacks.

Gifford[8] described the digging sticks used for tubers and roots as being eighteen to thirty-six inches long and one to two inches thick. The Cibecue and White Mountain sticks were chisel bladed; at times they were driven into the earth with a cobble. Western Apache mescal digging sticks were all chisel bladed and cobble driven. They varied from three to six feet in length.

All Western Apache used a special knife for trimming mescal leaves.[9] One I examined was of reddish chert, oval in shape, three and three-fourths inches long, one and seven-eighths inches across the short diameter, and three-eighths of an inch thick.

Knives were also used in seed gathering. The Northern Tonto used an ash-wood knife for severing sunflower heads. The Southern Tonto had a single-bladed (edged) wooden knife, six to eight inches long, that was used only for sunflower heads; a stone knife was used for the same purpose. Cutting was by pressure, not sawing. For sunflower heads the Cibecue used a stone knife.[10]

All Western Apache used long straight poles for reaching the branches of trees. For hooking saguaro fruit, poles with diagonal crosspieces were used.[11] The crosspiece was attached in such a way that it formed two acute angles; the fruit could then be caught and pulled off with one inside angle or pushed off with the other.[12] The poles were often of saguaro ribs lashed together to attain sufficient length. Both the White Mountain and the San Carlos used a stick for acorns, the latter an ocotillo stalk. Both collected piñon nuts, however, after these had fallen to the ground. The Cibecue used a stick to dislodge both acorns and piñon cones.[13]

Fruits of the small cacti were picked with tongs made from a split stick bent double.

Receptacles used in gathering included the twined burden basket, buckskin sacks, and occasionally old pitched baskets or basket trays, the latter being used to catch seeds as they were beaten from bushes.

Gifford[14] said the Northern Tonto beater was made of sumac stems. A White Mountain informant described the beater as being something like a tennis racket, only smaller, about eight inches wide, rather flat, and curved at the end. It was made of woven bear grass.

A Tonto tool that served a multiple purpose was described by Smart.[15] It was a stick about five feet long, hooked at one end, but otherwise straight. It resembled the Old World shepherd's staff. This was used to hook the fruit "leguara" and for loosening the earth in breaking into a rat's nest or rabbit's burrow. In the 1940s, such sticks were still carried by elderly White Mountain and Cibecue men and women, who used them as an aid in walking; no other use was described for them. The Southern Tonto and Cibecue sometimes climbed trees by means of a sapling leaned against the trunk. Among the Cibecue, both men and women climbed trees. The men of the two Tonto groups did most of the climbing, while the women did most of it among the San Carlos and White Mountain.[16]

Gifford[17] reported that patches of grass and brush were burned over to ensure a better crop of seeds by the Northern Tonto,

Southern Tonto and White Mountain. No more information was obtained on this except that among the Cibecue patches of wild tobacco were burned over. Both the Cibecue and the White Mountain burned trees (probably willow and sumac) to bring out the young shoots desired for basket making.

Ownership and Marking

Trees and wild plants growing on farm land belonged to the owner of that farm among the White Mountain and the Cibecue. Other than this there was no restriction as to where one might gather or hunt so long as he remained in his group's territory. A case of ownership of wild plants at Spring Creek among the second semiband of the Southern Tonto was reported by Gifford.[18] There a large patch of an edible seed plant was owned, and only four women (of four families) were permitted to gather.

Although wild plants were not ordinarily owned, certain plants or products were frequently marked in some manner to indicate the claimant's right to gather them. This applied only for a single season. The discoverer of a honey tree could establish a claim to it by placing a pile of rocks by it. Groups of people claimed sunflowers by tying a bunch of heads together before the seeds ripened. A stick set in the ground or hung on a tree would mark a patch of plants or acorns. An individual could designate only a limited number of trees for use, "just five or six," and only the tree where the stick was placed was reserved. Even then aggressive people would sometimes throw the stick away and harvest the products. Other individual methods of marking acorn trees were the use of grass, soapweeds, and stones. In the 1940s a dress, shawl, or ribbon was customarily used.

Division of Products

Although the poor frequently asked the rich and chiefs for agricultural products or for meat, they did not usually ask for wild plants because there was enough available for everyone. The few who begged continually, even for wild plant food, were likely to be given it but were regarded with mild contempt as lazy and worthless.

People were very generous with their gathered foods. The first family to gather a newly matured wild plant crop distributed a portion to others. "Whoever got the acorn or mescal first, pretty soon everybody had it." Such donors would be remembered at another time by those who received food from them.

In one local group at Cedar Creek the chief sent designated families to procure mescal; others were sent to hunt or told to plant. The produce was divided among all.

Trade

Wild food products were not infrequently traded or exchanged with other groups or with non-Apache. The Cherry Creek people traded mescal (together with burros, baskets, and buckskins) to the Tontos and Yavapai. The White Mountain traded mescal (and also burros and baskets) to the Pueblo for blankets. The Navajo gave blankets to the White Mountain for mescal, wild berries, salt, and baskets.

San Carlos Apache visited Diablo, an Eastern White Mountain chief, and gave him mescal and saguaro fruit. When they departed, they bore presents of blankets, corn, and buckskins. [19]

Storage

Some wild food crops were stored in caves near the place where they were gathered, but most were carried home for winter use. Here they were stored in a ground or tree cache or a wickiup. The largest and most permanent wickiups were always built here and were called by a special name, "ripe fruits wickiup," which referred to the plants stored in them. [20]

The White Mountain scattered their caches in case of emergency. There were as many as five or ten to a family, some large, some small, some for agricultural products, some filled with wild products. Some were near the permanent agricultural home sites, others near the winter gathering grounds.

Fig. 22. *Bland Tessay stands at the site of a nineteenth-century ground cache in the Cibecue area.*

Tree caches were used for dried meat, berries, cactus and yucca fruit, and mescal. At the home site a platform cache might be built in a tree. Elsewhere the cached products might simply be hung from the branches.

Rock shelters and caves were often used for storage. Goodwin[21] noted that such storage was usually in olla-shaped baskets among the White Mountain. According to Gifford,[22] pottery and baskets were used for such storage. Among the baskets used by the Northern Tonto was a coiled storage basket with a three-rod foundation, the design in Martynia. Its top was covered with grass. The Cibecue used a twined storage basket "so large that a woman had to get inside to make it." The Cibecue granary was on a platform in a cave. To store seeds, the Cibecue sometimes piled them on a cave floor.[23]

In the ground caches were stored, in addition to agricultural products, piñon nuts, acorns, and sometimes dried mescal. The pits were lined with slabs, juniper bark, or grasses and were sealed with grass or bark, slabs, and earth. The White Mountain, at least, tended to place them where the morning sun would keep them dry. Seeds were stored in pottery vessels or old pitched water baskets or gourds. Buckskin sacks or bags, storage baskets, and even old burden baskets were also used.

Mescal

The most important wild food plant was mescal (*Agave* sp.).[24] Edible species of agave grew close to Cedar Creek and in the area between Cibecue and Canyon Creeks. However, the preferred plants were obtained in lower country. One Cedar Creek informant stated that "the real good and big mescal is at Bylas Mountain." A Canyon Creek man said the best mescal was "where the big cactus grows" south of the Salt River. Goodwin[25] reported that the southern slopes of the Natanes Rim and Mount Turnbull and the Graham Mountains were favored spots for mescal gathering by the White Mountain Apache. According to Castetter,[26] the species used by the Western Apache must have been *Agave parryi, Agave palmeri,* and *Agave couesii.*

When other foods were not available, life was often sustaineed for weeks at a time by mescal. The Chiricahua were said by informants to have lived on nothing else for long periods. Bourke[27] wrote: "Mescal was to the aborigines of that region [Fort Grant?] much what the palm is to the nomads of Syria." The crown of the mescal provided food, the juice was fermented into a drink, the thorn with its adhering filament served as needle and thread, the stalk was used for a lance shaft, and even a "fiddle" was fashioned from the stalk.

The agave plant could be used at any season. Customarily, after the corn harvests, groups went to areas where the agave grew to prepare mescal for the winter. If the supply on hand was small, a new supply was gathered and prepared during the winter. In the fall and winter, good edible plants could be selected by observing the leaf bases and the terminal shoot, a thickening of which indicated that the plant would bloom the following spring. The best time for gathering was in the early spring, usually in April, at which time some of the plants blossomed. At this season enough mescal was prepared to last through the summer or longer.

Because of the difficulty of preparation, mescal gathering and roasting was usually a cooperative enterprise involving five to eight women. The party might be composed of neighbors or of an extended maternal family or group of relatives. Small parties frequently left their local group for a few days for the express purpose of preparing mescal. Often, however, nearly a whole group wintered in an agave area, the parties spreading out around their winter camps to gather the agave crowns.

A roasting place was selected in an area where there was a good stand of agave. From this the women of the party fanned out in groups of two or more, frequently searching a radius of a mile or more from the roasting pit to find suitable plants.

Implements needed in gathering were a mescal chisel and a mescal knife. The chisel was a straight stick of oak or other suitable wood two and a half to three or more feet long, one and a half to two inches in diameter, with a wedge-shaped end. The chisel end was placed under the crown of the agave and the shaft driven with any convenient stone to sever the root of the plant. After the plant had been cut or pried loose, the leaves were trimmed with the mescal knife. Before metal tools were introduced, this was an unhafted chert blade (described under skins in the section on hunting).

When severed, the crowns, sometimes weighing twenty pounds each, were carried to the roasting pit. A head was carried in each hand by the leaf bases. The burden basket was not used for this because the sticky juices of the plant would penetrate a sack or basket and cause the packer's body to swell and itch. However, Curtis[28] implied that the White Mountain women carried the heads in burden baskets. Several days might be required to gather the requisite number of plants, depending, of course, on the amount desired and the accessibility of the plants. Forty or more crowns were commonly roasted in a pit at one time.

The labor of preparing the roasting pit was considered men's work. While the women gathered the plants, the men dug an earth oven or cleaned an old one, the dimensions varying from three to twelve feet in diameter and from two to four feet in depth. After digging or clearing the pit, they filled it with wood laid in a crisscross pattern. The fuel was invariably oak, for pine or other woods were said to spoil the flavor of the mescal. Over the wood was placed a layer of stones. These were round, not flat, and five to eight inches in diameter. Although any available stone could be used, vesicular lava was preferred, for it was thought to retain the heat.

When preparations had been completed, the fire pit was ignited in a prescribed ritual manner. This was done exactly at sunrise by a lucky person (one whose participation ensured success). This man or woman prayed that the mescal might be well cooked, then lighted the wood successively at the east, south, west, and north sides of the pit. According to Curtis,[29] it was necessary to make fire with a fire drill, not with matches. Goodwin[30] recounted a White Mountain myth that purported to give the origin of the lighting ceremony and prayer. Coyote set fire to the wood in the pit and said the prayer now used: "I am going to light this fire from the Sun. Fire which never goes out, Black Sun, his fire, he sets fire to it." Black symbolized holiness.

It was the belief of all Western Apache that if any of the participants indulged in sexual intercourse while the mescal was being cooked, it would be underdone and inedible.[31] A White Mountain woman reported that the old people who lighted the fire at the mescal pit or corn-roasting pit, where the same taboo applied, invariably enjoined those present not to break the taboo. They apparently delighted in embarrassing the younger onlookers, who would turn red in the face and squirm on such occasions.

Gifford[32] stated that among the Northern Tonto, Southern Tonto, and White Mountain the fire was lighted by a summer-born person. Gifford[33] also noted that the Northern Tonto women used a scratching stick for two days while cooking mescal.

When the fire was lighted, it was allowed to burn until the fuel was consumed. Mescal could not be placed in the pit if the fire were still smoking. When the fuel had burned, green or wet vegatation, brush, grass, rushes, or leaves were hastily placed in layers over the white-hot stones; the mescal crowns were placed on these and in turn covered with other layers of vegetation. The whole was covered with a foot or more of earth. Informants agreed that a surface fire was never placed on an earth oven and that mescal was always cooked two days and nights, a total of nearly forty-eight hours. However, Reagan[34] stated that a fire was built on top of this mound and kept burning and that the cooking time was about twenty-four hours. Gifford[35] recorded that a fire was used on top of the oven by the Cibecue during part of the cooking time.

On the second morning after the fire lighting, the mound was opened and the cooked mescal heads removed. The means by which each woman recognized her own mescal varied. Sometimes each threw her plants into a different part of the pit. The San Carlos, according to Gifford,[36] marked a place in the mescal pit. A White Mountain man told me that the women marked their mescal with different kinds of grass, some using blue grass, some bear grass or other grasses. A Cibecue man stated that the women did not attempt to separate their mescal in the ovens but "branded it, just like cutting the ear of a cow," by trimming their heads in characteristic patterns, one leaving one leaf on, another two leaves, and so forth.

The cooked mescal was pounded flat with stones into sheets an inch or two thick and two or three feet in diameter. It was dried by placing it near a fire and turning it, or by placing it on specially constructed drying racks or stones to dry in the sun. A mescal drying frame was constructed like a miniature ramada. It was about two feet high and had a surface of about three by four feet. Bear grass was placed on top of the rack.

The dried sheets of mescal were rolled and tied with bear grass, some five or six sheets to a bundle. When dried in this manner, it was said to keep well for a year. One man said it would keep six years. When mescal was transported, bundles were wrapped in grass and carried in a network of yucca. Two bundles were attached by cords of yucca and placed across the back of a horse in the manner of a pack saddle. Four bundles were carried on a horse.

Mescal was said by more than one informant to have been his favorite food. While preparing it, the Apache always chewed a piece. The heart of the crown, the sweetest part of the plant, was usually reserved for children, who were given slices of it to eat "like candy."

Mescal was eaten both fresh and dried. Curtis[37] said it was usually made into a gruel and that berries of aromatic sumac and walnuts were crushed and added to give it flavor.

Palmer[38] stated that one of the choice dishes of the White Mountain Apache consisted of ground walnuts and dried, roasted mescal. This was eaten with corn bread.

A fermented drink made from the heart of the mescal plant was described by Curtis[39] and Reagan.[40] According to them, the cooked mescal crowns were left in a heated pit until they began to ferment. Then they were ground and boiled or boiled first and then ground, and the liquor was poured off and allowed to stand until fermented. A Canyon Creek man stated that it was fermented entirely in a vessel, not in a pit. He also described a mescal drink in which the juice of the mescal was strained and mixed half and half with tiswin water (the liquor of fermented maize) and allowed to stand in a vessel for five or six days. At the end of this time it was a stronger drink than tiswin. The younger generation, he said, was not familiar with this process.

A sweetish liquid was shaken from the flowers of agave after a rain, usually in mid-June. This liquid could be used with tortilla bread or coffee or it could be drunk. The fluid was emptied from the flowers into a basketry or pottery cup.

The agave flower stalk was baked when young, but not too young, and chewed for juice. During the 1940s, a few Apache grew sugar cane and used the stalk in the same manner. It was said to taste the same. The agave stalk, used at one time for lance shafts, was frequently fashioned into hoe handles in the 1940s.

A light brown paint was obtained from the hardened mescal juice that covered the pit stones after a baking. This was used by young girls to daub on their cheeks and was also occasionally used to paint stripes on buckskin. Bourke[41] noted that the Apache scouts painted their faces with the juice of the roasted mescal or with red ocher or deer's blood as ornamentation and protection from sun and wind. The hardened juice had only to be moistened before being applied.

Gifford[42] stated that the stalk and butt of sotol (*Dasylirion* sp.) were roasted and eaten by all the Western Apache. Other uses noted by him were the eating of the flowers by the San Carlos, eating of the seeds by Northern Tonto and Southern Tonto, and use as a detergent by the San Carlos. My only information was that "the mescal with thorns" was not used when "other mescal" was available.

Acorns

The acorn (*Quercus* sp.), if not as important as mescal among most of the Western Apache groups, was at least second to it. The Northern Tonto, according to Gifford,[43] rated it their most important wild crop.

Several varieties of acorns were used. Among the Southern Tonto there were four oaks, according to the native classification, these being, in order of preference, Gambel's (*Quercus gambelii*), Emory's (*Quercus emoryi*), scrub (*Quercus undulata*), and another type (*Quercus* sp.), the last two being about equally the third choice. The San Carlos used the scrub-oak acorns (*Quercus arizonicus*) but did not like the acorn of the "blue oak" (*Quercus* sp.).[44] Reagan identified the acorn used on the Fort Apache Reservation as from *Quercus undulata* var.[45] Acorn "coffee" was made by the White Mountain from the parched acorn of an unidentified oak. It was said to be less greasy than the former. Acorn "tea" was made in May from the leaves of still another unidentified oak.

The acorn matured in late July and August. In 1947–48 it was the only wild plant for which large gathering excursions were made; many families at Cibecue still traveled to Pleasant Valley, west of the reservation boundary, and remained there for a week to gather acorns. This area was always a favorite acorn ground of the Cibecue Apache. The Cedar Creek and East Fork groups of the White Mountain gathered acorns along the Black River or south of it. Goodwin[46] said the best acorn grounds were along the southern face of Natanes Rim from Blue River to Arsenic Tubs in the vicinity of the Eagle Creek farm site and in the gap between the Graham and Santa Teresa Mountains. Trees with promising crops frequently were reserved by marking them.

Straight long poles were used to dislodge acorns. The White Mountain and Cibecue also climbed the trees and shook the acorns to the ground.[47] Large parties usually participated in the acorn harvest, sometimes whole local groups.[48] Women and children usually did the gathering, transporting the nuts to camp in sacks or baskets.

Acorns were stored, shelled or unshelled, in burden baskets, pitched baskets, buckskin sacks, and gourd or pottery vessels. Gifford[49] stated that none of the Western Apache stored acorns in skin bags, but a White Mountain tale recorded by Goodwin[50] indicated storage in buckskin sacks, and this was confirmed by informants.

Acorns, as were other foods, were cached at times in rock shelters but not in ground caches because they easily became damp and rotted. Although Gifford[51] reported that the White Mountain stored their acorns shelled, lest they become wormy, two White Mountain informants indicated a preference for storing them unshelled, stating that if they were shelled before storing they developed a bad taste. If the unshelled acorns were dried in the sun three days to a week before storage, they would not become wormy.

The sweet variety of acorn was eaten whole and raw. Usually, however, acorns were ground on a metate for use without further preparation. Although metates of vesicular lava were preferred for other uses, sandstone metates were regarded as most desirable for acorns. Stone mortars were also used to grind acorns, at least by the Southern Tonto[52] and the White Mountain. Acorn flour was eaten dry or moistened, mixed with soups, pounded into meats, and sprinkled on foods.

Whole acorns were boiled like beans by the Southern Tonto, according to Gifford,[53] who also reported that acorn meal was boiled in soup by the Northern and Southern Tonto. White Mountain and Cibecue informants gave no recipes in which acorns were boiled and stated that boiling them produced a disagreeable taste.

Acorn bread was reported for the Southern Tonto by Gifford[54] and for the White Mountain or Cibecue (probably Cibecue) by Reagan,[55] who stated that acorn meal was mixed with wheat flour in a proportion of one to five. Confirmation of Reagan's acorn-bread recipe was not obtained.

Gifford[56] reported that there was no roasting of acorns on coals or parching in wooden or pottery bowls. However, parching was reported by the White Mountain.

A universal Western Apache dish was meat stew, to which was added uncooked acorn meal. This was said by some to have been their favorite food and was so regarded in the 1940s. The recipe had only to be mentioned, particularly among a group of old men, to start a nostalgic reminiscing on the tastiness of traditional foods.

Acorns and corn were sometimes parched, then ground, and eaten dry by the pinch. Ground acorn meal, unparched, was eaten dry or moistened, mixed with soups, and mixed with boiled meat or ground with it. Ground cooked meat and acorn meal was as popular as the stew mentioned above and was indeed only a dry variation of it.

Mesquite

The pods of the mesquite (*Prosopis chilensis*)[57] were esteemed as food, but they were secondary in importance. Goodwin[58] stated that they were not sufficiently important to induce a concentrated harvest movement.

Mesquite grew abundantly only at lower elevations along the Gila and Salt River valleys. Scattered specimens were to be seen at Cibecue (elevation 5,000 feet), but all were said to be near old camp sites and to have originated from seeds spat out or thrown away after people brought pods from the Salt River. The Cibecue beans were not plentiful and were said to be of poor quality. The plants themselves were described as growing "here like a bush— down at the Salt River like a tree."

The mesquite ripened in late August. Parties from Cibecue and Canyon Creek went to the valley of the Salt in September and October to gather the pods and brought them back in skin sacks. Goddard[59] wrote of the pods' falling from the tree and being picked up by the San Carlos Apache, and Hrdlicka[60] reported that the partial spoiling of the pods by worms did not prevent their use by these people.

After being gathered, the pods were either reduced to flour by pounding while fresh or were dried and stored. Accounts in the literature of Apache usage are brief and confusing, and the accounts of informants were equally so. However, it appears that when the fresh pods were pounded, the seeds were left in and pulverized with the pod and that if the pods were dried before being used, the seeds were discarded.

An informant from Cherry Creek stated that the mesquite beans were pounded in a hole in the earth, the bottom being lined with slabs of stone. A long stone pestle was wielded with two hands, and pods and seeds were ground together. In the pounding process as described by an upper Canyon Creek informant, a bedrock mortar was used ("they made a well in a flat rock"). Pounding was done with a round stone pestle, and the seeds were discarded before pounding.

Reagan[61] stated that the pods and seeds were crushed on metates. Hrdlicka[62] reported that the San Carlos pounded the pods to a pulp in a rock cavity or dried the beans, discarded the seeds, and pounded the pods. Gifford[63] noted that the beans were pounded in a stone mortar and the seeds were removed by all Western Apache. He also stated that no Western Apache ground the pods on a metate. However, a White Mountain informant averred that this was sometimes done.

Palmer[64] reported that the ripe beans were ground fine on a metate, mixed with water, and made into cakes, which were baked in ashes or dried in the sun. He did not indicate whether this was for storage or for use.

The pounded pulp of newly gathered beans was often squeezed for the juice, which was drunk, and the fiber was discarded. The pounded bean was said to make "pretty heavy food." It was drunk "thick and white, just like milk."

Stored dried beans of the mesquite were chewed and the pulp and seeds expectorated; children liked to chew them between meals. They might be pounded into flour. Mesquite flour could be "eaten as candy" or mixed into a mush and eaten. A drink also was made from the flour by mixing it with "warm water, not too hot."

If mesquite flour was to be stored, it was moistened and allowed to harden into cakes in a basket tray, then stored in a large basket. These cakes would keep a year or two. The White Mountain frequently made a hole in the center of the mesquite cakes and strung them on a cord so that they could be transported conveniently.

Mesquite pitch was chewed as a substitute for gum, especially by children. It was also used to attach arrow points to shafts. The San Carlos were said to have used mesquite almost exclusively for firewood, for which it was excellent.

The screw bean (*Prosopis pubescene*) did not grow in Western Apache territory. A Cibecue informant had long preserved a bean brought back from Mexico by his father, a scout, and placed it in his ear for earache. This remedy, he believed, had been recommended to his father by Mexicans or Chiricahua hostiles. Gifford[65] said the juice of the screw bean was used by the Eastern Chiricahua for earache and that the Eastern Chiricahua, Mescalero, and Lipan gathered it from the Río Grande area and prepared it like mesquite.

Cacti

Saguaro (*Carnegiea gigantea*)[66] was a relatively unimportant wild crop, and few people went to gather it. In the low country in the Gila Valley, it ripened in July.[67] The White Mountain often went to the Arivaipa territory in the San Pedro Valley, where the Arivaipa chiefs allotted them part of the gathering grounds.[68] According to Hrdlicka,[69] the San Carlos stayed two or three months at the saguaro grounds until all the fruit was matured and gathered. Bourke[70] stated that the Apache went out to gather pitahaya and at the same time make war on the Pima and Papago.

A long pole, usually fashioned by lashing together saguaro ribs, was used to remove the fruit. Usually a crosspiece was tied at one end so that two acute angles were formed with the pole; the upward projection of this crosspiece was pushed and the downward projection pulled to detach the fruit. The Southern Tonto and San Carlos used a pole with an end hooked to an acute angle.[71]

The saguaro fruit was often eaten raw, but most of it was prepared for other uses. The juice was first expressed by squeezing; the juice was saved to drink, and the seeds were washed and dried.

Bourke[72] stated that the Apache women made a preserve by boiling saguaro pulp.

The Cibecue parched the seeds in a basket. Sometimes they pulverized them with maize.[73]

The squeezed pulp was placed on a rock to dry, after which it was made into cakes. These dried fruit cakes were kept throughout the year and used as a sweet or were mixed with mescal juice.

Hrdlicka[74] stated that the dried cakes became wormy after six or seven months but still retained good color and odor and that they were eaten by the women and children. The seeds were roasted by the San Carlos, ground, mixed with water, and eaten as a mush.

Gifford[75] noted that the Cibecue and White Mountain wrapped saguaro cakes in willow bark for transport and for cleanliness. A White Mountain woman stated that mesquite bark, not willow bark, was used to wrap saguaro and mescal.

The saguaro burls were used, two together, by the Cibecue as containers for caked dried fruits and also as vessels in which to soak dried fruit.[76] The burls were very hard and shaped like a cup, for which they were often used.

A drink was made from the saguaro fruit by the White Mountain. The whole fruit, seeds and all, was mashed with the hands, water was added, and the mixture was placed in a jar and buried in a dry place for two days. When removed, it was drunk immediately and was said to be better than tiswin. Seeds were saved and ground with corn into a pudding.

The fruits of many kinds of cacti were used by the Apache. A White Mountain woman named nine kinds used in the East Fork area. Of these nine varieties, five were early ones, four were large ones, one was designated as "eagle" prickly pear, and there were five different colors of fruit. Reagan[77] wrote "a great variety of cactus fruit is found in the (Fort Apache) region, ranging from sour to sweet." Gifford[78] recorded the fruit of two kinds of cacti used by the Northern Tonto, four by the San Carlos, seven by the Cibecue, and eight by the White Mountain.

At one time, long journeys were made to gather cactus fruit. The women gathered the fruit with tongs of split sticks and removed the spines with a grass brush, with weeds, or by rolling it about on the ground. Reagan[79] reported that the spines were rubbed off with a piece of buckskin; my informants had not seen or heard of this method. The gathered fruit was packed in a burden basket.

The fruit of the prickly pear was peeled and eaten raw, except for a sweet variety that was made into a kind of butter.[80] Seeds were eaten with the fruits. The seeds of some varieties were so large that children who ate them often had difficulty with elimination; an informant shook with laughter as he told how a boy, after eating these, would "cry and cry."

The fruit was also "split like peaches" and dried on a rock, then stored for later use. Curtis[81] stated that seeds and pulp were ground together into a paste. Gifford[82] noted that the Northern Tonto dried the fruit and stored it in round, thick cakes similar to cheese.

All White Mountain and Cibecue informants denied the grinding of prickly pear seeds except a Cherry Creek man who said cactus seeds were used; but it is not certain whether his statement applied only to saguaro or also to prickly pear. Gifford[83] indicated that the Southern Tonto ground opuntia seeds and mixed them with acorn meal but denied the use of the seeds by the other Western Apache.[84] Hrdlicka[85] stated that a high branching cactus that he tentatively identified as *Opuntia arborescens* Engelm? or *Opuntia whipplei* Engelm? was used by the San Carlos. They parched, ground, and boiled the seeds into a mush or ate the flour of the seeds, washed down with water.

The sap from prickly pears reputedly was a cure for sores. The "leaves" were opened and placed on burns.

One variety of small-seeded prickly pear was said to have been brought north to the Cibecue area from the Salt River Valley and to have obtained its start from seeds expectorated by people eating the fruit.

Bourke[86] stated that "the Apaches say that the use of this fruit (tuna or nopal) must be attended with some precautions, as it predisposes to fevers."

Cholla (*Opuntia* sp.) was reported by Gifford[87] not to be used by the Western Apache, although the Northern and Southern Tonto were not included in his inquiry. However, its use was affirmed by both White Mountain and Cibecue informants.

A White Mountain woman stated that the yellow cholla fruit was usable if gathered during a certain limited season. It was pit-baked for one day, water being added to the pit to steam it in the same manner as green corn was baked. When dried, it would keep for a year. It was boiled with fat or in soup. The seeds were left in the fruit and were never used separately.

A Canyon Creek man stated that cholla fruit was picked when it became yellow and fully ripe in the fall. The fruits were placed in a fire and cooked, then dried, cracked, and the seeds removed. The seeds were then roasted in an open pan "like roast coffee," mixed with soft corn, and ground. Cholla seeds were never ground alone, always with corn. The ground meal was placed in the mouth dry or after it had been moistened with a little water and salt.

Informants had never heard of the use of cholla "joints" for food, only the fruit and buds, but cholla had some medicinal uses among the Canyon Creek band, where the peeled stalks were applied to burns. The boiled roots were said to make the best laxative for a baby or small child. A tablespoonful of the liquid extract would cause the bowels to move; on the other hand, if movements were thin and frequent, it was also used.

A small, multiple-barrel cactus fruit that was said to look and taste like a long strawberry was gathered by the basketful in mid-July. It was eaten raw and never preserved. This plant was another cactus used in treating burns.

Barrel cactus was cut and pounded to obtain water, according to informants, but was never used as an improvised cooking vessel.

Hrdlicka[88] reported that the San Carlos parched, ground, and boiled into mush the small black seeds in the yellow fruit of *Echinocereus wislizeni* and that when extremely thirsty they used the insipid juice of the plant.

Yucca Baccata

The fruit of the *Yucca baccata*[89] matured in early September.[90] Informants said the fruit had to be cooked before drying or it would spoil. After roasting the fruit was split, the whole seed ribbon removed, and the fruit dried on bear grass. When stored, it was wrapped in bear grass and tree-cached. With such open storage it would keep indefinitely. Dried yucca fruit was prepared for use by soaking and working in water. An informant denied that it was ever boiled, as was reported by Reagan.[91] Gifford[92] reported that in general the very ripe fruit was peeled, split, seeded, and the pulp eaten fresh. It was also sun-dried and stored. The fruit, if not very ripe, was roasted in ashes, then immersed in water, peeled, seeded, and either eaten or dried and stored.

The roots of the *Yucca baccata* were preferred as a soap over other species of yucca; however, because these roots caused the skin and eyes of some people to swell, they were used less than the roots of bear grass (*Nolina microcarpa*). *Nolina* or *Yucca baccata* roots were still the preferred source of soap on the Fort Apache Reservation in the 1940s.

The seeds of the *Yucca baccata* were never used for food, and neither were the blossoms or the flower stalk. The leaves were split for cordage. This cordage and that made from the leaves of other yucca species was the most commonly used on the Fort Apache Reservation. Split sections were tied together by square knots to make the desired lengths.

Yucca fruit and juniper berries were pounded together to make a gravy. Goddard[93] recorded a San Carlos tale in which ripe fruit was boiled and stirred with water, apparently to make a beverage.

Yucca Other Than *Baccata*

Yucca elata grew throughout the Fort Apache Reservation at elevations below 6,000 feet. The fruit of this species was not used, but the plant was esteemed for other purposes.

The blossoms were used for food and were said to be bitter unless picked by a lucky person who knew the proper time to gather them. They were boiled, often with a small black seed (unidentified); they were also boiled with fat or with bones. For storage they were dried on the top of a wickiup and then sacked and kept in a dry place, such as the ceiling of the wickiup.

The leaves of *Yucca elata* were used for the headshade of the cradleboard and for cordage. They were better suited to the latter purpose than *Yucca baccata*, for the leaves were longer.

The fruit stalk of *Yucca elata* was often charred over a fire and eaten like sugar cane. A curing rite was described in which the religious practitioner fashioned a peeled yucca stalk into the shape of a short snake, heated it in the fire, and ate it, spitting fragments at the sick person as he chewed.

Yucca elata roots were used for soap, although they were not so well liked for this purpose as those of *Yucca baccata* and *Nolina microcarpa*. The red roots of this species also were used in basket decoration.

Gifford[94] stated that the flowers of the "narrow-leafed yucca" were eaten boiled by the Cibecue, White Mountain, and both Tonto groups and that the Northern Tonto, Cibecue, and White Mountain ate the roasted stalk and butt.

Reagan[95] reported that the leaves of the *Yucca glauca* and those of *Yucca baccata* were used for strings, cords, and game counters and that its roots were pounded for soap. *Yucca glauca* appears to be the plant identified by Kearney and Peebles[96] as *Yucca elata*.

Palmer[97] stated that *Yucca augustifolia* was used as an emulsion in the cure of insect and snake bites.

Nolina

The young stalks of bear grass (*Nolina microcarpa*) were cut in May and June when they had reached a height of about thirty inches. They were placed in the fire for about half an hour, then peeled and eaten. They were said to taste like "some kind of fruit, soft and sticky." This was the only information obtained as to the use of *Nolina* for food. Gifford[98] said the stalk and butt were eaten by the Cibecue, White Mountain, and both Tonto groups, and he also[99] noted that the fruit was eaten by the San Carlos, the seeds parched by the White Mountain, and the flowers eaten by the Southern Tonto.

Nolina was said to provide "the best soap used." For this the crown and base of the leaves were pounded together and mixed with water.

Spoons were frequently fashioned of bear grass leaves. The leaf had only to be detached from the crown, for the base had a small spoonlike depression. Only dry grass was used for this purpose because the green grass tasted like soap. Yucca leaves also were used as spoons in this manner.

Bear grass was much esteemed as a thatching material for wickiup or ramada and as wrapping material for foods to be transported or stored. Women gathered the plant by severing the crown and leaves from the roots with a sharp rock. In later times an ax or pick was used. Sharpened chisel sticks, such as were used for mescal, were ineffective because the bear-grass roots were too tough. The detached plant was carried home intact. For thatching, green grass and dry were equally good, and a thatch of this material would last ten to fifteen years. The whole temporary cradleboard was made of *Nolina* leaves.

Sunflowers

Groups of people established ownership of a stand of wild sunflowers (*Helianthus* sp.) [100] by tying bunches of the heads together before they ripened. Then in the fall, when birds began to flock around the ripened heads, they were picked.

Fig. 23. *Large-headed sunflowers in the garden of Mrs. John Lupe south of Cibecue.*

A person gathering this plant beat the seeds into a basket hung over the shoulder, using a two-foot beating stick with an oval-shaped baskethead about four to six inches long on the beating end. Another method of gathering was to pick the whole heads and sun-dry them, later shaking the seeds loose.

Gifford[101] stated that knives were used by some Apache to sever sunflower heads. For this the Northern Tonto used an ash-wood knife, the Southern Tonto a stone knife and a single-edge hardwood knife six to eight inches long, and the Cibecue a stone knife. According to Gifford,[102] the Southern Tonto tied sunflower stems into bundles, sun-dried them, and shook out the seeds; only the San Carlos dried the heads over a fire before shaking them out.

Palmer[103] said parched grass seeds and sunflower seeds were made into flour and prepared either as a porridge or shaped into cakes and baked in hot ashes.

Informants described several preparations. After being parched in a basket tray, the seeds were rough-ground in a first grinding, then ground into a fine meal. This meal, mixed with corn meal, was put into hot water, then eaten as a pasty bread, not too moist, without salt. An industrious woman could prepare such a dish in about an hour. Sometimes, mixed corn and sunflower meal was boiled with salt into a cereal "just like oatmeal."

Sunflower seeds and corn were ground together into a flour that was eaten by the pinch. Children were not allowed to play or laugh while eating whole sunflower seeds for fear they would choke on them.

Army scouts, when preparing to leave on an expedition, had their wives grind about twenty-five pounds of sunflower seeds for rations.

Another method of eating sunflower was to parch the seeds, then grind them with mescal. This mixture was said to taste "just like candy."

Piñon

The piñon (*Pinus edulis* and *Pinus monophylla*) furnished one of the staple foods of the Apache.

Piñon was plentiful north of the Natanes Rim but less common in the Graham Mountains.[104] Late fall was the season when the nuts ripened. Informants claimed they were harvested from October to as late as December. Large parties, sometimes a whole local group, would gather them in the areas where trees were bearing.

The nuts were gathered from the ground and shaken or knocked from the trees. They were usually gathered in the cone unless it was late in the season, cones being dried or fired to dislodge the seeds. One family expedition was described in which the green cones were roasted in a brush fire, pulled out with a stick, then pounded between two stones and shaken to free the seeds. A labor-saving means of gathering was to rob the caches of rodents in the ground or in the piled brush.

The nuts were eaten raw or were roasted. Piñon nuts were parched with corn and ground into flour, which was eaten by the pinch. Gifford[105] said they were hulled on the metate and winnowed by the Northern Tonto, Cibecue, and White Mountain; these groups and the Southern Tonto, he reported, made a butter of the mashed hulled seeds, while the Tonto groups made a butter of the whole mashed seeds. Reagan[106] reported that piñon nuts were ground to a flour, hulls and all, and made into soups and baked like bread cakes. Both the grinding of the hulls and the use in soups or as bread cakes were categorically denied by a Cibecue and a White Mountain informant. The nearest thing to a soup they knew was a mixture of piñon and corn flour cooked into a mush.

Nuts were stored in baskets or pottery jars and also, according to Goodwin,[107] in buckskin sacks.

Piñon pitch was the favorite chewing gum, at least among the White Mountain. This pitch was also used to waterproof baskets. Heated pitch, or a heated pitched basket, was applied to the face by some to remove facial hair.

Piñon pitch was gathered in June. This was also the time for gathering piñon pollen, which was often used to supplement the supply of tule pollen.

Curtis[108] stated that the Apache, probably the White Mountain, made a drink from the green or dried inner bark of the piñon tree.

Walnuts

Walnuts (*Juglans* sp.) were considered by the Cibecue to be better if they fell naturally, but people sometimes climbed trees and shook them loose.[109] Among the White Mountain, the hulls were removed by pounding with a rock or, according to Gifford,[110] in a bedrock mortar. Then they were washed in a basket in a running stream. Washing was also practiced by the Cibecue.

The White Mountain used the juice of walnut hulls "like sheep dip" on their horses and cattle. It was also considered good for clearing maggots from wounds. A dose of one or two tablespoonfuls was administered internally to dogs as a cure for worms.

Walnuts were never boiled, according to informants. They were pulverized and mixed with mescal juice, producing a liquid of light creamy color having the consistency of tomato juice and said to taste like sweetened milk. It was eaten by dipping corn bread into it. Walnuts were said to be the only nuts eaten with the sweet mescal drink. They were also parched with corn, ground, and eaten by the pinch.

Reagan[111] reported that walnuts were mashed fine—kernels, hulls, and all—then boiled in water. From this a milky liquid was filtered and drunk.

Palmer[112] said walnuts were ground with dried mescal. The inner partition shells were ground in this dish and were said by Palmer to act as an aid to digestion.

Reagan[113] noted that walnut kernels and green corn were mashed together on metates and baked in cake form.

Juniper

Juniper (*Juniperus* sp.) berries were an important food. They were plentiful in the intermediate elevations north of the Natanes Rim.[114] The gathering season extended from October to December.

The berries were picked from the tree when fully ripe or were gathered after they had fallen and dried on the ground. According to informants, only the meat of the berry was used, not the seed, and this was boiled and eaten unseasoned.

Goodwin[115] recorded that the berries were partly dried, boiled until soft, then ground to a pulp on a metate or flat stone; the pulp thus obtained was molded into a ball and stored. Palmer[116] stated that at times the whole fruit, including the seed, was pounded and made into bread. One of Goodwin's tales[117] included an incident in which yellow juniper berries were parched in a basket.

Juniper ashes were mixed with corn mush for color and flavor. Particularly favored was the greenish color imparted by the ashes.

To cure pneumonia, juniper branches were heated, placed in a protective wrapping to prevent a burn, an applied to the back of a patient.

Torches were made of dried juniper bark. The bark was rubbed between the hands until the fibers were separated. From these a thick strand was produced by twisting. This was then wrapped from top to bottom and tied up and down its length with yucca string. The torch made a light like a small camp fire and would last four or five hours. If it died down, it had only to be shaken to flare anew.

A nonintoxicating, greenish-colored drink was made of juniper berries. The berries were soaked overnight, then pounded with the fruit of *Yucca baccata*. After mixing with water, the seeds and heavy part of the pulp were screened and the fluid drained into vessels. The juniper berries and yucca fruit could also be pounded together to produce a gravy. Juniper berries were mixed with dried or roasted agave crowns, similar to their use with yucca fruit, to make a beverage.

Miscellaneous Seeds

Aside from seeds specifically treated here, such as piñons, acorns, cactus, and sunflower seeds, the Apache used many other small seeds for food. Curtis[118] said many such seeds were gathered in baskets, ground on a metate, and shaped into an oily ball with the hands. It was said that a lump twice the size of a fist, when eaten with wild greens, could sustain a man for two days.

Informants mentioned that in general the seeds of many grasses and herbs were eaten. Such small seeds apparently were not gathered after the mid-1930s and were known only to older people in the 1940s. Specifically mentioned was a two-foot grass the stem of which was used as comb and broom material. This plant Reagan[119] identified as *Bouteloua gracilis* Lag. The reddish seeds of a two-foot "feather" grass, possibly the same plant as that identified by Reagan, were ground with corn and eaten.

Reagan[120] named several grasses the seeds of which were once ground and made into bread. These included, besides *Bouteloua gracilis* Lag., such grasses as *Eriocoma cuspidata* Nutt., *Sporobolus strictus* (Scribn.) Merrill, and *Epicompes rigens* Benth. The grass seeds enumerated by Reagan[121] as being edible, together with seeds from other unnamed bunch grasses, were ground and made into bread. The ground seeds were also mixed with corn meal and water and made into a mush or into a pone which was baked in husks or in ashes.

A number of foods were mentioned in the tales collected by Goodwin:[122] "iya ai" seeds were ground and made into a mush and "na djicyu je" seeds were parched and ground;[123] "na djilba ye" was another edible seed.[124]

Hrdlicka[125] noted two seeds used by the San Carlos. One called *kloh-tzo,* was said to look like rye but to be smaller. It was a grass that grew in the mountains where pines were found. After being ground, it was boiled a short time, then eaten with salt, like mush. The other, named *nap-tzi,* was also a mountain grass. It was roasted, ground fine, mixed with hot water, and eaten as a mush.

Gifford[126] stated that *chia* was basket-parched by the San Carlos, Cibecue, and White Mountain and was eaten dry by all the Western Apache; it was also eaten wet, at least by the Cibecue. It was called *nadiskit* by the Northern Tonto.[127] Possibly this was a species of *Salvia.*

Seeds of the devil's claw (*Martynia* sp.) were cracked and chewed for the juice, which was "just like milk."

When gathered, seeds were shaken into a basket or detached with a beater. Women normally did the gathering, but Goodwin[128] said boys and girls went off in groups to gather seeds, making a social event of it.

Seeds were stored in pottery, gourd, or old pitched water-basket receptacles and cached under ground or in caves and rock shelters. Gifford[129] said the Cibecue sometimes piled seeds on a cave floor.

Berries and Fruits

A plant with red berries (possibly *Rhus trilobata*) was said to grow "everywhere" but to be larger and more abundant at elevations above 5,000 feet. The red berry of this plant was gathered in June. It was usually ground but was sometimes chewed raw for the juice. The seeds were never used. The ground berries were stirred in warm water to make a colored nonintoxicating drink. A drink was made by adding dried mescal juice. After American supplies became available, sugar often was substituted for the mescal juice. The drink, when mixed with mescal, was said to taste like sugared tomatoes and to look like canned tomatoes. The stalks were used for baskets, being split into three sections or else peeled directly of the bark. The pitched water basket was always made of this material, which was also used, although infrequently, for making the round burden basket. The berry was gathered in sacks and would keep two or three years.

There appear to be several references in the literature to the plant described above. Gifford[130] stated that the San Carlos made a beverage of crushed sumac berries. Hrdlicka[131] reported that a red berry used by the San Carlos was washed, crushed and dried, ground, stirred with water, and drunk or eaten as thin mush. Palmer[132] noted that "squaw berries" were washed to get rid of an acid exudation, insects, and so forth, then dried and pounded for food.

Palmer[133] stated that cooking and carrying baskets were made of the twigs of *Rhus aromatica*.

A "wild grape" (*Vitis arizonica*) was picked when ripe and eaten raw. The berry was also pounded, dried on the ground in the sun, and stored in sacks; it was never stored in a vessel. Another use was to boil the juice from the berries to make wine.

Among the White Mountain Apache, both wild plums (*Prunus* sp. ?) and wild cherries (*Prunus virginiana*) were eaten raw, although Gifford[134] stated that neither was used by the Western Apache. According to Bourke,[135] however, Apache foods included the wild cherry and the wild strawberry (*Frageria* sp.?).

A six-foot shrub was shown near Grasshopper from which brown berries "just like a little apple" were obtained. These were ground—the seeds were discarded—and mixed with mescal juice. The pulp was also eaten raw and was said to make one "fat and happy." They were preserved with or without grinding.

Manzanita (*Arctostaphylos pungens*) flowers and fruits were used. Gifford[136] said the Southern Tonto digging stick was made of manzanita wood.

Hrdlicka[137] noted two berries eaten by the San Carlos. One, *Canotia holocantha,* was called "soft wood." The other was a small, black berry called *chi-ln-tlezh* (unidentified and not translated).

Reagan[138] stated that there were not many berries in the Fort Apache region. Those available were gathered by the women and usually were served raw.

An old Cedar Creek man stated that the Navajo at one time used to bring rugs to the Whiteriver area to trade for "baskets, mescal, and wild berries."

The same man named mescal and venison as his favorite foods and added that he had never cared much for berries, although when extremely hungry he had often eaten them.

Greens

The Apache were fond of greens. Gifford[139] said all the Western Apache ate greens boiled and that the Cibecue and White Mountain also ate them raw.

Palmer[140] noted that the White Mountain women gathered large baskets of greens daily when in season, primarily species of Amaranthus and Chenopodium. Dried mescal was soaked, beaten and added to the greens when they were almost cooked. Salt was added to all green vegetables, but they were never cooked with meat. Formerly they were stone-boiled in baskets.[141]

The White Mountain and Cibecue used wild onions, wild potatoes, and Indian spinach (lambsquarter, *Chenopodium leptophyllum* (Moq.) Nutt. and *Chenopodium incanum* Watson).[142] Although lambsquarter grew wild in abundance, the black seeds were broadcast around the camps so that they would come up thickly near at hand. The plant was still widely used on the Fort Apache Reservation in the 1940s. Probably this was the plant mentioned by Hrdlicka[143] as used by the San Carlos, who ate it raw or chopped up, mixed with a little fat and salt, and boiled.

The Rocky Mountain bee plant (*Cleome serrulata*) leaves and whole young plant were used as greens by the Carrizo and Cibecue bands. An informant said it was brought to Cibecue before 1900 by Indian Cooley, who obtained seeds from the Carrizo and threw them on a sandy place near Lower Cibecue Mission. The plant spread along the roads but was not abundant in the 1940s. It was not used for dye and was said to have no use other than for "spinach." The plant was evident in scattered stands on the road between McNary and Whiteriver. Mr. Schroeder, the forester at Whiteriver Agency, believed the plant to be a recent introduction. Kearney and Peebles[144] said it appeared to have been introduced into Arizona.

Roots, Fungi, and Miscellaneous

The inner bark of pine (*Pinus* sp.) was used as a food.[145]

Many varieties of fungi furnished food,[146] although only corn smut and mushrooms were mentioned by informants.

A White Mountain woman stated that at one time very young and green wild gourds were eaten. A statement by Goodwin,[147] that the Wild Gourd Growing People were named for their habit of eating wild gourds, indicated that the Tonto possibly once ate gourds. Dr. E. F. Castetter[148] believed it improbable that wild gourds were ever eaten because they are very bitter. A wild gourd (*Cucurbita foetidissima*) was used "like sheep dip." It was mashed—stem, leaves, and roots—and soaked in hot water until soapy. The liquid was then applied to the sores on a horse's back. It was said to sting like turpentine and was never used on humans. Reagan[149] said the leaves of a gourd that grew on the surface of the ground and that he tentatively identified as *Cucurbita perennis* Gray was ground and used as a green paint in sand paintings.

Blossoms from a number of plants were eaten. The use of *Yucca elata* blossoms has been discussed elsewhere. Wild-rose blossoms were dried or "barbecued" by the White Mountain. Although informants denied that pumpkin blossoms were ever eaten, a White Mountain tale in which the mother of Slayer of Monsters sent her daughter-in-law out to gather squash blossoms for boiling indicates that they were once used.[150]

The White Mountain said that from the mountaintops they gathered small wild potatoes (*Solanum fendleri* or *Solanum jamesii*), which smelled and tasted like the commercial Irish potato. They also gathered wild onions (*Allium* spp.). Wild tomatoes (*Lycopersicum* sp.?) were found plentifully along the Black River.

For rheumatism and colds, the White Mountain fried greasewood in fat until it began to turn green, then rubbed it over the patient.

Hrdlicka[151] stated that *"Dickleostemma,* var. Bordiaca, *Capitata pauciflora,"* which grew on the San Carlos Reservation, was eaten in the spring. The small blue flower of the plant was eaten raw; the bulbs were eaten either raw or cooked.

Reagan[152] reported that the dried root of *Euphorbia serphyllifolia* was preserved in sacks and used, after being chewed, as yeast for the "green corn ash wedding cake." My informants did not know of this use.

Bourke[153] stated that the bulb of the wild hyacinth (?) was eaten either raw or cooked and tasted like raw chestnuts. He also noted that the tule (*Tule amarilla?*—probably *Typha* sp.) bulb was eaten, being always roasted between hot stones. Bourke[154] thought tule pollen was an ancient food of the Apache and was offered or sacrificed and used with prayer for this reason. Gifford[155] recorded that the tips of tule shoots were eaten by the White Mountain and by the Northern Tonto and that the stem bases were eaten by the San Carlos, Cibecue, and White Mountain. The Cibecue ate the tule-flower buds and the blue-flowered corn raw; the tule-stem bases were eaten by the San Carlos children.[156] Tule (*Typha* sp.) pollen was regularly gathered in June north of Cibecue in the 1940s and at the swampy lakes in the McNary area. Because the gathering places were somewhat distant and snakes were said to be numerous in the tule areas, many did not gather pollen but preferred to pay others twenty-five cents or more for a small bottle of it.

Honey

Several Cibecue and White Mountain informants spoke of honey gathering. The oldest said the White Mountain were not familiar with honey until white Americans arrived.

Only men gathered honey. When wild honey was discovered in a hollow tree, the observer marked it with a pile of rocks. This designation of prior rights would be respected; if another person, failing to notice the pile of rocks, cut the tree down, the honey would be divided if the original discoverer claimed it. In early times the Apache built a fire to smoke the bees out and then detached the comb from the outside of the tree. When metal axes became available, the tree was cut down. The honey was transported in ordinary or pitched water baskets. It was eaten immediately, not stored.

Chief 01 in the 1890s used to harvest the honey systematically from four or five rock hives near the winter camping grounds south of the Salt River. At one hive he would remove a rock from the sandstone crevice in which the bees nested, dig out the honey, then replace the rock. At another he would make a yucca brush fire to smoke out the bees, placing a rock over the fire so that it would burn slowly and make a great deal of smoke.

Honey was also gathered from big black bees (bumblebees?) that made their hives in agave or sotol stalks. The stalks were punctured and then split open to expose the honey. This was removed in the form of little lumps of "candy," which was "sometimes sweet, sometimes not, and tasted like chocolate." It was often eaten on the spot.

Bumblebee honey was gathered from the ground by the Northern Tonto, San Carlos, and Cibecue.[157] When a Northern Tonto stepped on a bumblebee nest and was stung, he told a chief, who sent men and boys with digging sticks to take the honey. Only the honey was eaten, not the grubs.[158]

A sweet substance was sucked from the large red flower of a small herb by the Cibecue and White Mountain. It was never gathered, but the interior of the flower was pulled out and sucked where found. Children would hunt for this.

Salt

Salt was gathered by a few volunteers and shared with others upon their return. The Cibecue obtained it from two caves near the Salt River on the north side. Probably these were the two caves mentioned by Gifford[159] as being on Salt River near the confluence of the Cibecue Creek, where he said the Southern Tonto obtained it, and near the confluence of the Salt River and Carrizo Creek, where he said the Cibecue and White Mountain got it.

A Cibecue informant reported that all the Western Apache, but no other people, used the two caves on the Salt River. The Salt stalactites were knocked off with a stone axe or the salt was scraped off into a sack or basket. About fifty pounds was gathered at a time, and this supply was said to last two years. Gifford[160] stated that the stalactites were shot down with arrows by the Cibecue, who also obtained a reddish salt from the cave floor.

The salt was ground on a metate, then moistened and made into a ball, flattened on one side. It was placed on grass and dried by the fire. About twenty-four hours' time was required to harden it.

The San Carlos obtained salt from a cave on the Black River and also at a point about twelve miles east of San Carlos.[161] The Southern Tonto got crystallized salt from the damp soil near the edge of the Little Colorado River. This salt was molded into a cylindrical cake around a stick and carried by yucca cords. The White Mountain obtained crystallized salt on the ground near a salt spring on Carrizo Creek. It was molded around a stick, which was then removed and a carrying rope inserted in the hole.[162]

Ritual attended the gathering of salt. A special prayer was said at the cave on the Salt River, accompanied by the offering of a red, yellow, blue, white, or black stone. This stone had to be tossed into the cave before entering. An individual dared not enter the cave alone, for it was thought an old man with a dog would appear to unaccompanied persons. At one time the cave was said to contain a footprint of Changing Woman, which people who went there were required to lick.

Bourke[163] said a goddess sometimes called Maria Santissima as well as by her Apache name was probably the goddess of salt; that such a goddess was adored by the Zuñi; and that the most sacred ceremonies of the Apache ritual were celebrated in caves at the Salt Springs on the Río Prieto (Salt River). A White Mountain informant on the salt ritual, a Catholic, translated the name Changing Woman as "Our Blessed Mother."

Gifford[164] reported that, when obtaining salt from the Salt River–Carrizo Creek cave, the Apache prayed to Changing Woman, to her son, and to "the one who made salt." He said there were timbers in the cave, which indicated an old ruin.

Salt was occasionally traded by the White Mountain to the Navajo for blankets and rope.

Salt was sometimes stored in a gourd vessel, but a more common method was to retain it in ball form. In this way it could he beld over a vessel of cooking food and the desired quantity scraped off with a rock.

Comestible Clay

The eating of clay was reported briefly by Bourke,[165] who stated that comestible clay was used only as a condiment to relieve the bitter taste of the wild potato in the same manner as it was known to the Zuñi and Hopi. In the same place, he mentioned that clay was scarcely used any longer by the Navajo.

Gifford[166] noted that the Southern Tonto goddess Changing Woman forbade the eating of clay or other "dirt" with the crops she gave mankind.

Condiments Other Than Salt and Clay

Juniper ashes were mixed in corn meal mush by the White Mountain and the Cibecue to give it a greenish color and to add flavor.

Gifford[167] said the leaf ash of *Yucca baccata* was added to maize mush by these people.

The leaves of a two-foot plant with a purple daisylike flower somewhat resembling the Rocky Mountain bee plant were used by the Cibecue for seasoning boiled meat. Possibly this plant was a mint. It was said to be "like pepper."

Another plant boiled with meat was also said to season it like "black pepper." Two or three of these plants were boiled and the liquid used for cough medicine, taken mixed with water.

Summary and Conclusions

The amount of wild plant foods that were used by the Apache fluctuated with the abundance of agricultural harvests and with the success of hunting and raiding expeditions. Wild plant foods were gathered more intensively if there was a shortage of other foods. More use was made of wild plants by the Northern Tonto, Southern Tonto, and San Carlos groups than by the more agricultural White Mountain and Cibecue groups. Before American occupation, the Western Apache probably depended on wild plants for approximately 40 percent of their food. This figure is an estimate based on informants' recollections of the 1870s and traditions of earlier times. Naturally, it varied considerably from group to group, year to year, and season to season.

From the standpoint of volume used and continuous dependability, mescal was the most important Western Apache wild plant food. The Northern Tonto must be excluded from this statement; to these Indians the acorn was a more important food than mescal, which was procured through trade or by long gathering excursions outside their territory. Among the White Mountain and Cibecue—and probably also the Southern Tonto—the acorn was a close second to mescal in importance. The San Carlos made as much or more use of mesquite and saguaro fruit as they did of acorns.

In the order of their relative economic importance, wild plant foods used by the White Mountain and Cibecue were mescal, acorns, sunflower seeds; other wild seeds and nuts, including piñon and walnut; yucca fruit, prickly pear fruit, juniper berries, mesquite, and saguaro. In addition to these, various roots, greens, and berries were used. Favorite foods, or at least the foods spoken of most often, were mescal and acorns, although sunflower seeds and piñon nuts were close behind in favor. Some foods, such as the saguaro, were relished but were more in the nature of seasonal luxuries or occasional foods that provided a change of diet. Juniper berries, although enjoyed, were something of a hard-times staple.

Goodwin[168] estimated that 35 to 40 percent of all prereservation White Mountain food was from wild plants, staples being mescal and acorns (the two most important), saguaro fruit, mesquite beans, yucca fruit, sunflower seeds, fruit of the prickly pear, piñon nuts, and juniper berries.

Opler[169] estimated that the prereservation diet of the White Mountain and Cibecue consisted of 65 percent vegetable products, but he did not differentiate between wild and cultivated plants.

Bourke,[170] undoubtedly writing of both Chiricahua and Western Apache, named mescal, yucca fruit, the mesquite bean, Indian fig (cactus fruit), sunflower seeds, several unidentified grass seeds, wild potatoes, wild cherries, and wild strawberries as the principal wild plant foods of the Apache. Of these, he considered mescal the most important. Bourke's observations were made in the eighth and ninth decades of the nineteenth century.

In 1890, Palmer[171] listed the following as White Mountain Apache plant foods: greens (mostly species of Amaranthus and Chenopodium), sunflower seeds, grass seeds, mesquite pods, acorns, squaw berries, juniper berries, mescal, walnuts, and wild potatoes.

Reagan,[172] who made his observations in 1901–1902, included walnuts, mesquite beans, mescal, berries, cactus fruit, piñon nuts, yucca fruit, and acorns in the wild plant foods used on the Fort Apache Reservation. In his "Plants Used by the White Mountain Apache Indians of Arizona,"[173] Reagan listed forty-eight species of wild plants used for food or beverages by the White Mountain and Cibecue Apache.

Hrdlicka[174] said in 1908 that wild plants used by the San Carlos were cactus seeds, cactus fruits (of which saguaro was the most valuable), mescal, yucca fruit, berries, seeds, acorns (which were but little used), and a few roots, bulbs, and leaves.

Goodwin[175] wrote in 1935 that a good many wild plant foods were still in use among the White Mountain Apache, especially acorns

Fig. 24. *The old guardhouse at Fort Apache as it looked in 1947.*

and mescal. The use of such foods declined to the point where in 1947 only a few families with a taste for some of the traditional foods made an effort to gather them. The one wild crop still harvested to any extent was the acorn. Women gathered greens or berries or fruits growing conveniently near at hand, but distant trips requiring overnight camping or expeditions by large parties were made only to the acorn grounds. Even the knowledge of the uses of plants was rapidly being lost. Part of the disuse of wild plants might be attributed to the concentration of population and the restriction of movement enforced by the soldiers when the Apache were being pacified; part to the enforcement of compulsory school attendance, which prevented winter migrations; part to an increasing familiarity with and fondness for American foods; and part to removal, through cattle checks, government work, and off-reservation jobs, of the necessity for gathering.

Before the coming of the white Americans, the Apache appeared to have made excellent use of the natural plant resources in their territory. Because of the great ecological diversity of their region, there was a wide variety of plants that matured at different seasons and in widely separated places. This made the Apache migratory from spring until fall.

Chapter 5

FOODS

Utensils and Implements

UTENSILS and implements used in the preparation and consumption of foods by the Western Apache were few and simple.

Water was usually obtained and stored in small-mouthed baskets coated with piñon resin. Bourke[1] recorded the use of cow entrails by the Chiricahua for this purpose. Occasional use was also made of gourds as water containers, or even deerskin bags, according to informants, although the last-named does not seem very practicable.

For boiling, plain black pottery, tall in proportion to diameter and pointed at the base, was used. The only decoration was a narrow band of diagonal indentations an inch or two below the lip of the jar. This was the only pottery made. Informants declared that stone boiling in baskets was practiced only by men on raids and hunting trips, since pottery was too much of an encumbrance to carry along. However, Palmer[2] stated that stone boiling was done and Smart[3] reported that he saw no earthenware among the Tonto, the only utensils used in preparing food being "shallow vessels of closely netted straw." Use of pottery was reported among the Tonto by the surviving Oatman girl.[4] There was no stone boiling in skins.

Cooked food was transferred to baskets for serving. Goddard's tale "The Deer Woman"[5] relates that corn-meal mush was dipped into a basket and that boiled deer meat was taken from a pot and put in a basket. In even earlier times, corn mush and other foods were eaten from a basket with the fingers or with the base of a beargrass leaf, which served as a spoon.

200

Informants denied the use of horn for vessels. Goddard,[6] however, recorded a tale in which an eagle offered a horn vessel of boiled corn to a man.

Small wooden bowls were made for soups. Soups were also drunk from gourd dippers.

Basket trays were used for parching grain and seeds; fast movement prevented burning. Palmer[7] stated that parching trays were moistened thoroughly before they were used.

Metates were not carried on trips. Some were cached in several places in the winter grounds. Small manos were carried on trips to grind seeds, using a slab of bedrock as a base. Usually a woman was equipped with but one mano and one metate. The Western Apache used no stationary grinding bin such as that of the Pueblos. Women ground from a kneeling position on a metate propped up with stones at an angle of about fifteen degrees.

The metate was still being used in the 1930s and 1940s, although apparently it was no longer manufactured. In 1939, I saw Apache men readily trade old Pueblo fetish stones they were wearing for one of the many beautifully made metates excavated at Kinishba.

To stir cooking food, two small sticks were held together in the hand. It was believed that the use of only one stick would cause death to a member of the family. Wooden skewers were used to hold meat or ears of corn over the fire, to remove meat or dumplings from the pot, or to turn food in the coals.

Kitchens and Fires

The camp was kept supplied with wood and water by the women, although men helped gather the heavy logs needed for the pit ovens. Water, at one time carried in a pitch-coated water basket, was commonly carried and kept in large metal containers or in milk cans during the 1940s. Possibly the Apache woman's most prized possessions were the little burros on which wood and water were packed. The women successfully resisted several strong efforts by government stockmen to rid the range of these animals.

Cooking was by broiling over open fires or in hot coals or ashes; by pit-baking; by parching; and by boiling. As the Apache were fond of soups, cooking by boiling was a favorite method. According

Fig. 25. *Many of the minority of Indians who owned frame houses used the house for storage and lived in an adjacent wickiup. They complained they could not breathe inside a house.*

to a White Mountain woman, her people used four-stone pot rests, the Chiricahua only three stones. Gifford[8] recorded three stones used by the San Carlos, none by the other Western Apache groups.

For parching, a basket tray and hot coals were used, with corn cobs the preferred fuel for charcoal. Gifford[9] recorded pot-parching among the Southern Tonto.

Pit ovens for green corn were located near the permanent agricultural sites.

In inclement weather, cooking was done over a small rock-enclosed fire pit in the center of the wickiup. In good weather, it was accomplished outdoors, often within a brush windbreak or under a ramada. Apache who had frame houses, a minority, usually furnished them with very cheap tin cookstoves. Griddles and Dutch ovens changed the manner of making bread, but some women still made "ash bread" in hot coals and ashes. Even families with frame houses and stoves usually moved into a wickiup or ramada for the summer season. One woman whose family was fonder than most of the old Indian recipes cooked all her Indian foods in her wickiup or ramada, even though she had one of the best-furnished houses on the reservation.

Fire was made with a drill. A stalk of yucca or bear grass as thick as a finger was split and grooved on one edge to form the hearth. This was placed on a rock. Juniper bark and grass were shredded between the hands, then placed with a little dust and dirt into the groove of the hearth. The drill consisted of yucca or wood. The end was placed in the bark and earth in the hole of the hearth, and the drill was twirled between the palms with a strong downward pressure. Fire-making tools were carried in the quiver or in a buckskin bag attached to the back of the belt.

A "strong man" could start a fire with one twirl of the drill (that is, without readjusting the hand position to the top of the drill). After one twirl, the smoking bark could be picked up and blown into flames. Others required as many as six twirls; these would laugh at their lack of proficiency. As late as the 1890s, schoolboys wagered marbles or other objects on how well they could make fire, proficiency being measured by the number of times they had to move their hands back to the top of the drill to twirl it.

Grown men wagered belts of cartridges or money on the number of twirls it would take them to make fire. Hough[10] stated that the Apache could make fire within three-fourths of a minute and added that Bourke had said the Apache could grind out fire in ten seconds.

Flint and steel were used for fire making after the acquisition of metal. This method was often preferred because the materials did not get wet and because a piece of flint, a small bit of file, sponge-wood, and juniper bark could easily be carried in a small buckskin bag at the belt. Tinder was obtained from the heart of a dead oak. This was compressed in the fingers and held in the left hand next to a piece of flint. Sparks were struck off the flint onto the tinder with steel held in the right hand.

Children's Foods

Children were nursed whenever they cried. There was no apparent embarrassment about nursing in public places. Hrdlicka[11] reported that the Apache baby for the first five or six months received only mother's milk, then a little food. Nursing continued until the child was able to walk or until another pregnancy occurred. Pregnancy, however, did not always cause an interruption of nursing, and on rare occasions a mother nursed both her latest and a previous infant at the same time. Red pepper was placed on the nipple when it was desired to wean a child.

Apparently, as soon as Apache children were able to eat solid food, they were fed the same foods adults ate. They were at times given tiswin, a mildly intoxicating corn beer. Indian Service officials frequently were appalled at the heavy, starchy diet given infants. Efforts to promote the use of milk or canned milk for children or for babies whose mothers were unable to nurse the children did not meet with success except in the Cedar Creek area, where a much-

Fig. 26. *An Apache infant was quite comfortable in a cradleboard. This one is well shaded from the sun.*

loved and respected schoolteacher induced the Apache to use canned milk in great quantities, not only for children but for adults as well. Parents were very indulgent with their children, buying them soda pop and candy at the stores even when they could ill afford to do so.

Ownership

Food was generally considered the property of the wife because she had gathered it or prepared it. A husband could not dispose of wild plant foods without consulting his wife, as he had had little or no part in procuring them. However, he might give away farm produce, for he often participated in the farm work. Meat brought to camp by the husband became the property of both spouses and either could dispose of it without consulting the other. In the husband's absence a wife could have one of his animals slaughtered without his permission if she needed meat. If he was at home, she could ask him to butcher an animal.[12]

Theft was not common. It was said that only those who were poor stole food. Usually, cases of theft involved stealing from a food cache or field. Men were not inclined to participate in arguments over stolen food, for these were regarded as women's quarrels. Boys who filched products from the fields might be caught by the owner in the field and whipped, or their parents might be told.[13]

Social Customs

The Apache ate when they were hungry. There was no set time for meals. Usually, hot meals were eaten in the morning and evening. If people became hungry during the day, they chewed dried berries or mescal or other readily available foods. In the 1940s meals were prepared in the morning and evening and also, by many, at midday. Apache who worked for the government and those who had close contact with the whites regularly ate a midday meal.

In early times children were said to have eaten apart, while man and wife ate together. Twentieth-century children ate with their

Fig. 27. *Bland Tessay and a ramada.*

parents unless there were guests, in which case the children waited
and ate what was left. Children were always given as much as they
desired of what the family could provide. Stratton[14] said the Tonto
meted out their foods when these were in short supply and that
food was always meted out to captives. He noted further that the
Tonto were "disbelievers in the propriety of treating female youth
to meat."

Meals were eaten in the wickiup during inclement weather. At
such times a man and wife would sit together on one side of the
fire, with the children across from them. If there were many, a
third group might be placed to form a triangle around the fire.
Meals were always taken outdoors during good weather, sometimes within a windbreak or under a ramada.

Small individual bowls were used for eating soups. Solid foods,
such as corn-meal mush, meat, or meat-mush combinations, were
dipped with the fingers from a common basket. Even in late times

food often was eaten from a common vessel of metal or crockery. Meat was placed in the mouth and held with one hand while a bite was cut off with a knife. Grease was rubbed from the hands on the arms and legs and was believed to impart strength by "feeding" them.

The Western Apache were a hospitable people. Friends and relatives made frequent visits, and they were welcomed and fed as long as they cared to remain. Even strangers could expect to be received well and to be fed and allowed to spend the night. Goodwin[15] described the great consideration with which guests were received; they were usually spared conversation until they had satisfied their hunger. Bourke[16] noted that scouts, as they prepared their meals, invited neighboring Americans to partake of their food. Palmer[17] stated, "It is always customary for one who has anything which others have not, to share as long as it lasts," and said that the more thrifty found it difficult to accumulate anything because their hungry friends visited them at all hours.

During the 1940s the Western Apache did not eat with one another as they once did; hospitality was not so freely extended. The only occasions on which large numbers of people ate together were

Fig. 28. *Social dancing near baskets of food.*

the girls' puberty ceremonies, at which times the families of the participating girls provided all visitors with food.

It was not clear just what, if any, indications of appreciation of a meal or of a host's hospitality were considered proper. Apparently, a guest ate as much as he desired, there being no compulsion that he either partake sparingly or consume everything set before him. A Cibecue informant stated that there was no manner of showing appreciation or of expressing thanks. A White Mountain informant (through a female interpreter) said appreciation was tendered by the expression "I thank you ever so much." I suspect that formerly there was no equivalent of the English "thank you."

Since women did the cooking, they also set the food before their husbands, thereby waiting on them to some extent.[18] Women took food to men at the sweat house. Large meetings were accompanied with sweat baths and food.[19]

There were special occasions when the Western Apache were expected to provide food. The puberty ceremony, mentioned above, was one. Food was also provided for helpers at planting time. Food had to be provided for all who offered their services upon a death in the family, and such individuals were feasted again on the first annual anniversary of the death.

Relative Importance, Preferences, Attitudes

Food had social and religious significance in the life of the Western Apache. "Superficial veneration" was accorded mescal, corn, beans, pumpkins, mesquite, yucca, and sunflowers.[20] Bands and local groups were sometimes named in accordance with their predominant food. The Cibecue band were often called Corn-Feeds-the-People Folk; the San Carlos, Wheat-Field Indian; and the Cherry Creek local group, variously, Wheat-Feeds-the-People Folk (from the wheat they raised) and Meat-Feeds-the-People Folk (because of the large number of livestock they captured from the Mexican settlements, to which they were closer than any other Cibecue group).

There was much stress on diligence in procuring food supplies.[21] Prestige was acquired from ability to procure food and also from generosity in giving it away.[22] The exchange of food between families of newly married couples and the ability of a man to provide meat for his in-laws were of great importance.[23]

A woman sometimes tested her new daughter-in-law by giving her corn to grind. Failure in such a test might be used as a reason for separation.[24]

The Western Apache believed that the spirits of the dead attempted to entice the living with food. Once a mortal partook of such food, there could be no return to the land of the living. A witness told of a dying Cedar Creek girl's lapsing into a coma in 1948, then reviving long enough to say that she had talked with her dead grandfather, who had wanted her to eat, but "she did not want to eat their food."

Foods contaminated by such animals as bears, coyotes, hawks, and eagles were believed capable of causing illness and death. One man told of an opportunity he had to attend school at Carlisle in 1893. Many older people urged him not to go, saying, "You're too small to go; people back there eat all kinds of snakes and fish— you'll come back and make everybody sick."

The Western Apache evaluation of other peoples was colored by the attitude of such people toward native foods and food customs. A man who had been at Fort Apache when Negro troops were stationed there was asked how the Negro was regarded. He replied that his people had said, "The Negro is a pretty good friend of the Indian. Some white people are different. Indian like the Negro, Negro like the Indian. The Negro eats everything; he eats the Indian food and likes it."

Informants usually mentioned venison, mescal, and corn as being among the most important and highly favored of the pre-reservation foods, although often they spoke of such delicacies as wood rats and combination foods prepared with acorns and sunflower seeds and walnuts as favorites.

Livestock taken in raids on sedentary peoples once were an important source of animal food. Horse and burro meat, especially burro, was preferred to beef if the animals were plump. Cozzens[25] observed meat being cut from live burros by the Chiricahua in the belief that meat taken from a live animal was more tender than that from a dead one.

Although practically all the meat from game animals was used, the entrails were especially esteemed. In describing a fight in which Chiricahua women tore and scratched at each other, Bourke[26] wrote: "The entrails were the coveted portions, for the possession of which the more greedy or more muscular fought with frequency." Santee[27] also noted the Apache fondness for entrails, describing a feast on them and an affray in which two old men drew knives over a paunch. In 1892[28] the San Carlos agent wrote: "Brutality in the butchering of beef cattle has been done away with; women are not allowed near the slaughter-house while the butchering is in progress, and the animals' intestines are not permitted to be given to the Indians, but are destroyed." The White Mountain in 1948 still ate the entrails of a beef first because they relished those parts most.

Santee[29] stated that twentieth-century Western Apache of the decade after 1910 had voracious appetites. He observed that they feasted all day and far into the night when meat was made available to them in plenty. Hrdlicka[30] noted that San Carlos schoolchildren did not eat immoderately. Workmen who ate at Kinishba in 1939 were in no way gluttonous. Their meager lunches, eaten amid the ruins during a noon break, might consist of a piece of heavy wheat tortilla, a bit of stew or some other mushy-looking food wrapped in a piece of tortilla, or perhaps only a small piece of fruit. Every two or three days, one of them would show up at the screen door to the small kitchen quarters where Dean Byron Cummings was preparing his lunch and stand silently until Cummings, knowing the man had nothing to eat, took a sandwich to him.

During the late 1940s on the Fort Apache Reservation, the principal article of food, when the Indians could afford it, was beef. On the reservation it was one of the comparatively cheap foods, being sold at reservation trading posts 50 percent cheaper than in Phoenix or Albuquerque. On the other hand, most canned goods and bulk foods sold 10 to 12 percent higher on the reservation.

Beef invariably was ordered by the Western Apache in terms of money value rather than by weight. The usual purchase was "fifty cents worth of beef" or "a dollar's worth of beef." It was only rarely that a customer requested a special cut rather than just plain beef. Mutton and pork, the latter in the form of chops or bacon, were sold on the reservation, but not in any quantity. Tinned beef and fancy canned beefs were purchased if the Indians had the money.

They cared very little for mutton. All efforts to introduce sheep in the early 1900s failed, and the Whiteriver agent unhappily reported: "They can not be induced to take care of sheep."[31] The only sheep on the reservation in the 1940s were those run by whites who had permission to do so. There were perhaps half a dozen goats in 1948.

Aside from beef, the most important item in the 1940s Apache diet was the wheat-flour tortilla. Potatoes were used to some extent, as were beans, particularly canned beans. Western Apache with very small cash income bought fancy canned fruits, candy, and watermelon at twelve cents a pound. They paid ten cents a bottle for soda pop, preferably of a red color, which was usually purchased during their shopping trips.

They were not fond of fresh vegetables, although they picked wild greens and used green squash. Few of them cared for milk, fresh or canned; in the Cedar Creek area, however, the trader sold many cases of evaporated milk, and adults there drank it directly from the can. One man, a cattle owner who had been to boarding school, liked milk but would not keep a cow because it was "too much bother; people come home tired and late and no milk—cow run away." One couple who had learned to like milk at school kept a cow for a brief time but stopped when neighbors taunted them with "trying to be like white people." In still another case a progressive woman with considerable property had kept and milked cows and said she would do so again; she did not care what others thought and was probably never troubled with reproaches of any kind, for she was notably independent and also respected as a generous giver of food.

Most elderly people expressed a preference for old-time foods— mescal, acorn, sunflower seeds, walnut, yucca fruit, and corn dishes—over modern American foods. The old chief Baha once spoke with great appreciation of all the new and appetizing foods the whites had brought, and R 25 stated that when the Western Apache were dependent on wild foods their diet was often meager and monotonous, but these were exceptional attitudes.

An old scout at East Fork, who for years received the largest government pension on the Fort Apache Reservation and who frequently carried several hundred dollars around in his pockets, refused to buy the packaged and easily prepared American foods he could so easily afford. Instead, he made his wife grind corn daily and prepare Apache dishes. This angered her so much that she sometimes told other women, "I would like to kill that man."

Upon returning home from World War II, a young veteran of the New Guinea and Philippines campaigns expressed a great distaste for American foods and made his wife prepare only Indian dishes. This she did, grinding corn on a metate, although she possessed a metal grinder, because "it tastes better if the iron doesn't touch it." Other young people said their favorite dish was boiled meat with acorn meal mashed in it, but most had not tasted a large variety of the old Western Apache recipes.

Although generosity in giving away food no longer prevailed in the 1940s, people with property, particularly cattle, and those steadily employed usually felt an obligation to help support their indigent relatives and in-laws. Employed Indians with good credit at the trading posts were eternally pestered by relatives and friends for permission to charge on their accounts. The pleas would be "All I want is a little flour" or "All I want is a little coffee." Some of the traders stated that a large percentage of such charges were paid not by those who obtained the goods but by the individuals in whose names the accounts stood.

A young war widow with four minor children received insurance and pension checks totaling more than two hundred dollars a month. Her local trader said her relatives ate up practically all of it each month, leaving her little for personal needs.

Most Western Apache were said by the Whiteriver home extension agent and by traders to spend their whole income, no matter what the amount, as soon as they received it. The largest portion was spent on food, as would be expected of a people with low income. The trading posts carried many good credit risks for months at a time until cattle checks were distributed. Elderly and middle-aged Indians had an enviable reputation for integrity and dependability with the traders. Their word was accepted as a contract. The younger people were not considered so reliable; many were poor credit risks, if not deliberate defaulters.

For a man to have to cook for himself was considered something of a misfortune. Aside from the inconvenience of performing an un-accustomed task, cooking placed a man in the awkward position of doing women's work and subjected him to the pitying ridicule of his fellows. At Cibecue a number of widowers were in this predica-ment. One, an elderly scout, had tried repeatedly to find a wife, offering his seventy-five-dollar pension to a woman who would feed him and take care of him, but all had laughingly refused his proposals.

The Western Apache rarely questioned or quibbled over prices at the trading posts. On one occasion when a man protested that sugar was too expensive, an old Indian clerk rebuked him, saying, "What's a little piece of metal when you can get *sugar*? Where else would you get anything so sweet and good for your coffee?"

Miscellaneous Ritual Associated With Foods

Bourke[32] stated that the Apache had a taboo against tasting fish, fish-eating birds, domesticated dogs, and, at times, porcupines and peccaries. Various food taboos and dislikes have been discussed in the section on particular classes of animals.

Food taboos among the Western Apache changed within histori-cal times. The elk, once a food animal, was no longer hunted or eaten after a group of people became sick from eating elk flesh. Fish, once untouchable, were relished by some of the younger men, although by no means all, at mid–twentieth century. Because of the issue of military pork rations in the 1870s and 1880s, the Indians gradually lost their repugnance for pork. Some taboos ap-parently were restricted to local groups or families, such as the taboo against the bear, the flesh of which was eaten by some and refused by others. Goodwin[33] described several taboos that had varying force from family to family. Among these were several that prohibited newlyweds from using certain foods lest their use affect their children unfavorably.

Goddard[34] stated that menstruating women could not eat the head or heart of deer, for such an act would make the hunter un-able to kill the animal in the future.

Goodwin[35] wrote: "In the old days on the first war party a boy was not allowed to eat the insides of any animal, only the good

Fig. 29. *A World War II veteran celebrates the Fourth of July, 1947. Proudly flying his flag, he shows the effects of the American acculturation. He and the other Apache draftees had been sent off with war dances, the first since the hostilities of 1917–18. They had almost forgotten how to do the dances.*

meat." If the boy ate intestines, it was believed that something would happen to him and he would not be able to travel well. It might be suspected that this taboo was imposed because the viscera were regarded by older hunters as the good meat.

Food bitten or even visited by a coyote or a dog was thought to give the eater coyote sickness.[36]

Only elderly people among the White Mountain could eat corn that had been chewed by bears, coyotes, or predatory birds. It was thought that young people who ate such food would become sterile. For the same reason, only the old ate the carcasses of animals that had been killed by predators.

The Cibecue were careful not to eat corn from a locality in the field where eagles or hawks had eaten their prey. Children were thought to die from this breach.

Goodwin[37] reported that unmarried girls did not slice meat unless they happened to be orphans. The reason for this restriction was not learned.

Other taboos are mentioned in Chapter 3, "Hunting."

Meals and Menus

The Western Apache said they had no preference for certain foods at certain periods of the day comparable to the American preference for bacon and eggs for breakfast or for soup at dinner. Anything available was prepared for the hot meals, and berries or dried foods were eaten at other times.

On the whole, spring was the time when grass and weed seeds, stored acorns, and jerked meat were eaten, although there might be fresh meat to boil.

During the summer there were quanitites of green corn, green-corn tortillas, beans, pumpkins, watermelons, mesquite, and acorns but not much meat.

In the fall there was an abundance of acorns and other wild food plants in addition to the harvested crops.

During the winter there was more use of mescal and meat. Stored acorns, walnuts, berries, and corn were also eaten. An attempt was made to have some corn with every meal, or at least once a day. Dried summer berries were also made to last through the winter.

The menu for a typical day might consists of hot corn-meal mush in the morning, corn bread and boiled deer meat in the evening, and perhaps snacks of sunflower meal, berries, mescal, corn bread, or liquefied mescal and walnuts during the day. Other daily menus described by informants included every native recipe, alone or combined with other foods.

Drinks

Coffee was drunk by practically all Western Apache, young and old, when they were able to obtain it. The army issued coffee as part of the Indian rations in the nineteenth century. One old man recalled when coffee beans were first issued. They were boiled for hours without result, and it was not until a year later that a soldier showed them how to grind and use the beans. Milk was not often used with coffee, and because the people did not have much sugar, they drank coffee readily without it.

Tea rarely was drunk. An informant could think of only two men, neither of whom drank coffee, who liked cocoa.

In early days milk from the udders of fresh does was cooked, usually in the udders. Goodwin[38] recorded a tale in which a grandmother sucked the milk out of fawns' stomachs when her grandsons brought them from the hunt.

The Western Apache were fond of the white man's intoxicants. An old informant told how, as a sick man fifty years earlier, he had visited relatives on the San Carlos Reservation. These had kept him liberally supplied with whiskey to "make him strong," and they loaded him down with several bottles for his return trip. The whiskey, he believed, had cured his illness.

The most common intoxicating drink of the Western Apache was tiswin, made of corn with frequent additions of such ingredients as wheat, sugar, yeast, and wild roots. Other items occasionally added to give "kick" or "medicine" were Copenhagen snuff and canned mincemeats that advertise a rum or brandy flavor.

Tiswin, from the Spanish word *tesvino,* was commonly called tulapai by whites on the reservation and by the Apache themselves. *Tulapai* is an Anglicization of the Apache term for the drink. Informants all claimed that the White Mountain and Cibecue obtained the drink from the Chiricahua, who in turn had received it from the Mexicans. A Cibecue man said the first Western Apache use of it "must have been 1850, maybe." Hrdlicka[39] said it was introduced within the memory of White Mountain men of middle age (in 1904) by a fellow tribesman called Brigham Young, who brought it from the Chiricahua. It is possible that the use of tiswin dates back further. An old White Mountain informant stated that it was obtained from the Chiricahua and that the story dated back four or five generations.

A Cibecue informant described the manufacture of tiswin as follows: Corn was soaked for one day, then placed in a gunnysack and hot water was poured on it. After two or three days, it sprouted and was ground on a metate. It was then placed in a pot or five-gallon can of water and boiled until the liquid was reduced to a level within about five inches of the bottom. Water was added. It was then strained, and the corn particles either were fed to horses or thrown away. The strained liquid was kept in a vessel for one day and then drunk. The Cibecue sometimes added sugar to increase alcoholic content. About a half-inch of the root of *Datura metaloides* (Jimson weed) invariably was added. Another root added by some was not identified, but from the description it was obtained in the Salt River Valley from a "four-square cactus." An old root was said to be bigger than the arm or hand, while a young root was as large as a finger. The roots of still another unidentified plant were used in tiswin by some of the Cibecue, who learned about the plant, which had no other use, from the Chiricahua. Two or three roots were crushed very lightly, then boiled in the drink. The plant was called "gan arrow."

Hrdlicka's[40] description of Western Apache tiswin was the most complete published. He said the White Mountain soaked their corn overnight, put it in a hole in the ground blanketed with yucca leaves, covered it with a gunnysack, and sprinkled it once a day for about a week. By the end of this time the corn had sprouted about two inches. It was then spread on a blanket for one day to dry somewhat, and the next day it was ground, mixed, and kneaded like dough. About ten pounds of corn dough was mixed in an earthen pot with about four gallons of water. This was stirred and boiled until reduced to half its original quantity. While the liquid was cooking, roots of *Datura metaloides* were added. After the first boiling, water was added to replace that lost through evaporation; the new liquid was again boiled and reduced by half. It was then strained through a perforated can, cooled until lukewarm, and poured into a pot that was never washed and was used for no other purpose. Coarsely ground wheat was added and allowed to float on top. In about eighteen hours it was ready to drink, and if not consumed in a short time, it would soon take on a strong and acid taste.

Reagan[41] mentioned in his description of tiswin that after the first boiling of several hours the corn mash was strained and recrushed on the metates, then returned to the liquid for reboiling. At the end of this time it was set aside to ferment for sixteen to twenty-four hours. The recrushing process was confirmed by a White Mountain woman who said the second boiling continued for only about half an hour.

The same woman stated that "real" tiswin was not intoxicating but was a nutritious corn-food beverage and that it was made intoxicating by the addition of sugar, raisins, prunes, and yeast. She added that the Apache of the East Fork area no longer used *Datura* root in their tiswin.

Reagan[42] stated that various perennial plants and roots were added to tiswin, including that of the *Euphorbia serphyllifolia* Pers., the root bark of the "lignum-vitae" tree,[43] some "loco weed" (not *Datura*, which is in the same place given separate mention), the peyote "bean," and the juice of *Datura metaloides* or the powdered root of the plant. Inquiries failed to confirm that the peyote button or any part of a cactus plant, except possibly the roots, had ever been used in tiswin or that the Cibecue or White Mountain had ever used peyote.

The bad effects of tiswin drinking were described at length by Reagan.[44] Hrdlicka[45] stated that the effects of tiswin might induce vomiting and produce headache and weakness for half a day. He saw nursing infants that became ill from the milk of mothers who had been drinking. On the Fort Apache Reservation in the 1940s, tiswin drinking was recognized by both whites and Indians as economically wasteful and as a cause of most of the quarrels resulting in bodily injury.

Summary and Conclusions

The Western Apache were catholic in their food tastes. They liked a variety of foods, a mixed diet composed of meat, agricultural products, and wild plants. They were so fond of all these three classes of food that they missed any type when it was not available. Although no type of food was strongly favored over another, meat must be listed first among their food preferences, with agricultural products a close second and wild plant foods third.

Food preparation was comparatively simple. The dome-shaped oven, batteries of metates, and elaborate bread recipes of the

Pueblo were lacking. Even the pit ovens were constructed on a simpler principle. Western Apache techniques of food preparation, although adequate, lacked the refinements and elaborations of more sedentary societies.

The early-day foods were partly replaced by American foods obtained from the traders. Women preferred the easily prepared canned and packaged store foods over the laboriously gathered and prepared traditional foods.

Chapter 6

CONCLUSIONS

I. The Cultural Position of the Western Apache in the Southwest

Distribution and comparative studies and other ethnological papers, although still very incomplete, have provided enough data to place the Western Apache as a tribe sharing many cultural traditions with all the Southern Athapascans, but with a closer affinity to the neighboring Mescalero and Chiricahua than to the others in most respects. In one area, the agricultural complex, they affiliate most closely with the Navajo.

Additional information in this study does not change the picture, but it does strengthen our perception of the Western Apache as a tribe sharing an older agricultural complex with the Navajo or perhaps with a group of formerly existing Athapascan tribes. A minor Yuman influence is also detected.

The nonagricultural aspects of food economy link the Western Apache more closely with Rancheria and Basin peoples than with the Pueblo. This is exemplified in their more extensive use of wild plants and game, in the use of the seed beater, and in the pit-baking and seed-parching techniques of food preparation.

In traits associated with hunting, the Western Apache share many elements with the Navajo and other Southern Athapascans. General Athapascan traits are the use of a corral windbreak by hunting parties, dreams indicating good or bad fortune, cries of animals bringing luck or indicating direction of game, proprietary hunting rituals passed on by religious practitioners for pay, and the performance of camp chores by grown-boy apprentices.

220

Possible influences from tribes to the west and south are to be seen in the restriction on mountain-sheep hunting and the use of sheep pelts. The circumspection surrounding the hunting of sheep becomes stronger as one goes from the Apache to the Maricopa and the Pima-Papago and on to the Yaqui. The Western Apache used a knife, rather than a hatchet, for trimming mescal, seemingly a trait shared only with the Maricopa and Papago.

The idea of the mourning ceremony appears to have been adopted in a very minor way from the Yuman and reworked into the Apache pattern of payment in food for services or favors performed. Among the Western Apache, the mourners are fed by the bereaved family when they arrive to offer sympathy and help, and the same mourners must be fed again on the first anniversary of the death.

Trapping and snaring techniques were weakly developed throughout the Southwest, but in all this region such techniques are particularly lacking among the Western Apache. The throwing stick for rabbits was also absent in this tribe.

The origins of the Western Apache agricultural complex are obscure. It is possible that they brought agriculture with them into east-central Arizona or that they took it over from the Salado Pueblo peoples who once inhabited the area. The Apache disclaim any knowledge of the people who once lived (until about A.D. 1350) in the extensive pueblos of Kinishba and Grasshopper.

Comparative ethnological material would indicate that the Western Apache derived their agriculture from the Navajo or from a Southern Athapascan agricultural complex that was at one time continuous from the Navajo country to the Gila, including the upper tributaries of the Gila.[1] Additional evidence indicates a well-developed agriculture among the northern Navajo and Apache groups—probably Jicarilla and groups later destroyed or amalgamated with the Jicarilla—in northern New Mexico and adjacent Colorado about 1600 to 1650.[2]

Agriculture diminished in importance among the Southern Athapascans as groups were displaced under Comanche and other pressures. It is possible that as the Mescalero and Eastern Chiricahua acquired horses, increasing dependence on buffalo hunting and excursions and raids on the Spanish and Mexican settlements led them to abandon agricultural activities; agriculture then persisted only in the isolated country of the Navajo and the comparatively horseless Western Apche. Ethnological material also appears to indicate some Pima-Papago contacts and some Pueblo contacts that may date back to the origin of the Western Apache agricultural complex but are probably more recent.

Western Apache agricultural traits that seem to derive from the Navajo or from a source common to both are corn colors associated with sex; chewing and spitting of first hailstones to stop hail; prayers of evil or jealous persons believed to damage crop; piling of corn harvest on ritual seed; location of field boundaries by arrow shoot; corn pollen believed to turn into cutworms if not shaken from the plants; corn hit by lightning not eaten; stones thrown by night watchers into field to frighten animals; ceremonies to remove worms; taboo on pregnant women in a field; soaking of seeds with drought-resistant plants; corn touched or contaminated by bear or coyote not used; helical planting.

One trait, the association of the cricket with agriculture, links the Mescalero and the Western Apache.

Pueblo resemblances relate the Western Apache so specifically to neighboring Pueblo that the traits seem to be special borrowings rather than developments from a general Pueblo agricultural complex. Western Apache traits that are similar to Hopi are distance racing to make the sun move more slowly, planters working barefooted, female inheritance of land, clan ownership of lands, and the planting of prayer plumes in fields to avert flood (Hano). Zuñi traits shared by the Apache are female inheritance of land and eagle, hawk, turkey, and road-runner, but never owl, feathers planted in corners of fields.

Some Western Apache traits indicate diffusion from or to the Pima. Among these are high regard for flat-headed corn, use of weed smoke to drive grasshoppers from a field, sprinkling of ashes on plants to drive off insects, soaking of seeds to aid sprouting, use of pumpkin seeds for cosmetic grease, and the cultivation of Martynia.

In several respects the Western Apache differ from their neighbors. In the Southwest they were almost unique, at least within historic times, in that women conducted most of the agricultural activities. The reason for this was probably that agriculture was not the principal base of subsistence, hunting requiring much more of a man's energies than among other southwestern groups. Other distinctive features were the proprietary agricultural rituals exercised for pay and an excessive fear of the contaminating influences of lightning, predatory birds, and some animals on crops or farm lands.

In Western Apache agriculture there was a lack of any ritual connected with beans, possibly indicating their late introduction as a crop plant. Less use was made of the pumpkin than in neighboring agricultural groups. Food preparation was on the whole simpler (at least as it concerns agricultural products) than among other agricultural peoples of the Southwest. The domed oven, hominy, and wafer bread were lacking.

Several factors make it hazardous to attempt to place the Western Apache precisely in their Southwest cultural setting. Among these are the incompleteness of the record, the historical displacements of the Western Apache, and the doubtful antiquity of many traits, particularly those relating to the use of food plants and certain agricultural techniques. Such evidence as there is would appear to indicate a Navajo derivation of Apache hunting and agricultural complexes or, perhaps, a general Southern Athapascan origin of these complexes for both the Western Apache and Navajo. Definite contacts with Pueblo and Pima and Yuman peoples are indicated, but these appear to have been of only secondary importance in their influence on Western Apache subsistence economy.

II. General Summary

The Western Apache included agriculture as a part of their subsistence economy for more than two centuries, its importance varying from group to group. It was practically negligible among the Northern Tonto, of considerable importance to the Southern Tonto and San Carlos, and during the period just before the American occupation it furnished approximately 25 percent of the subsistence of the White Mountain and Cibecue.

The origin of Western Apache agriculture is highly problematical. Evidence would indicate that it was derived either from a once widespread Southern Athapascan agricultural complex or specifically from the Navajo, which it closely resembles. Whatever the origin, accretions were made through contacts in trade and war with neighboring peoples: Pueblo, Pima, Yuman, Spanish and Mexican.

Principal crop plants were corn, pumpkins, beans, and wheat. Of these, corn and pumpkins were planted for more than 200 years, beans for at least 150, and wheat for 90. Minor crops occasionally planted or broadcast were melons, sunflowers, gourds, devil's claw, tobacco, lambsquarter, and possibly cotton. Corn may be said to have been the only crop of major importance.

Agriculture played a significant role in social values and attitudes. Farm lands gave added economic security and prestige to their owners. Landless people worked on the farms of chiefs and rich men, thereby building up a patron-client relationship.

Women performed the greater part of the agricultural tasks, since much of the time and energies of the men were expended in hunting and raiding. However, men assisted in these labors when they were available, and in some groups the heavy labor of clearing land and planting was recognized as work proper for men. Women were recognized as better farmers. Both men and women possessed proprietary agricultural ritual, which at times was performed for pay.

Agriculture did not force a sedentary life upon the Western Apache. Crops were planted and thereafter given a minimal amount of care while groups migrated to wild-plant gathering grounds.

In the period immediately preceding the advent of American troops, agriculture appears to have been in a state of static balance with gathering and hunting. Evidence does not indicate that there was any shift in the direction of more dependence on agriculture. The Western Apache apparently were well satisfied with their diverse subsistence and seminomadic way of life.

Approximately 35 percent of White Mountain and Cibecue food was meat. Among the other groups, especially the Northern Tonto, meat provided a larger proportion of the diet. In the order of their importance, the meat foods were large game (deer being outstandingly important), small game (principally rodents), and livestock taken in raids on Spanish and Mexican settlements.

Hunting carried with it considerable prestige. All men hunted, but some had outstanding skill or possessed proprietary hunting ritual that brought them social and economic benefits.

Attitudes toward foods changed. Elk, once an esteemed game animal, became taboo after the turn of the century because of an outbreak of sickness following the eating of elk. Fish, once taboo, slowly became accepted as an edible food.

Before the coming of the Americans, about 40 percent of White Mountain and Cibecue foods were from wild plants. Staples, in order of importance, were mescal, acorn (of first importance among the Northern Tonto), sunflower seeds, other wild seeds and nuts (including piñon and walnut), yucca fruit, prickly-pear fruit, juniper berries, mesquite, and saguaro.

In order of quantitative importance, wild plants rank first among the Western Apache foods, then meat, with agricultural products last. Their preferences for staple foods were, in order, venison, other meat, corn, mescal and acorns, sunflower seeds, and piñon nuts.

A great dislocation in economic life accompanied creation of the Apache reservations. Hunting and gathering ceased to have their former importance and in the 1940s furnished but a negligible fraction of Western Apache subsistence. Agricultural activity fluctuated with the policies of agents, opportunities for off-reservation employment, and government relief efforts. The introduction of cattle breeding furnished a source of food and cash income. Beef supplanted venison as the favorite food and by 1949 constituted perhaps 50 percent of the Western Apache diet. White flour, purchased at the trading posts, replaced corn meal in the cereal portion of the diet. Fresh plant foods were little used.

Probably the most significant environmental factor affecting Western Apache economy was the great ecological diversity of the Apache habitat. The Western Apache occupied a territory varying in elevation from two thousand to eleven thousand feet and in vegetation from tall cactus to spruce. Within the general area itself there was great diversification rather than gradual change, for it was broken into deep valleys and high ranges. This environment provided a wide variety of plant products growing at different seasons of the year. An opportunity was thus offered for the fairly continuous exploitation, from spring to autumn, of a series of wild plant products ripening at staggered intervals. It was an opportunity that, when taken, forced a continual series of moves over most of the growing season.

With reference to farming opportunities, the White Mountain and Cibecue were perhaps more favored than other groups by a suitable combination of irrigable terrain and climate. However, agricultural opportunities were available to all. Minor variations of elevation and terrain caused differences in planting and harvest times in order to avoid frosts. In only a few areas of exceptionally favorable rainfall, such as Forestdale, was agriculture without irrigation attempted and the benefit of underground seepage used.

Variations in hunting and gathering opportunities were probably not as limiting in their effects as those in agricultural opportunity, for the range of most bands included a wide variety of life zones, and the Apache migrated to favorable areas rather than depending on their own immediate neighborhoods. However, the Northern Tonto, who lived far from the best agave areas, were forced to obtain their mescal either by long gathering expeditions or through trade with more fortunately situated bands to the south; actually, they placed more dependence on other foods, such as acorns. Such foods as saguaro fruit and mesquite beans, which grew in the lower elevations, were used to a greater extent by the San Carlos than by the more northerly groups, who had to travel farther to obtain them.

In early times the Western Apache made reasonably full use of their environmental resources and possibilities. Most edible plants and animals were used. Two notable exceptions in the animal world were bear and fish. Bear were hunted and eaten, but not by all and with ritual limitations. Fish, although abundant in the streams flowing through the Apache territory, were ignored. Some of the canines and felines were not eaten by all groups, and certain birds were shunned by all. The Western Apache did not cultivate their territory intensively, although it was climatically better suited to farming than most areas of the Southwest.

After livestock had been introduced into the New World by the whites, the Western Apache failed to accept domestic animals except as beasts to be kept temporarily until needed, then slaughtered. Even in the 1940s most of the Apache who owned cattle were not true stock breeders. A minority had become successful growers; most left their animals in the care of government employees and collected a semiannual check from their sale.

Full advantage was never taken of the farming opportunities offered by the Fort Apache Reservation. The greater part of the land developed lay fallow each year. Modern American scientific techniques of farming were not widely adopted.

Gathering practically ceased with the restrictions imposed upon seasonal migrations by compulsory school attendance. Game no longer was abundant.

Considering the cultural possibilities and limitations of both the pre-American and post-American periods, the Western Apache made more complete use of their natural environment before the whites came than afterward.

A most intriguing question is why, given the comparatively favorable area they occupied, did the Western Apache not greatly increase their agricultural activities or even adopt a sedentary agricultural way of life as did so many of the southwestern tribes known to them? Or, after the coming of the Spaniards, why did they not take to stock breeding as did the Navajo and others? This of course, is one of the central problems of anthropology: Why do people, given a clear choice, choose this instead of that?

Possibly the very abundance of environmental possibilities in the Western Apache habitat led the Apache to follow them all instead of concentrating on one. It appears that the Western Apache had preferred their varied economic pursuits from as far back as we have knowledge of them until the army occupation forced a change.

Their seminomadic lifestyle may have been a deep-seated cultural tradition, something acquired as one of the almost unconscious values of life almost from birth. A change of scene, a change of climate, different foods, new activities may have been exhilarating. From an early age the Apache child learned this way and accepted it and perhaps valued it above all others. A deep conservatism also may have been involved. We can only speculate.

NOTES

Chapter 1. **Introduction**

1. For a short comparative summary of Southern Athapascan cultures, see Goodwin, "The Southern Athapascans." As of 1949 the best general descriptions of individual Apache groups were Kluckhohn and Leighton, *The Navaho,* for the Navajo; Opler, "A Summary of Jicarilla Apache Culture," for the Jicarilla; McAllister, "Kiowa-Apache Social Organization," for the Kiowa-Apache; Castetter and Opler, "The Ethnobiology of the Chiricahua and Mescalero Apache," and Hoijer, *Chiricahua and Mescalero Apache Texts,* for the Mescalero; Opler, *An Apache Life Way,* for the Chiricahua. No general ethnological summary of Lipan Apache culture had then been published.

2. Opler, "The Kinship Systems of the Southern Athabaskan-speaking Tribes," p. 620.

3. Ibid., p. 629.

4. Hoijer, "The Southern Athapaskan Languages," p. 86.

5. Goodwin, The *Social Organization of the Western Apache,* pp. 4, 12 *et seq.*

6. Opler, *An Apache Life Way,* pp. 1–3.

7. Geographical data are from unpublished materials placed at my disposal by Robert Holtz, Superintendent of the Fort Apache Indian Reservation.

8. Data on vegetation are adapted from Kearney and Peebles, *Flowering Plants and Ferns of Arizona;* Nichol, "The Natural Vegetation of Arizona"; Benson and Darrow, "A Manual of Southwestern Desert Trees and Shrubs"; and from information supplied by William Schroeder, the forester at Whiteriver Agency.

9. Goodwin's basic papers, "The Social Divisions and Economic Life of the Western Apache," *The Social Organization of the Western Apache,*

229

"White Mountain Apache Religion," "Myths and Tales of the White Mountain Apache," have been followed for all general Western Apache data.

10. The Fossil Creek, Bald Mountain, and Oak Creek bands of the Northern Tonto were intermingled with Yavapai who shared their territory.

Chapter 2. **Agriculture**

1. Goodwin, *The Social Organization of the Western Apache,* p. 12 and map on p. 652. Nearly all the locations mentioned on the pages that follow are from Goodwin, who before his early death had old Apaches take him on camping trips to the areas of pre-American encampments and farming sites.

2. Emory, *Notes of a Military Reconnaissance,* p. 579.

3. Goodwin, *The Social Organization of the Western Apache,* p. 15.

4. Ibid., pp. 17–19.

5. Ibid., p. 21.

6. Ibid., pp. 22–23.

7. Ibid., p. 61.

8. Opler, *Report on the Fort Apache Indians of Arizona,* p. 9.

9. Goodwin, *The Social Organization of the Western Apache,* p. 24.

10. Ibid., p. 28.

11. Ibid., pp. 30–31.

12. Ibid., p. 33.

13. Ibid., pp. 60–61.

14. Ibid., pp. 36–41.

15. Ibid., pp. 43–45.

16. Ibid., p. 43.

17. Ibid., p. 673.

18. Ibid., p. 19.

19. Hough, "Archaeological Field Work in Northeastern Arizona," pp. 389–90.

20. Bourke, *On the Border With Crook,* p. 179.

21. Opler, *Report on the Fort Apache Indians of Arizona,* p. 34.

22. Clum, *Apache Agent,* p. 163.

23. Goodwin, *The Social Organization of the Western Apache,* pp. 9–10.

24. Ibid., pp. 97, 152–55; Goodwin, "Characteristics and Functions of Clan in a Southern Athapascan Culture," pp. 401–402.

25. Goodwin, *The Social Organization of the Western Apache,* p. 374.

26. Ibid., p. 334.

27. Ibid., p. 128.

28. Gifford, "Culture Element Distributions: XII, Apache-Pueblo," p. 100.

29. Goodwin, *The Social Organization of the Western Apache,* pp. 151–52.

30. Ibid., pp. 376–77.

31. Goodwin, "Myths and Tales of the White Mountain Apache," p. 76; *The Social Organizations of the Western Apache,* pp. 154–55.

32. Goodwin, *The Social Organization of the Western Apache,* p. 655.

33. Ibid., p. 151.

34. Ibid., pp. 130–31, 138–44, 630–50.

35. Ibid., pp. 153–54.

36. Ibid., pp. 150–51.

37. Ibid., p. 424.

38. Ibid., p. 9.

39. Gifford, "Culture Element Distributions: XII, Apache-Pueblo, p. 168.

40. Goodwin, "The Social Divisions and Economic Life of the Western Apache," p. 63.

41. Opler, *Report on the Fort Apache Indians of Arizona,* p. 34.

42. Ibid., p. 34.

43. Thomas, *Forgotten Frontiers,* pp. 32–33.

44. Goodwin, *The Social Organization of the Western Apache,* p. 156.

45. Goodwin, "Experiences of an Indian Scout," Part 1, pp. 32–33.

46. Goodwin, *The Social Organization of the Western Apache,* p. 156.

47. Goodwin, "Experiences of an Indian Scout," Part 1, p. 33.

48. Goodwin, *The Social Organization of the Western Apache,* p. 682.

49. Ibid., p. 388.

50. Ibid., pp. 30–31.

51. Opler, *Report on the Fort Apache Indians of Arizona,* p. 34.

52. Goodwin, *The Social Organization of the Western Apache,* p. 166.

53. Ibid., p. 156.

54. Ibid., p. 192.

55. Goodwin, "The Social Divisions and Economic Life of the Western Apache," p. 57; *The Social Organization of the Western Apache,* p. 356.

56. Goodwin, *The Social Organization of the Western Apache,* p. 356.

57. Goodwin, "Myths and Tales of the White Mountain Apache," p. 99n.; *The Social Organization of the Western Apache,* pp. 288, 330–31.

58. Goodwin, "Myths and Tales of the White Mountain Apache," p. 71n.

59. Goodwin, *The Social Organization of the Western Apache,* p. 372.

60. Ibid., p. 473.

61. Ibid., p. 288.

62. Ibid., pp. 151–52.

63. Ibid., p. 166; "Myths and Tales of the White Mountain Apache," p. 99n.; "Experiences of an Indian Scout," Part 1, p. 33.

64. Goodwin, "The Social Divisions and Economic Life of the Western Apache," p. 63.

65. Palmer, "Customs of the Coyotero Apache," p. 161.

66. Goodwin, *The Social Organization of the Western Apache*, p. 387.

67. Goodwin, "Myths and Tales of the White Mountain Apache," p. 71.

68. Bourke, "The Medicine-Men of the Apache," p. 529.

69. Gifford, "Culture Element Distributions: XII, Apache-Pueblo," p. 18.

70. Bourke, "Diary," 22 December 1872.

71. Gifford, "Culture Element Distributions: XII, Apache-Pueblo," pp. 18, 103.

72. Goodwin, *The Social Organization of the Western Apache*, p. 157.

73. Goodwin, "Myths and Tales of the White Mountain Apache," p. 71.

74. Barnes, *Apaches and Longhorns*, pp. 112–16.

75. Goodwin, *The Social Organization of the Western Apache*, p. 333.

76. Ibid., p. 472.

77. Goodwin, "Myths and Tales of the Western Apache," p. 61.

78. Goodwin, *The Social Organization of the Western Apache*, p. 116.

79. Ibid., pp. 600–613.

80. Barnes, *Apaches and Longhorns*, p. 114.

81. Castetter and Bell, *Pima and Papago Indian Agriculture*, pp. 79–80; Castetter and Bell, "Agriculture Among the Yuman Tribes of the Lower Gila and Colorado Rivers."

82. Goodwin, "Myths and Tales of the White Mountain Apache," p. 98.

83. Ibid., pp. 51–52.

84. Goodwin, "White Mountain Apache Religion," pp. 32–33.

85. Curtis, *The North American Indian*, p. 38.

86. Reagan, "Notes on the Indians of the Fort Apache Region," p. 292.

87. Goodwin, "Myths and Tales of the White Mountain Apache," p. 71.

88. Reagan, "Plants Used by the White Mountain Apache of Arizona," p. 148.

89. Ibid., p. 148.

90. Reagan, "Notes on the Indians of the Fort Apache Region," p. 295.

91. Ibid., pp. 292–93.

92. Palmer, "Customs of the Coyotero Apache," p. 168.

93. Reagan, "Notes on the Indians of the Fort Apache Region," p. 295.

94. Goodwin, *The Social Organization of the Western Apache*, p. 472.

95. Bourke, *An Apache Campaign in the Sierra Madre*, pp. 27–28.

96. Santee, *Apache Land*, p. 7.

97. Reagan, "Notes on the Indians of the Fort Apache Region," p. 292.

98. Whipple, Eubank, and Turner, "Report Upon the Indian Tribes," p. 120.

99. Bourke, *On the Border With Crook*, pp. 457–58.

100. Goodwin, *The Social Organization of the Western Apache,* p. 330.
101. Goodwin, "Myths and Tales of the White Mountain Apache," pp. 71–76.
102. Gifford, "Culture Element Distributions: XII, Apache-Pueblo," pp. 20, 105.
103. Dorsey, *Indians of the Southwest,* p. 185.
104. Gifford, "Culture Element Distributions: XII, Apache-Pueblo," p. 105.
105. Goodwin, *The Social Organization of the Western Apache,* p. 623.
106. Bourke, *On the Border With Crook,* pp. 457–58.
107. Goddard, "San Carlos Apache Texts," pp. 364–65.
108. Gifford, "Culture Element Distributions: XII, Apache-Pueblo," p. 150.
109. Bourke, "The Folk-Foods of the Rio Grande Valley and of Northern Mexico," pp. 47–48.
110. Gifford, "Culture Element Distributions: XII, Apache-Pueblo," p. 20.
111. Ibid., p. 665.
112. Clum, *Apache Agent,* p. 163.
113. Reagan, "The Cliff Dwellers of Arizona," p. 296.
114. Lockwood, *The Apache Indians,* p. 99.
115. Bourke, *On the Border With Crook,* pp. 457–58.
116. Reagan, "Notes on the Indians of the Fort Apache Region," p. 299.
117. Ibid., p. 299.
118. Ibid., p. 292.
119. Whipple, *Report on the Indian Tribes,* p. 14.
120. Gifford, "Culture Element Distributions: XII, Apache-Pueblo," p. 20.
121. Reagan, "Plants Used by the White Mountain Apache of Arizona," p. 156.
122. Ibid., p. 156.
123. Bourke, *On the Border With Crook,* pp. 457–58.
124. Goodwin, *The Social Organization of the Western Apache,* p. 157.
125. Curtis, *The North American Indian,* p. 133.
126. Bourke, "The Medicine-Men of the Apache," p. 502.
127. Ibid., pp. 476–77.
128. Palmer, "Customs of the Coyotero Apache," p. 165.
129. Goddard, "Myths and Tales from the White Mountain Apache," p. 123.
130. Curtis, *The North American Indian,* pp. 46–47.
131. Cummings, "Apache Puberty Ceremony for Girls."
132. Goodwin, "White Mountain Apache Religion," p. 26.
133. Espinosa, *First Expedition of Vargas into New Mexico, 1692,* p. 238.

134. In *Documentos para la historia de México,* Series 3, Part 4, p. 564.

135. Ibid., p. 503.

136. Guiteras, "Rudo Ensayo," p. 126.

137. "Relación de Todas las Cosas Que en el Nuevo México se Han Visto y Sabido," *Documentos para la historia de México,* Series 3, Part 1, p. 97.

138. Bolton, *Kino's Historical Memoirs of Pimaría Alta,* I, map.

139. *Documentos para la historia de México,* Series 4, Part 1, p. 95.

140. Thomas, *Forgotten Frontiers,* p. 12.

141. Letter in *Documentos para la historia de México,* Series 4, Part 1, p. 92.

142. Ibid., p. 95.

143. Thomas, *Forgotten Frontiers,* pp. 155–56.

144. Ibid., p. 156.

145. Bourke, "The Early Navajo and Apache," pp. 289–90.

146. Dorr, "A Ride with the Apaches," p. 45.

147. Bolton, *Kino's Historical Memoirs of Pimaría Alta,* II, p. 257.

148. Cook, "Journal," p. 137.

149. Gregg, *Commerce of the Prairies,* pp. 193–94.

150. Sapir, "Internal Linguistic Evidence Suggestive of the Northern Origin of the Navaho," pp. 228–31.

151. Goodwin, "The Social Divisions and Economic Life of the Western Apache," p. 61.

152. *Report of the Commissioner of Indian Affairs for 1874,* pp. 286–87.

153. Frazer, *The Apaches of the White Mountain Reservation, Arizona,* p. 14.

154. Ibid., p. 14.

155. *Report of the Commissioner of Indian Affairs for 1886,* p. 41.

156. Ibid., 1892, pp. 802–803.

157. Ibid., 1899, pp. 582–83.

Chapter 3. **Hunting**

1. Goodwin, *The Social Organization of the Western Apache,* p. 475.

2. Ibid., p. 332.

3. Ibid., pp. 149–50.

4. Ibid., p. 150.

5. Ibid., pp. 12–44.

6. Eastman, *Seven and Nine Years Among the Comanches and Apaches, passim.*

7. Goodwin, *The Social Organization of the Western Apache,* p. 158. Goodwin has been followed on most of the Western Apache hunting and gathering areas and bounds.

8. Goodwin, "The Social Divisions and Economic Life of the Western Apache," p. 61.

9. Ibid., p. 61.

10. Goodwin, *The Social Organization of the Western Apache,* pp. 157–58.

11. Ibid., p. 475.

12. Ibid., p. 475.

13. Ibid., p. 476.

14. Goodwin, "Experiences of an Indian Scout," Part 1, p. 35.

15. Gifford, "Culture Element Distributions: XII, Apache-Pueblo," p. 9.

16. Ibid., p. 30.

17. Ibid., p. 29.

18. Palmer, "Customs of the Coyotero Apache," p. 165.

19. Bourke, "Vesper Hours of the Stone Age," p. 57.

20. Gifford, "Culture Element Distributions: XII, Apache-Pueblo," p. 9.

21. Ibid., p. 119.

22. Möllhausen, *Diary of a Journey from the Mississippi to the Coasts of the Pacific with a United States Government Expedition,* II, p. 211.

23. Smart, "Notes on the 'Tonto' Apaches," p. 418.

24. Gifford, "Culture Element Distributions: XII, Apache-Pueblo," p. 30.

25. Ibid., p. 119.

26. Ibid., p. 30.

27. Ibid., p. 31.

28. Mason, "Arrows and Arrow-Makers," p. 73.

29. Ibid., p. 71.

30. Gifford, "Culture Element Distributions: XII, Apache-Pueblo," p. 30.

31. Ibid., pp. 31, 121.

32. Ibid., pp. 30, 120.

33. Ibid., p. 120.

34. Ibid., p. 31.

35. Smart, "Notes on the 'Tonto' Apaches," p. 418.

36. Gifford, "Culture Element Distributions: XII, Apache-Pueblo," pp. 31, 121.

37. Ibid., p. 120.

38. Smart, "Notes on the 'Tonto' Apaches," p. 418.

39. Ibid., p. 419.

40. Mason, "Arrows and Arrow-Makers," p. 71–72.

41. Bourke, "Vesper Hours of the Stone Age," p. 57.

42. Gifford, "Culture Element Distributions: XII, Apache-Pueblo," p. 30–31.

43. Ibid., p. 121.

44. Ibid., p. 31, 121.

45. Ibid., p. 32.

46. Ibid., p. 32.

47. Ibid., p. 32.

48. Ibid., pp. 32, 121.

49. Ibid., pp. 121–22.

50. Smart, "Notes on the 'Tonto' Apaches," p. 418.

51. Ogle, "Federal Control of the Western Apaches, 1848–1886," Part 4, 15 (1940), p. 329.

52. Gifford, "Culture Element Distributions: XII, Apache-Pueblo," pp. 32, 122.

53. Ibid., p. 35.

54. Ibid., p. 6.

55. Bourke, *On the Border With Crook,* pp. 129–30.

56. Gifford, "Culture Element Distributions: XII, Apache-Pueblo," p. 33.

57. Ibid., p. 123.

58. Ibid., p. 31.

59. Mason, "Arrows and Arrow-Makers," p. 69.

60. Palmer, "Customs of the Coyotero Apache," p. 167.

61. Gifford, "Culture Element Distributions: XII, Apache-Pueblo," pp. 31, 121.

62. Mason, "Arrows and Arrow-Makers," p. 74.

63. Ibid., p. 69.

64. Goodwin, "Myths and Tales of the White Mountain Apache," p. 54n.

65. Goodwin, *The Social Organization of the Western Apache,* p. 112.

66. Gifford, "Culture Element Distributions: XII, Apache-Pueblo," p. 86.

67. Goodwin, "Myths and Tales of the White Mountain Apache," p. 130–31.

68. Gifford, "Culture Element Distributions: XII, Apache-Pueblo," p. 7.

69. Ibid., p. 84.

70. Ibid., p. 85.

71. Cremony, *Life Among the Apaches,* pp. 28–29.

72. Ibid., pp. 291–92.

73. Ibid., pp. 204–205.

74. Personal communication from William Schroeder, forester.

75. Goddard, "Myths and Tales from the San Carlos Apache," p. 51.

76. Goodwin, "Myths and Tales of the White Mountain Apache," p. 90n.

77. Gifford, "Culture Element Distributions: XII, Apache-Pueblo," p. 5.

78. Ibid., p. 81.

79. Ibid., p. 84.

80. Ibid., p. 85.

81. Ibid., pp. 6, 82.

82. Ibid., p. 7.

83. Bourke, "Notes Upon the Religion of the Apache Indians," p. 438–39.

84. Gifford, "Culture Element Distributions: XII, Apache-Pueblo," p. 8.

85. Ibid., p. 82.

86. Ibid., p. 88.

87. Ibid., p. 9.

88. Ibid., p. 88.

89. Bourke, "Notes Upon the Religion of the Apache Indians," p. 440.

90. Hoijer, *Chiricahua and Mescalero Apache Texts*, p. 217.

91. Bourke, "Notes Upon the Religion of the Apache Indians," p. 440.

92. Bourke, "The Medicine-Men of the Apache," p. 505.

93. Ibid., p. 505.

94. Gifford, "Culture Element Distributions: XII, Apache-Pueblo," p. 82.

95. Ibid., p. 5.

96. Ibid., p. 84.

97. Ibid., pp. 82–83.

98. Bourke, *On the Border With Crook*, pp. 129–30.

99. Davis, *The Truth About Geronimo*, pp. 64–65.

100. Goddard, "Myths and Tales from the San Carlos Apaches," pp. 47–49.

101. Ibid., p. 65.

102. Gifford, "Culture Element Distributions: XII, Apache-Pueblo," p. 90.

103. Bourke, *An Apache Campaign in the Sierra Madre*, pp. 30–32; Palmer, "Customs of the Coyotero Apache," pp. 167–68.

104. Cremony, *Life Among the Apaches*, pp. 27–28.

105. Cruse, *Apache Days and After*, p. 45.

106. Gifford, "Culture Element Distributions: XII, Apache-Pueblo," p. 6.

107. Ibid., p. 5.

108. Goodwin, *The Social Organization of the Western Apache*, p. 475.

109. Bourke, *An Apache Campaign in the Sierra Madre*, p. 28.

110. Bourke, "Vesper Hours of the Stone Age," p. 59.

111. Gifford, "Culture Element Distributions: XII, Apache-Pueblo," pp. 10, 90.

112. Stratton, *Life Among the Indians, or The Captivity of the Oatman Girls*, p. 98.

113. Goodwin, *The Social Organization of the Western Apache*, pp. 332–33; Goodwin, "Myths and Tales of the White Mountain Apache," p. 163n.

114. Gifford, "Culture Element Distributions: XII, Apache-Pueblo," p. 9.

115. Ibid., p. 121.

116. Ibid., p. 87.

117. Reagan, "Notes on the Indians of the Fort Apache Region," p. 296.

118. Goodwin, *The Social Organization of the Western Apache,* p. 333.

119. Goodwin, "Myths and Tales of the White Mountain Apache," pp. 42–43.

120. Ibid., p. 41.

121. Goddard, "Myths and Tales from the San Carlos Apache," pp. 47–49.

122. Goodwin, "Myths and Tales of the White Mountain Apache," p. 115.

123. Bourke, "The Medicine-Men of the Apache," p. 580.

124. Gifford, "Culture Element Distributions: XII, Apache-Pueblo," p. 84.

125. Goodwin, "Myths and Tales of the White Mountain Apache," pp. 130–31.

126. Bourke, "Notes Upon the Religion of the Apache Indians," p. 440.

127. Ibid., pp. 438–39.

128. Goodwin, *The Social Organization of the Western Apache,* p. 676.

129. Gifford, "Culture Element Distributions: XII, Apache-Pueblo," p. 98.

130. Ibid., p. 98.

131. Reagan, "Notes on the Indians of the Fort Apache Region," p. 292.

132. Bloom, "From Lewisburg to California in 1849: Notes from the Diary of William H. Chamberlin," p. 169.

133. Gifford, "Culture Element Distributions: XII, Apache-Pueblo," p. 99.

134. Bourke, *An Apache Campaign in the Sierra Madre,* p. 27–28.

135. Goodwin, "Experiences of an Indian Scout," Part 1, p. 35.

136. Santee, *Apache Land,* pp. 11–12.

137. Palmer, "Customs of the Coyotero Apache," pp. 169–70.

138. Goodwin, "Experiences of an Indian Scout," Part 1, pp. 67–68 and n.

139. Gifford, "Culture Element Distributions: XII, Apache-Pueblo," p. 9.

140. Ibid., p. 89.

141. Goodwin, "Myths and Tales of the White Mountain Apache," p. 94 and n.

142. Ibid., pp. 76, 97, *et passim.*

143. Goodwin, *The Social Organization of the Western Apache,* p. 264.

144. Goodwin, "Experiences of an Indian Scout," Part 1, p. 35.

145. Goodwin, *The Social Organization of the Western Apache,* p. 475.

146. Hoijer, *Chiricahua and Mescalero Apache Texts,* p. 217.

147. Goodwin, *The Social Organization of the Western Apache*, p. 332.

148. Bourke, "Notes Upon the Religion of the Apache Indians," p. 438–39.

149. Bourke, "The Medicine-Men of the Apache," pp. 501–502.

150. Ibid., p. 504.

151. Ibid., p. 505.

152. Goddard, "Myths and Tales from the San Carlos Apache," pp. 62–64.

153. Ibid., pp. 62–63.

154. Goodwin, "Myths and Tales of the White Mountain Apache," p. 91n.

155. Ibid., p. 41.

156. Goodwin, *The Social Organization of the Western Apache*, p. 304.

157. Ibid., p. 476.

158. Gifford, "Culture Element Distributions: XII, Apache-Pueblo," p. 86.

159. Ibid., p. 8.

160. Ibid., p. 88.

161. Ibid., p. 87.

162. Ibid., p. 87.

163. Ibid., p. 9.

164. Ibid., p. 88.

165. Ibid., p. 8.

166. Goodwin, "The Social Divisions and Economic Life of the Western Apache," p. 61.

167. Opler, *Report on the Fort Apache Indians of Arizona*, p. 35.

Chapter 4. **Gathering**

1. Goodwin, *The Social Organization of the Western Apache*, p. 158.

2. Ibid., p. 159.

3. Goodwin, "Myths and Tales of the White Mountain Apache," p. 123 and n.

4. Goodwin, "The Social Divisions and Economic Life of the Western Apache," pp. 62–63.

5. Ibid., p. 65.

6. Goodwin, "Experiences of an Indian Scout," Part 1, p. 36.

7. Santee, *Apache Land*, p. 7.

8. Gifford, "Culture Element Distributions: XII, Apache-Pueblo," pp. 11, 91.

9. Ibid., p. 11.

10. Ibid., pp. 95–96.

11. Ibid., p. 11.

12. Ibid., pp. 91–92.

13. Ibid., p. 91.

14. Ibid., p. 136.

15. Smart, "Notes on the 'Tonto' Apaches," p. 418.

16. Gifford, "Culture Element Distributions: XII, Apache-Pueblo," p. 92.

17. Ibid., pp. 14, 96.

18. Ibid., p. 167.

19. Goodwin, *The Social Organization of the Western Apache,* p. 54.

20. Ibid., p. 160.

21. Goodwin, "The Social Divisions and Economic Life of the Western Apache," p. 62.

22. Gifford, "Culture Element Distributions: XII, Apache-Pueblo," pp. 93, 99, 100.

23. Ibid., p. 99.

24. For the distribution and use of agave in the Southwest, see Castetter, Bell, and Grove, "The Early Utilization and Distribution of Agave in the American Southwest."

25. Goodwin, *The Social Organization of the Western Apache,* pp. 12–13, 15–16, 156.

26. Castetter et al., "The Early Utilization and Distribution of Agave in the American Southwest," p. 33.

27. Bourke, *On the Border With Crook,* p. 10.

28. Curtis, *The North American Indian,* pp. 17–18.

29. Ibid., pp. 17–18.

30. Goodwin, "Myths and Tales of the White Mountain Apache," pp. 56–57.

31. Gifford, "Culture Element Distributions: XII, Apache-Pueblo," pp. 12, 93.

32. Ibid., p. 12.

33. Ibid., p. 93.

34. Reagan, "Notes on the Indians of the Fort Apache Region," p. 293.

35. Gifford, "Culture Element Distributions: XII, Apache-Pueblo," p. 15.

36. Ibid., p. 12.

37. Curtis, *The North American Indian,* pp. 17–18.

38. Palmer, "Customs of the Coyotero Apache," p. 168.

39. Curtis, *The North American Indian,* p. 20.

40. Reagan, "Notes on the Indians of the Fort Apache Region," pp. 293–94.

41. Bourke, *An Apache Campaign in the Sierra Madre,* pp. 26–27.

42. Gifford, "Culture Element Distributions: XII, Apache-Pueblo," p. 13.

43. Ibid., p. 92.

44. Ibid., p. 92.

45. Reagan, "Plants Used by the White Mountain Apache of Arizona," p. 148.

46. Goodwin, *The Social Organization of the Western Apache*, pp. 156–57.

47. Goodwin, "Experiences of an Indian Scout," Part 1, pp. 33–34.

48. Goodwin, *The Social Organization of the Western Apache*, pp. 156–67.

49. Gifford, "Culture Element Distributions: XII, Apache-Pueblo," p. 12.

50. Goodwin, "Myths and Tales of the White Mountain Apache," pp. 60–61.

51. Gifford, "Culture Element Distributions: XII, Apache-Pueblo," pp. 92–93.

52. Ibid., p. 12.

53. Ibid., pp. 11, 12.

54. Ibid., p. 12.

55. Reagan, "Notes on the Indians of the Fort Apache Region," pp. 294–95.

56. Gifford, "Culture Element Distributions: XII, Apache-Pueblo," pp. 11–12.

57. For the distribution and use of mesquite in the Southwest, see Bell and Castetter, "The Utilization of Mesquite and Screwbean by the Aborigines of the American Southwest."

58. Goodwin, *The Social Organization of the Western Apache*, p. 157.

59. Goddard, "San Carlos Apache Texts," pp. 364–65.

60. Hrdlicka, "Physiological and Medical Observations Among the Indians of Southwestern United States and Northern Mexico," p. 258.

61. Reagan, "Plants Used by the White Mountain Apache of Arizona," p. 145.

62. Hrdlicka, "Physiological and Medical Observations Among the Indians of Southwestern United States and Northern Mexico," p. 258.

63. Gifford, "Culture Element Distributions: XII, Apache-Pueblo," pp. 12, 93.

64. Palmer, "Customs of the Coyotero Apache," p. 169.

65. Gifford, "Culture Element Distributions: XII, Apache-Pueblo," p. 93.

66. For the distribution and use of saguaro in the Southwest, see Castetter and Bell, "The Aboriginal Utilization of the Tall Cacti in the American Southwest."

67. Goodwin, *The Social Organization of the Western Apache*, p. 156.

68. Ibid., p. 54.

69. Hrdlicka, "Physiological and Medical Observations Among the Indians of Southwestern United States and Northern Mexico," p. 257.

70. Bourke, "The Folk-Foods of the Rio Grande Valley and of Northern Mexico," p. 52.

71. Gifford, "Culture Element Distributions: XII, Apache-Pueblo," pp. 11, 91.

72. Bourke, "The Folk-Foods of the Rio Grande Valley and of Northern Mexico," p. 52.

73. Gifford, "Culture Element Distributions: XII, Apache-Pueblo," p. 94.

74. Hrdlicka, "Physiological and Medical Observations Among the Indians of Southwestern United States and Northern Mexico," p. 257.

75. Gifford, "Culture Element Distributions: XII, Apache-Pueblo," p. 94.

76. Ibid., p. 94.

77. Reagan, "Notes on the Indians of the Fort Apache Region," p. 294.

78. Gifford, "Culture Element Distributions: XII, Apache-Pueblo," p. 94.

79. Reagan, "Notes on the Indians of the Fort Apache Region," p. 294.

80. Ibid., p. 294.

81. Curtis, *The North American Indian,* p. 19.

82. Gifford, "Culture Element Distributions: XII, Apache-Pueblo," p. 95.

83. Ibid., p. 95.

84. Ibid., pp. 13, 94.

85. Hrdlicka, "Physiological and Medical Observations Among the Indians of Southwestern United States and Northern Mexico," p. 257.

86. Bourke, "The Folk-Foods of the Rio Grande Valley and of Northern Mexico," p. 44.

87. Gifford, "Culture Element Distributions: XII, Apache-Pueblo," p. 13.

88. Hrdlicka, "Physiological and Medical Observations Among the Indians of Southwestern United States and Northern Mexico," p. 257.

89. For the use of yucca in the Southwest, see Bell and Castetter, "The Utilization of Yucca, Sotol, and Beargrass by the Aborigines in the American Southwest."

90. Goodwin, "The Social Divisions and Economic Life of the Western Apache," p. 62.

91. Reagan, "Notes on the Indians of the Fort Apache Region," p. 294.

92. Gifford, "Culture Element Distributions: XII, Apache-Pueblo," p. 94.

93. Goddard, "San Carlos Apache Texts," pp. 362–64.

94. Gifford, "Culture Element Distributions: XII, Apache-Pueblo," p. 94.

95. Reagan, "Plants Used by the White Mountain Apache of Arizona," pp. 147–49.

96. Kearney and Peebles, *Flowering Plants and Ferns of Arizona,* p. 198.

97. Palmer, "Customs of the Coyotero Apache," p. 164.

98. Gifford, "Culture Element Distributions: XII, Apache-Pueblo," p. 13.

99. Ibid., p. 94.

100. For the cultivation of sunflowers, see the section on this plant in the chapter on agriculture.

101. Gifford, "Culture Element Distributions: XII, Apache-Pueblo," pp. 95–96.

102. Ibid., p. 96.

103. Palmer, "Customs of the Coyotero Apache," p. 169.

104. Goodwin, *The Social Organization of the Western Apache,* p. 157.

105. Gifford, "Culture Element Distributions: XII, Apache-Pueblo," p. 13.

106. Reagan, "Notes on the Indians of the Fort Apache Region," p. 294.

107. Goodwin, "Myths and Tales of the White Mountain Apache," pp. 54–55.

108. Curtis, *The North American Indian,* p. 19.

109. Gifford, "Culture Element Distributions: XII, Apache-Pueblo," p. 91.

110. Ibid., p. 95.

111. Reagan, "Notes on the Indians of the Fort Apache Region," p. 292.

112. Palmer, "Customs of the Coyotero Apache," p. 168.

113. Reagan, "Plants Used by the White Mountain Apache of Arizona," pp. 148–49.

114. Goodwin, *The Social Organization of the Western Apache,* p. 157.

115. Goodwin, "Experiences of an Indian Scout," Part 1, p. 34.

116. Palmer, "Customs of the Coyotero Apache," p. 169.

117. Goodwin, "Myths and Tales of the White Mountain Apache," pp. 54–55.

118. Curtis, *The North American Indian,* p. 15.

119. Reagan, "Plants Used by the White Mountain Apache of Arizona," p. 155.

120. Ibid., p. 149.

121. Ibid., pp. 148–49.

122. Goodwin, "Myths and Tales of the White Mountain Apache," *passim.*

123. Ibid., pp. 54–55.

124. Ibid., pp. 51–52.

125. Hrdlicka, "Physiological and Medical Observations Among the Indians of Southwestern United States and Northern Mexico," p. 259.

126. Gifford, "Culture Element Distributions: XII, Apache-Pueblo," p. 14.

127. Ibid., p. 96.

128. Goodwin, "Myths and Tales of the White Mountain Apache," p. 123 and n.

129. Gifford, "Culture Element Distributions: XII, Apache-Pueblo," p. 99.

130. Gifford, Ibid., p. 96.

131. Hrdlicka, "Physiological and Medical Observations Among the Indians of Southwestern United States and Northern Mexico," p. 258.

132. Palmer, "Customs of the Coyotero Apache," p. 169.

133. Ibid., p. 169.

134. Gifford, "Culture Element Distributions: XII, Apache-Pueblo," p. 14.

135. Bourke, *On the Border With Crook,* pp. 129–31.

136. Gifford, "Culture Element Distributions: XII, Apache-Pueblo," p. 91.

137. Hrdlicka, "Physiological and Medical Observations Among the Indians of Southwestern United States and Northern Mexico," p. 258.

138. Reagan, "Notes on the Indians of the Fort Apache Region," p. 294.

139. Gifford, "Culture Element Distributions: XII, Apache-Pueblo," p. 14.

140. Palmer, "Customs of the Coyotero Apache," pp. 169–70.

141. Ibid., p. 169–70.

142. Reagan, "Plants Used by the White Mountain Apache of Arizona," p. 156.

143. Hrdlicka, "Physiological and Medical Observations Among the Indians of Southwestern United States and Northern Mexico," p. 258.

144. Kearney and Peebles, *Flowering Plants and Ferns of Arizona,* p. 371.

145. Bourke, *An Apache Campaign in the Sierra Madre,* pp. 30–32.

146. Curtis, *The North American Indian,* p. 19.

147. Goodwin, The Social Organization of the Western Apache, p. 623.

148. Personal communication.

149. Reagan, "Plants Used by the White Mountain Apache of Arizona," p. 148.

150. Goodwin, "Myths and Tales of the White Mountain Apache," p. 28.

151. Hrdlicka, "Physiological and Medical Observations Among the Indians of Southwestern United States and Northern Mexico," p. 258.

152. Reagan, "Plants Used by the White Mountain Apache of Arizona," p. 148.

153. Bourke, "The Medicine-Men of the Apache," p. 520.

154. Ibid., p. 518 *et seq.*

155. Gifford, "Culture Element Distributions: XII, Apache-Pueblo," p. 14.

156. Ibid., p. 96.

157. Ibid., p. 10.

158. Ibid., p. 90.

159. Ibid., p. 96–97.

160. Ibid., p. 96–97.

161. Ibid., p. 96–97.

162. Ibid., p. 97.

163. Bourke, "Notes Upon the Religion of the Apache Indians," p. 446.

164. Gifford, "Culture Element Distributions: XII, Apache-Pueblo," pp. 96–97.

165. Bourke, "The Medicine-Men of the Apache," p. 540.

166. Gifford, "Culture Element Distributions: XII, Apache-Pueblo," p. 97.

167. Ibid., p. 15.

168. Goodwin, "The Social Divisions and Economic Life of the Western Apache," p. 62.

169. Opler, *Report on the Fort Apache Indians of Arizona,* p. 35.

170. Bourke, *On the Border With Crook,* pp. 129–31.

171. Palmer, "Customs of the Coyotero Apache," pp. 169–70.

172. Reagan, "Notes on the Indians of the Fort Apache Region," pp. 292–95.

173. Pp. 155–160.

174. Hrdlicka, "Physiological and Medical Observations Among the Indians of Southwestern United States and Northern Mexico," pp. 257–59.

175. Goodwin, "The Social Divisions and Economic Life of the Western Apache," p. 64.

Chapter 5. **Foods**

1. Bourke, *An Apache Campaign in the Sierra Madre,* p. 100.

2. Palmer, "Customs of the Coyotero Apache," pp. 169–70.

3. Smart, "Notes on the 'Tonto' Apaches," p. 419.

4. Stratton, *Life Among the Indians, or The Captivity of the Oatman Girls,* p. 97.

5. Goddard, "Myths and Tales from the San Carlos Apache," p. 52.

6. Goddard, "Myths and Tales from the White Mountain Apache," p. 133.

7. Palmer, "Customs of the Coyotero Apache," pp. 169–70.

8. Gifford, "Culture Element Distributions: XII, Apache-Pueblo," p. 15.

9. Ibid., p. 15.

10. Hough, "Apache and Navaho Fire-Making," p. 585.

11. Hrdlicka, "Physiological and Medical Observations Among the Indians of Southwestern United States and Northern Mexico," pp. 76–77.

12. Goodwin, *The Social Organization of the Western Apache,* p. 334.

13. Ibid., p. 384.

14. Stratton, *Life Among the Indians, or The Captivity of the Oatman Girls,* p. 97.

15. Goodwin, *The Social Organization of the Western Apache,* pp. 545–46.

16. Bourke, *An Apache Campaign in the Sierra Madre,* pp. 27–28.

17. Palmer, "Customs of the Coyotero Apache," p. 168.

18. Goodwin, *The Social Organization of the Western Apache,* p. 335.

19. Goodwin, "Myths and Tales of the White Mountain Apache," p. 116.

20. Bourke, "Notes Upon the Religion of the Apache Indians," pp. 448–49.

21. Goodwin, "Myths and Tales of the White Mountain Apache," p. 142.

22. Ibid., p. 142; Goodwin, *The Social Organization of the Western Apache,* pp. 542–43.

23. Goodwin, "Myths and Tales of the White Mountain Apache," pp. 76, 94, 97, *et passim.*

24. Ibid., p. 108.

25. Cozzens, *The Marvelous Country,* p. 121.

26. Bourke, *An Apache Campaign in the Sierra Madre,* p. 90.

27. Santee, *Apache Land,* pp. 2–3.

28. *Report of the Commissioner of Indian Affairs for 1892,* p. 220.

29. Santee, *Apache Land,* pp. 2–3.

30. Hrdlicka, "Physiological and Medical Observations Among the Indians of Southwestern United States and Northern Mexico," p. 220.

31. *Report of the Commissioner of Indian Affairs for 1905,* Part 1, pp. 158–59.

32. Bourke, "Notes on the Gentile Organization of the Apaches of Arizona," p. 124.

33. Goodwin, *The Social Organization of the Western Apache,* p. 330.

34. Goddard, *Myths and Tales from the San Carlos Apache,* p. 63.

35. Goodwin, "Experiences of an Indian Scout," Part 1, p. 48.

36. Ibid., Part 2, pp. 33–34.

37. Goodwin, *The Social Organization of the Western Apache,* pp. 472–73.

38. Goodwin, "Myths and Tales of the White Mountain Apache," p. 41.

39. Hrdlicka, "Method of Preparing Tesvino Among the White River Apaches," pp. 190–91.

40. Ibid., p. 190–91.

41. Reagan, "Notes on the Indians of the Fort Apache Region," p. 298.

42. Reagan, "Plants Used by the White Mountain Apache of Arizona," p. 151.

43. This is doubtful according to E. F. Castetter; personal communication.

44. Reagan, "Plants Used by the White Mountain Apache of Arizona," pp. 151–52.

45. Hrdlicka, "Physiological and Medical Observations Among the Indians of Southwestern United States and Northern Mexico," p. 177.

Chapter 6. **Conclusions**

1. See the summary and conclusions section of Chapter 2, "Agriculture," where historical evidence is cited.

2. Hill, "Some Navaho Culture Changes During Two Centuries," *passim;* Thomas, *After Coronado,* pp. 17–21, 27.

BIBLIOGRAPHY

Bailey, Flora L. "Navaho Foods and Cooking Methods," *American Anthropologist,* 42: 270–90, 1940.

Barnes, Will Croft. *Apaches and Longhorns.* Los Angeles: Ward Ritchie Press, 1941.

Beach, W. W. *The Indian Miscellany.* Albany: J. Munsell, 1877

Beaglehole, Ernest. "Hopi Hunting and Hunting Ritual," *Yale University Publications in Anthropology,* No. 4, 1936.

———. "Notes on Hopi Economic Life," *Yale University Publications in Anthropology,* No. 15, 1937.

Beals, Ralph L., "The Comparative Ethnology of Northern Mexico Before 1750," *Ibero-Americana,* 2: 93–225, 1932.

———. "The Contemporary Cultures of the Cahita Indians," *Bureau of American Ethnology Bulletin 142,* 1945.

Bell, Willis H., and Edward F. Castetter. "The Utilization of Mesquite and Screwbean by the Aborigines in the American Southwest," *University of New Mexico Bulletin, Biological Series,* Vol. 5, No. 2, 1937.

———. "The Utilization of Yucca, Sotol, and Beargrass by the Aborigines in the American Southwest," *University of New Mexico Bulletin, Biological Series,* Vol. 5, No. 5, 1941.

Benson, Lyman, and Robert A. Darrow. "A Manual of Southwestern Desert Trees and Shrubs," *University of Arizona Biological Science Bulletin No. 6,* 1944.

Bieber, Ralph P., ed. *Exploring Southwestern Trails, 1846–1854.* Glendale, California: The Arthur H. Clark Co., 1938.

Bloom, Lansing B., ed. "Bourke on the Southwest, X," *New Mexico Historical Review,* 11: 217–82, 1936.

———. "From Lewisburg to California in 1849: Notes from the Diary of William H. Chamberlin," *New Mexico Historical Review,* 20: 144–80, 1945.

Bolton, Herbert E., trans. and ed. *Kino's Historical Memoirs of Pimaría Alta.* 2 vols. Cleveland: Arthur H. Clark, 1919.

Bourke, John Gregory. *An Apache Campaign in the Sierra Madre.* New York: Charles Scribner's Sons, 1886.

————. "Diary." Photostatic copy in University of New Mexico Library.

————. "The Early Navajo and Apache," *American Anthropologist, O.S.,* 8:287–95, 1895.

————. "The Folk-Foods of the Rio Grande Valley and of Northern Mexico," *Journal of American Folk-Lore,* 8:41–71, 1895.

————. "The Medicine-Men of the Apache," Bureau of American Ethnology *Ninth Annual Report,* 1892, pp. 443–603.

————. "Notes on the Gentile Organization of the Apaches of Arizona," *Journal of American Folk-Lore,* 3:111–26, 1890.

————. "Notes Upon the Religion of the Apache Indians," *Folklore,* 2:419–54, 1891.

————. *On The Border With Crook.* New York: Charles Scribner's Sons, 1891.

————. "Sacred Hunts of the American Indians," *Compterendu de la Huitieme Session Congres International des Americanistes.* Paris: 1892.

————. "Vesper Hours of the Stone Age," *American Anthropologist, O.S.,* 3:55–63, 1890.

Brand, D. D., chairman. "Symposium on Prehistoric Agriculture," *University of New Mexico Bulletin, Anthropological Series,* Vol. 5, No. 1, 1936.

Castetter, Edward F. "Early Tobacco Utilization in the American Southwest," *American Anthropologist,* 45:320–25, 1943.

———— and Willis H. Bell. "The Aboriginal Utilization of the Tall Cacti in the American Southwest," *University of New Mexico Bulletin, Biological Series,* Vol. 5, No. 1, 1937.

———— and Willis H. Bell, *"Agriculture Among the Yuman Tribes of the Lower Gila and Colorado Rivers."* Manuscript.

———— and Willis H. Bell. *Pima and Papago Indian Agriculture.* Albuquerque: University of New Mexico Press, 1942.

———— and M. E. Opler, "The Ethnobiology of the Chiricahua and Mescalero Apache," *University of New Mexico Bulletin, Biological Series,* Vol. 4, No. 5, 1936.

————, Willis H. Bell, and Alvin R. Grove. "The Early Utilization and Distribution of Agave in the American Southwest," *University of New Mexico Bulletin, Biological Series,* Vol. 5, No. 4, 1938.

Chamberlin, Ralph V. "The Ethno-Botany of the Gosiute Indians of

Utah," *American Anthropological Association Memoirs,* Vol. 2, Part 5, 1911, pp. 329–405.

Clum, Woodworth. *Apache Agent: The Story of John P. Clum.* Boston: Houghton Mifflin, 1936.

Cooke, Philip St. George. "Journal." In Ralph P. Bieber, ed., *Exploring Southwestern Trails.*

Cozzens, Samuel Woodworth. *The Marvellous Country.* Boston: Lee and Shepard, 1876.

Cremony, J. C. *Life Among the Apaches.* San Francisco: A. Roman, 1868.

Cruse, Brigadier General Thomas. *Apache Days and After.* Caldwell, Idaho: The Caxton Printers, 1941.

Cummings, Byron. "Apache Puberty Ceremony for Girls," *The Kiva,* Vol. 5, No. 1, 1939, pp. 1–4.

Curtis, Edward S. *The North American Indian,* Vol. I. Cambridge: The University Press, 1907.

Cushing, Frank Hamilton. "Zuñi Breadstuffs," Museum of the American Indian, *Indian Notes and Monographs,* Vol. 8, 1920.

Davis, Britton. *The Truth About Geronimo.* New Haven: Yale University Press, 1929.

"Descripción Geográfica, Natural, y Curiosa de la Provincia de Sonora." In *Documents para la historia de México,* Series 3, Part 4. Mexico: Vicente García Torres, 1856.

Documentos para la historia de México. Series 3 and 4. Mexico: Vicente García Torres, 1856.

Dorr, Herbert C. "A Ride with the Apaches." In W. W. Beach, *The Indian Miscellany.*

Dorsey, George A. *Indians of the Southwest.* N.p.: Santa Fe Railway System, 1903.

Eastman, Edwin. *Seven and Nine Years Among the Comanches and Apaches.* Jersey City: Clark Johnson, 1873.

Eggan, Fred. *Social Organization of North American Tribes.* Chicago: University of Chicago Press, 1937.

Emory, Lieutenant Colonel W. H. *Notes of a Military Reconnaissance.* Washington: Wendell and Van Benthryshi, 1848.

Espinosa, J. Manuel, trans. *First Expedition of Vargas into New Mexico, 1692.* Albuquerque: University of New Mexico Press, 1940.

Forde, C. Daryll. "Hopi Agriculture and Land Ownership," *Journal of the Royal Anthropological Institute of Great Britain and Ireland,* 61: 357–406, 1931.

252 THE WESTERN APACHE

Franciscan Fathers. *An Ethnologic Dictionary of the Navaho Language.* Saint Michaels, Arizona: The Franciscan Fathers, 1910.

Frazer, Robert. *The Apaches of the White Mountain Reservation, Arizona.* Philadelphia: Indian Rights Association, 1885.

Gifford, E. W. "Culture Element Distributions: XII, Apache-Pueblo," *Anthropological Records,* Vol. 4, No. 1, 1940.

———. "Northeastern and Western Yavapai," *University of California Publications in American Archaeology and Ethnology,* Vol. 34, No. 4, 1936, pp. 247–354.

———. "The Southeastern Yavapai," *University of California Publications in American Archaeology and Ethnology,* Vol. 29, No. 3, 1932, pp. 177–252.

Goddard, Pliny Earle. "Myths and Tales from the San Carlos Apache," *American Museum of Natural History Antropological Papers,* Vol. 24, Part 1, 1918, pp. 1–86.

———. "Myths and Tales from the White Mountain Apache," *American Museum of Natural History Anthropological Papers,* Vol. 24, Part 2, 1919, pp. 87–139.

———. "San Carlos Apache Texts," *American Museum of Natural History Anthropological Papers,* Vol. 24, Part 3, 1919, pp. 141–367.

Goodwin, Grenville. "Characteristics and Functions of Clan in a Southern Athapascan Culture," *American Anthropologist,* 29: 394–407, 1937.

———. "Experiences of an Indian Scout," *Arizona Historical Reviews,* Vol. 7, Nos. 1 and 2, 1936. No. 1, pp. 31–68; No. 2, pp. 31–73.

———. "Myths and Tales of the White Mountain Apache," *Memoirs of the American Folk-Lore Society,* Vol. 33, 1939.

———. "The Social Divisions and Economic Life of the Western Apache," *American Anthropologist,* 37: 55–64, 1935.

———. *The Social Organization of the Western Apache.* Chicago: University of Chicago Press, 1942.

———. "The Southern Athapascans," *The Kiva,* Vol. 4, No. 2, 1938, pp. 5–10.

———. "White Mountain Apache Religion," *American Anthropologist,* 40: 24–37, 1938.

Gregg, Josiah. *Commerce of the Prairies.* Dallas: Southwest Press, 1933.

Guiteras, Eusebio, trans. "Rudo Ensayo," *Records of the American Catholic Historical Society of Philadelphia,* Vol. 5, No. 2, 1894, pp. 112–264.

Hill, W. W. "The Agricultural and Hunting Methods of the Navaho Indians," *Yale University Publications in Anthropology,* No. 18, 1938.

———. "Navaho Warfare," *Yale University Publications in Anthropology*, No. 5, 1936.·

———. "Santa Clara Field Notes."

———. "Some Navaho Culture Changes During Two Centuries," *Smithsonian Institution Miscellaneous Collections*, 100: 395–415, 1940.

Hoijer, Harry. *Chiricahua and Mescalero Apache Texts*. Chicago: University of Chicago Press, 1942.

———. "The Southern Athapaskan Languages," *American Anthropologist*, 40: 75–87, 1938.

Hough, Walter. "Apache and Navaho Fire-Making," *American Anthropologist*, 3: 585–86, 1901.

———. "Archaeological Field Work in Northeastern Arizona. The Museum-Gates Expedition of 1901." In *Smithsonian Institution Annual Report for 1901*, 1903.

———. "The Hopi Indian Collection in the United States National Museum," *United States National Museum, Proceedings*, 54: 235–96, 1918.

Hrdlicka, Ales. "Method of Preparing Tesvino Among the White River Apaches," *American Anthropologist*, 6: 190–91, 1904.

———. "Physiological and Medical Observations Among the Indians of Southwestern United States and Northern Mexico," *Bureau of American Ethnology Bulletin 34*, 1908.

Jones, Volney H. "A Summary of Data on Aboriginal Cotton of the Southwest." In D. D. Brand, "Symposium on Prehistoric Agriculture."

Kearney, Thomas H., and Robert H. Peebles. *Flowering Plants and Ferns of Arizona*. Washington: Government Printing Office, 1942.

Kluckhohn, Clyde, and Dorothea Leighton. *The Navajo*. Cambridge: Harvard University Press, 1946.

Kroeber, A. L., ed. "Walapai Ethnography," *American Anthropological Association Memoirs*, No. 42, 1935.

Lockwood, Francis Cummins. *The Apache Indians*. New York: The Macmillan Co., 1938.

Lowie, Robert H., "The Northern Shoshone," *American Museum of Natural History Anthropological Papers*, Vol. 2, Part 2, 1909, pp. 165–306.

———. "Notes on Shoshonean Ethnography," *American Museum of Natural History Anthropological Papers*, Vol. 20, Part 3, 1924, pp. 185–314.

McAllister, J. Gilbert. "Kiowa-Apache Social Organization." In Eggan, *Social Organization of North American Tribes*, pp. 99–169.

Mason, Otis T. "Arrows and Arrow-Makers," *American Anthropologist, O.S.,* 4:45–74, 1891.

Möllhausen, Balduin. *Diary of a Journey from the Mississippi to the Coasts of the Pacific with a United States Government Expedition.* 2 vols. London: Longman, Brown, Green, Longmans, and Roberts, 1858.

Nichol, A. A., "The Natural Vegetation of Arizona," *University of Arizona Technical Bulletin No. 68* (reprint), 1943.

Ogle, Ralph H. "Federal Control of the Western Apaches, 1848–1886," *New Mexico Historical Review,* 14:309–365, 1939; 15:12–71, 188–248, 269–335, 1940.

Opler, Morris Edward. *An Apache Life Way: The Economic, Social, and Religious Institutions of the Chiricahua Indians.* Chicago: University of Chicago Press, 1941.

———. "The Kinship Systems of the Southern Athabaskan-speaking Tribes," *American Anthropologist,* 38:620–33, 1936.

———. *Report on the Fort Apache Indians of Arizona.* Washington: Government Printing Office, 1936. (Typed copy in office of superintendent, Fort Apache Reservation Schools, was used.)

———. "A Summary of Jicarilla Apache Culture," *American Anthropologist,* 38:202–223, 1936.

Palmer, Edward. "Customs of the Coyotero Apache," *Zoe,* 1:161–72, 1890.

Parsons, Elsie Clews, "Isleta, New Mexico," *Bureau of American Ethnology 47th Annual Report,* 1932, pp. 193–466.

———. *Pueblo Indian Religion.* 2 vols. Chicago: University of Chicago Press, 1939.

———. "The Social Organization of the Tewa of New Mexico," *American Anthropological Association Memoirs,* No. 36, 1929.

Reagan, Albert B. "The Cliff Dwellers of Arizona," *Indiana Academy of Science Proceedings,* 1904, pp. 295–96.

———. "Notes on the Indians of the Fort Apache Region," *American Museum of Natural History Anthropological Papers,* Vol. 31, Part 5, 1930, pp. 281–345.

———. "Plants Used by the White Mountain Apache of Arizona," *Wisconsin Archaeologist,* N.S., 8:143–61, 1929.

Report of the Commissioner of Indian Affairs for 1874. Washington: Government Printing Office, 1874. See also reports for 1886, 1892, 1899, and 1905.

Russell, Frank, "The Pima Indians," *Bureau of American Ethnology 26th Annual Report,* 1908, pp. 3–389.

Sanches, Padre Bartolome. "Letters." In *Documentos para la historia de México*, Series 4, Vol. 1. Mexico, Vicente García Torres, 1856.

Santee, Ross. *Apache Land*. New York: Charles Scribner's Sons, 1947.

Sapir, Edward. "Internal Linguistic Evidence Suggestive of the Northern Origin of the Navaho," *American Anthropologist*, 38: 224–35, 1936.

Simmons, Leo, ed. *Sun Chief: The Autobiography of a Hopi Indian*. New Haven: Yale University Press, 1942.

Smart, Charles. "Notes on the 'Tonto' Apaches," *Smithsonian Institution Annual Report for 1867*, 1868, pp. 417–19.

Spier, Leslie, "Cultural Relations of the Gila River and Lower Colorado Tribes," *Yale University Publications in Anthropology*, No. 3, 1936.

———. "Havasupai Ethnography," *American Museum of Natural History Anthropological Papers*, Vol. 29, Part 3, 1928, pp. 81–392.

———. "Klamath Ethnography," *University of California Publications in American Archaeology and Ethnology*, 30: 1–388, 1930.

———. "Problems Arising from the Cultural Position of the Havasupai," *American Anthropologist*, 31: 213–22, 1929.

———. *Yuman Tribes of the Gila River*. Chicago: University of Chicago Press, 1933.

Stratton, R. B. *Life Among the Indians, or The Captivity of the Oatman Girls*. San Francisco: Grabhorn Press, 1935.

Thomas, Alfred Barnaby. *After Coronado*. Norman: University of Oklahoma Press, 1935.

———. *Forgotten Frontiers*. Norman: University of Oklahoma Press, 1932.

Titiev, Mischa, "Old Oraibi: A Study of the Hopi Indians of the Third Mesa," *Peabody Museum of American Archaeology and Ethnology Papers*, Vol. 22, No. 1, 1944.

Whipple, A. W. *Reports of Explorations and Surveys, to Ascertain the Most Practicable and Economical Route for a Railroad from the Mississippi River to the Pacific Ocean*. 12 vols. Washington: A. O. P. Nicholson, 1855–60.

Whipple, Lieutenant A. W., Thomas Ewbank, and William W. Turner. "Report Upon the Indian Tribes." In A. W. Whipple, *Reports of Explorations and Surveys*, Vol. III, Part 3.

White, Leslie A., "Notes on the Ethnozoology of the Keresan Pueblo Indians," *Michigan Academy of Science, Arts, and Letters Papers*, Vol. 31, Part 3, 1947, pp. 223–43.

———. "The Pueblo of Santa Ana, New Mexico," *American Anthropological Association Memoirs*, No. 60, 1942.

Whiting, Alfred F. "Ethnobotany of the Hopi," *Museum of Northern Arizona Bulletin 15,* 1939.

Wissler, Clark. "Material Culture of the Blackfoot Indians," *American Museum of Natural History Anthropological Papers,* Vol. 5, Part 1, 1910, pp. 1–176.

Zarate Salmeron, Geronimo de. "Relación de Todas las Cosas Que en el Nuevo México se Han Visto y Sabido." In *Documentos para la historia de México,* Series 3, Part 1.

INDEX

Q